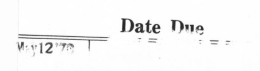

Date Due

May 12 '70

FUNDAMENTALS
of Psychotherapy

GLEN A. HOLLAND

HOLT, RINEHART AND WINSTON

New York   Chicago   San Francisco   Toronto   London

This book is dedicated to my mother,

GEORGIANNA MYERS HOLLAND

and to my father,

CLYDE ERVIN HOLLAND

PREFACE

In writing *Fundamentals of Psychotherapy* I have hoped to contribute to the solution of two problems, discussed below, in instructing students in psychotherapy. It is also my hope that psychotherapists with considerable training and experience, as well as specialists in fields such as counseling, guidance, pastoral counseling, and so on, will find their thinking about their work considerably clarified if recast in terms of the frame of reference suggested in *Fundamentals*.

The first problem is that while most students of psychotherapy have some background of training in general psychology, this background is of relatively little use to them when they approach the study of psychotherapy. The reason for this is that the concepts generally used in teaching or explaining psychotherapy are almost unique to the field of therapy and relatively unrelated to the rest of psychological and sociological knowledge. There is no good reason why this should be so, except that many of the pioneers in the field, especially the psychoanalysts, did not have any significant training in psychology, sociology, and so on. In the years since the founding of psychoanalysis and other forms of therapy, the fields of psychology and psychotherapy have developed to a considerable extent independently, with psychology being more influenced (perhaps) by psychotherapeutic concepts and findings than vice versa. At any rate, the student of psychology who wishes to learn about the field of psychotherapy often finds it difficult to correlate the terms and concepts that he finds being used in psychotherapy with analogous terms and concepts that he knows from his prior training in psychology. My efforts at solving this problem rest primarily in an attempt to develop a theoretical and practical approach to psychotherapy in which the explanatory and descriptive concepts are those of general psychology. This has been attempted before and has been done with considerable finesse by others. I hope, however, that my efforts will have some distinctive value of their own.

This leads us to the second problem that I am trying to cope with in *Fundamentals*. Clinical work with disturbed persons now involves four separate groups of concepts. The first comprises theoretical explanations of psychopathology and psychotherapy, such as the various forms of psychoanalysis, client-centered therapy (Carl Rogers), and directive psychotherapy (Frederick Thorne). The second group of concepts are classificatory concepts used for sorting patients into more homogeneous groups: for example, psychoses and neuroses, character disorders, emotional disorders, and organic defects. The third group of concepts are those relating to testing and formal evaluation, using test and projective techniques such as the Rorschach. Strangely enough, these are usually not closely coordinated with either the theoretical or the classificatory frames of reference. The final group of concepts are those that have to do with psychotherapy: for example, catharsis, analysis of the transference, and resistance. Although the examples that I have given happen to be related to psychoanalytic theory in general, there is no logic-tight chain of reasoning that leads from the psychoanalytic theory of psychopathology to the techniques of psychotherapy. To illustrate my point, a number of different forms of therapy have been advocated by Rank, Jung, Adler, Ferenczi, and others closely related to psychoanalysis. Although there were theoretical differences as well as differences in psychotherapeutic technique between each of these men and Freud, it would be extremely difficult to justify the differences in psychotherapeutic technique on the basis of their theoretical positions. I think it is only justified to say that they differed in theoretical points of view *and also* in their approach to psychotherapy.

So here we have the problem of four different sets of concepts used for purposes of theorizing about psychopathology, classifying patients, diagnosing patients through the use of test and projective techniques, and helping patients through psychotherapy. What I have attempted to do is to simplify the situation for the student by using one set of concepts for theoretical, diagnostic, and therapeutic purposes.

To further simplify the learning task for the beginning therapist, I have centered attention on three principal concepts: feeling and emotion, cognitive structure, and communication. These three areas are discussed first in terms of their importance in the theoretical understanding of psychopathology, they are discussed again in terms of their relevance for diagnostic evaluation, and they are used a third time when psychotherapeutic techniques are taken up. By the time the student has completed *Fundamentals*, he has at least received a thorough grounding in a basic set of concepts that will serve him well for all purposes of conceptualizing, diagnosing, and helping with human problems. Furthermore, he will have at his disposal a frame of reference to which he can readily relate whatever training he has had in psychology, social psychology, sociology, cultural anthropology, general semantics, and related subjects. In other words, he will be dealing with concepts not peculiar to the field of psychotherapy but rather with those he already knows from previous education.

I think all of us who are involved in psychotherapy have some interest in lifting the veils of ignorance and mystery from this subject for the interested layman. With this in mind I have made an especial effort to make the language and thinking as clear as possible. Some of my professional colleagues have protested that this tends to make *Fundamentals* sound unscholarly. I trust that those who read it will have the good sense to value clarity of exposition (insofar as I may have been able to achieve it) and will not be duped into confusing a simplified theoretical framework with oversimplification of the problems dealt with.

The writing of this manuscript was in a very real sense made possible by the interest and encouragement of my publisher, Holt, Rinehart and Winston, Inc. Theodore Sarbin, University of California at Berkeley, has tried valiantly to rescue the manuscript from its more glaring idiosyncracies and to make it more academically respectable. He should not be blamed if he has not altogether succeeded, since my efforts to foil him have been dedicated and persistent. As to my other indebtednesses, they include the faculties of my student days at Stanford and Yale, and all the excellent colleagues I have enjoyed on the faculties of Connecticut College for Women, Pomona College, and U.C.L.A., as well as my contemporaries in the field of clinical psychology in the Southern California area.

The writing of *Fundamentals* has been accomplished in the time left over from a busy practice in clinical psychology. It has, therefore, quite literally been taken from time and resources belonging to my immediate family. I can repay their generosity only by acknowledging the unflagging and uncomplaining encouragement of my wife, Marjorie Stanfield Holland, and the continuing inspiration provided by my children, Nancy Jean Holland and Glenn Stanfield Holland.

LOS ANGELES, CALIFORNIA   G.A.H.
DECEMBER 1964

CONTENTS

Part One | THEORY

Chapter 1 | *Theories of Psychotherapy*

INTRODUCTION

The purpose of this book is to provide those persons interested in the study of psychotherapy with an introduction to the subject that has its basis in general principles of psychology.

The reader who is new to the study of psychotherapy might possibly assume (as would seem reasonable) that all psychotherapeutic techniques are based upon general principles of psychology. If, however, by "general principles" are meant those principles or generalizations based on experimental evidence and generally taught in academic courses, then relatively little psychotherapeutic theory actually has such a basis. To explain why this is so, we must review, at least briefly, the origins and development of psychotherapy.

FREUDIAN THEORY

Freud's background and training.   Modern psychotherapy had its origins in the work and writings of Sigmund Freud. Although psychoanalysis, Freud's creation, is considered generally and correctly to be a psychological theory or a theory of psychology, Freud himself had no formal training as a psychologist. He was acquainted with the work of Helmholtz and Fechner and showed some interest in it, but only general traces of this interest remain in the basic philosophy of psychoanalysis (1). Freud's first love was neurology and research in neurology. His change of vocation was not of his own choosing but was partly due to anti-Jewish prejudice in the academic circles of the Vienna of the 1880s. This forced Freud into the practice of medicine, a pursuit with which he was never particularly happy, and into training as a specialist in "nervous diseases" (2). It was after the choice of this specialty that Freud obtained his psychiatric training from Charcot, Liebeault, and Bernheim. The immediate precursor of Freud's development of psychoanalytic theory was his collaboration with Breuer on a study of hysteria.

Freud as a psychologist.   The significance of this background for psychoanalytic theory is that it is, for all practical purposes, exclusively neurological, medical, and psychiatric. Although there was a considerable body of research and theory in psychology by 1900 (the publication date of Freud's *The Interpretation of Dreams*), and although scientific psychology flourished prodigiously during the remaining thirty-nine years of Freud's life, it is difficult to find clear evidence of Freud's awareness of this development of scientific psychology or evidence that it influenced the development of psychoanalytic theory.

Freud's disregard of scientific psychology would, of course, be irrelevant to our present concern if psychoanalysis were not considered a psychological theory itself but solely and exclusively a branch of medical theory. On this point we can do no better than to quote Zilboorg, who was the possessor of two medical degrees and a practicing psychoanalyst until his death in 1960.

Zilboorg says: "Freud was a doctor, a neurologist who strayed away from neurology early in his career and soon found himself isolated yet famous, a founder of a new type of medical psychology which was almost entirely the product of his own creative intuition" (3, p. 1).

Elsewhere Zilboorg repeats this conclusion regarding the psychological nature of psychoanalytic theory: ". . . psychoanalysis is, or legitimately strives to become, a system of individual psychology" (3, p. 2).

Regarding the relationship of psychoanalysis to psychiatry, Zilboorg points out: ". . . psychiatry, the field of the severer forms of mental illness, was never a strong point of Freud's own education or of his studies and fundamental formulations" (3, p. 16). On the question as to whether psychoanalysis is simply a branch of medicine, Zilboorg concludes: "Freud seems to have arrived ultimately at the unshakable conclusion that psychoanalysis is not exclusively a branch of medicine" (3, p. 12).

Although we have chosen to quote Zilboorg because of the aptness of his expressions on this point, any number of authorities on Freud and his work have substantiated the conclusion that Freud himself considered his theories to be psychological in nature and to be much more closely identified with the study of man than with the study of medicine.

Freud's development of psychoanalytic technique.   If Freud came into medicine rather late in his training, if his training in psychiatry was even more belated and rather cursory, and if his knowledge of scientific psychology was always meager and of little consequence to his formulation of psychoanalysis, then upon what was Freud's psychoanalytic theory based?

Psychoanalysis originated as a variation in methodology for the treatment of hysteria. Freud had learned the use of hypnosis as a method of treatment from Charcot, but he was reportedly not a particularly effective hypnotist and rather disliked the use of hypnosis in any event. He found that he could obtain much the same type of response and effect as was obtained by hypnosis by simply having his patients lie down and talk to him while he remained out of their field of direct vision.

In attempting to duplicate the kind of communication and emotional response that were obtainable under hypnosis, Freud instructed his patients to say whatever came into their thoughts, regardless of considerations of content, propriety, reasonableness, or emotionality. He was insistent upon this rule of "free association," since he believed that it was essential in order to achieve a therapeutic effect comparable to that obtained with the use of hypnosis.

Freud developed this method of treatment, which began as an alternative to hypnotic treatment, over a period of ten years before his first major publication (*The Interpretation of Dreams*). What happened in this period was that Freud became increasingly impressed with the essentially new information about human beings that he obtained from his patients by using the technique of free association. During this ten-year period he also decided that dreams were another source of information about the individual comparable with the results of free association. It was largely through an analysis of his own dreams that Freud was able to convince himself of the universality of the phenomena which he had originally associated with psychopathology. This was the origin of the psychological aspect of what was originally a treatment technique.

After 1900 Freud's interest in psychoanalysis was increasingly divided between its value as a source of psychological information and its value as a treatment technique. Later still his interest in the application of his psychological theory to such fields as art, literature, religion, and anthropology took up much of his creative effort.

The source of Freud's psychology. In the foregoing material we have tried to answer our own question regarding the source of Freud's psychological theories and principles. Freud's investigative method was the psychotherapeutic interaction between himself as the "investigator" and his patient as the "subject." (However, there is clear evidence that Freud was involved both as investigator *and* subject in some of the basic formulations of psychoanalytic theory [2].) The instructions to the subject were to free associate and to report dreams. The data were the verbalizations of Freud's patients combined with his own introspections and self-analysis. The evaluation of the data was what might be called "intuitive," rather than statistical. Validation, initially, was by replications conducted by Freud. Later others were taught the Freudian technique, but there seems to have been a tendency for investigators who consistently arrived at conclusions that differed from Freud's to eventually find themselves "beyond the pale" of Freudian psychoanalysis.

Freud's psychological methodology has been stated in this form in order to contrast it with the methods of experimental psychology. In experimental psychology, every effort is made to exclude the influence of the investigator from the determination of the subjects' behavior. The subjects are supposedly chosen for their ability to represent accurately some larger "universe" of subjects. Only a limited number of variables of behavior are investigated, using a careful experimental design to insure lack of bias and adequate control of variables irrelevant to the purpose of the experiment. Whenever possible the results of the experiment are expressed in mathematical terms and statistically analyzed. Only at this point may the investigator draw his conclusions. Replication of the experiment by other investigators is usually considered necessary for general acceptance of the original conclusions. If there is not essential agreement among investigators, still others may become involved, and the eventual resolution of the difference may be many years in the making.

The scientific status of Freud's psychology.   It is clear, therefore, that the sources of Freud's psychological theory had nothing in common with the experimental methods of psychology, nor were the common safeguards that would qualify his data as scientific used. Attempts to validate Freudian theory by the use of experimental methods have been rather sparse, partly because Freudian concepts are difficult to define in terms definite and concrete enough for experimental purposes. After a survey of all such attempts at experimental validation through 1941, Sears stated:

> So far, it must be concluded, the complicated interplay of psychological forces in the analytic interviews, i.e., in the fact-finding situation, remains a fascinating tangle for the experimental psychologist. The problems of the therapeutic process will have to be carefully formulated in objective terms, probably those of learning theory, before the *process of psychoanalysis itself* can be subjected to realistic and insightful investigation (4, pp. 328–329).

Aside from the scientific limitations of Freud's investigative methods, we should also consider the limitations of Freud's technique so far as the selection of "subjects" for investigation is concerned. It is obvious that Freud's subjects were patients suffering from certain kinds of emotional difficulty. Although many laymen and some experimental psychologists consider this enough to invalidate Freud's conclusions as applied to "normal" persons, we are not particularly disturbed by this limitation. This is because we can find no consistently valid basis for differentiating psychotherapeutic patients from nonpatients, except that nonpatients do not ask for appointments. The only question in this respect would be whether persons classified as hysterical, obsessive, and phobic in the Vienna of sixty years ago (such classifications representing the bulk of the persons whom Freud analyzed, apart from other psychotherapists), might have certain emotional characteristics or experiences common to them but not found so consistently in a more heterogeneous population.

What concerns us more regarding the nature of Freud's subjects is that they were predominently rather young, intelligent, educated, verbally facile adults of middle-class background. Freud himself did very little psychotherapy with children, with persons in psychotic or borderline-psychotic states, with the unintelligent, with lower-class subjects, with inarticulate subjects, or with older subjects. He considered many adjustment problems that were then regarded either as neurotic or as character disorders not amenable to psychotherapeutic treatment by psychoanalytic methods. In fact one of the things that Jones's biography of Freud makes clear is that Freud's active career as a therapist was cut short, first by the dearth of patients during and immediately after World War I, and later by old age and physical infirmity (he developed cancer of the jaw in 1923, at which time he was 67 years old). From this postwar period to the end of his life, his subjects were predominantly psychotherapists in training or "didactic" analyses.

Freud can hardly be held accountable, as some critics seem to do, for the fact that many of his early patients were Viennese and were a part of the Victorian era. In fact he is not accountable for the other limitations of his patient-informants, since these were determined by his own ideas as to which persons were most likely to benefit from analysis. Rather, our concern is that Freud did not limit his conclusions to the subjects he saw and to the universe or population that they represented. For example, Freud's theories concerning childhood and development were based almost exclusively on the retrospective accounts of adults. This led him into serious error very early in his theorizing when he concluded that all of his patients (mostly classified as hysterics or obsessives) had been seduced as children. When Freud later established that this was not literally true, he almost abandoned his psychological theorizing. However, this experience did not prevent Freud later from insisting upon the complete universality of developmental phenomena (such as the Oedipus complex) that he inferred from the same type of evidence.

Freud as a therapist.   Since we are primarily interested in Freud's psychology as a theoretical basis for psychotherapy, it is relevant to consider its value or validity from that point of view. In doing so, it is well to keep in mind that the effectiveness of a given therapy in producing "cures" is not highly regarded as evidence for or against the theory behind the therapy, especially when the original problem is functional rather than organic-structural.

Freud had a modest regard for his own method of treatment so far as its applicability was concerned. He believed it was most suitable for young, intelligent, educated, and verbal subjects. He considered it effective primarily in the treatment of cases diagnosed as hysteric, obsessive, or phobic.

Clara Thompson (5) suggests that Freud's enthusiasm for psychoanalysis as a therapeutic method waxed and waned at various times. It is apparent from Freud's letters to Fleiss (6) that he was alternatively encouraged and discouraged during the years between 1890 and 1900 when he was working alone. Aside from his papers between the period 1910–1915 and one in 1919, Freud wrote very little on the subject of psychotherapy per se until his modest summing up of the therapeutic potential of psychoanalysis in his paper, "Analysis Terminable and Interminable," published in 1937. In this paper (7) Freud indicated that he was not at all sure how complete a change in adjustment could be effected by means of psychoanalysis nor how invulnerable a person who had undergone psychoanalysis might be to further unusual demands upon his capacity to adjust.

Conclusions.   There are two points that we have tried to establish in this review of Freud's background and his work. The first is that although Freud thought of his psychoanalytic theory as a psychological theory and it has been accepted as such, it is a psychological theory *sui generis* rather than one based upon and integrated with general principles of psychology that have been developed through normal scientific procedures. Our position, as it will be developed in later chapters, is that a rationale for diagnosis (evaluation) and psychotherapy can also be based upon such general psychological principles.

Our second point has to do with whether such a rationale is necessary or desirable, even if possible. If psychoanalytic theory and technique were completely adequate for dealing with all types of problems in all types of patients, there would seem to be little practical reason for suggesting any other rationale for psychotherapeutic procedures, regardless of the origin of Freud's theory or his lack of formal psychological training. Some psychotherapists apparently believe that Freud's theories are sufficient as they stand for all psychotherapeutic purposes and that those who cannot be helped by psychoanalytic means cannot be helped by any form of psychotherapy. Rather than citing in detail all the many criticisms and revisions of psychoanalytic theory, we have in this introduction simply cited Freud's own opinions as to the limitations of psychoanalytic technique. These alone would suggest that Freud began, but did not finish, the task of developing effective psychotherapeutic techniques for the wide range of human problems to which psychotherapeutic procedures are now seen as applicable.

AN EVALUATION OF FREUDIAN THEORY

General appraisal.   We shall begin our evaluation of Freudian theory by saying that we find it difficult to conceive of anyone's functioning as a psychotherapist without the use of or reference to psychoanalytic theory and concepts. If this sounds too extreme a statement, it probably sounds extreme only to those who are not aware of the extent to which Freudian theory has infiltrated and influenced psychological thinking in such fields as child psychology, the psychology of adjustment, the psychology of personality, and social psychology. Often, however, the contributions of psychoanalytic theory to these fields has been but poorly digested and assimilated. Perhaps it would be better to say, "only partially digested and assimilated." There are good reasons for this "digestive" difficulty, and the reasons have to do with parts and aspects of Freudian theory that are basically irreconcilable with the principles of general psychology, at least as these principles have developed up to the present.

In this section of our chapter we shall present our own conclusions as to the assimilable and valuable contributions of psychoanalysis to general psychology and try to indicate what we consider the shortcomings or outright errors of Freudian theory.

Motivational theory.   There is a direct and obvious conflict between experimental studies of motivation and the motivational theory of psychoanalysis. In fact it is not always easy to determine which part of Freudian theory can be most legitimately equated with motivational research in psychology. Certainly the research psychologist finds nothing that he can readily equate with "libido."

As to "life" and "death" instincts, the motivational psychologist would probably reply that the concept of instinct as applied to human behavior has been passé since the time of William McDougall. He might suggest that instead of investigating a death instinct, we would derive more profit from the Yale studies of frustration and aggression (8), which strongly suggest that man's destructive proclivities stem from his inability to satisfy significant needs.

The psychologist who was also an expert on emotion and motivation would probably agree that "anxiety" or its operationally defined equivalent does play a large part in determining a person's mode of adjustment. He would recognize that anxiety is an unpleasant and therefore a motivating experience or condition. He would expect that behavior that tended to reduce anxiety would also tend to become habitual. However, he would not know what to say about the thesis that all anxiety is ultimately derived from "id" impulses and the conflict between "id" and "superego," except that since he doesn't know what an id or a superego is, he is hardly in a position to determine when they are in conflict with each other. He might point out that it is possible to produce all of the symptoms of anxiety in any kind of a subject from white rats to man simply by conditioning the subject to expect an unpleasant feeling (such as that produced by an electric shock) when a given signal is presented to him.

If now we described the "pleasure principle," to our experimentally minded psychologist, he might finally begin to nod his head in agreement. "Yes," he might say, "I understand the pleasure principle. It has been known in psychology for some fifty years or more as Thorndike's 'law of effect.' You might talk with the learning theorists about that. They have been having an argument about the matter for a long time. Look it up in the experimental literature yourself, if you like, under 'reinforcement' and 'reinforcement theory.' It has had its ups and downs of theoretical acceptance and rejection, but the majority of psychologists still seem to find some kind of use for it."

Developmental theory.   Freud reported only one prolonged therapeutic contact with a child (the case of "little Hans"). The bulk of his developmental theories was based on the retrospective accounts of patients. Considering these circumstances, the accuracy of Freud's contributions to the theory of child development is impressive. Perhaps his initial error in regarding the seduction phantasies of patients as realistic reports of childhood experiences motivated Freud to be especially cautious in this field.

We cannot help but wonder, for instance, how long scientific studies of the child would have ignored sexually motivated behavior in infancy and childhood if it had not been for Freud's formulations. Compared to the vistas of understanding that Freud's *Three Contributions to the Theory of Sex* opened up for psychotherapists and scientists alike, his error in describing a "latency" period for sexual motivation seems minor indeed. Freud's distinction between "phallic" and "genital" sexuality is still (and probably will continue to be) a basically useful distinction in any attempt to untangle some of the more perplexing problems concerning the emotional relations between persons and the complex interplay between sexual and emotional responses in any given relationship.

Similarly, we wonder how psychotherapists who are unwilling to accept Freud's account of the "Oedipus complex" and the corresponding emotional ties between father and daughter (and the resultant jealousies between like-sexed parent and offspring) go about the task of understanding the complex emotional relationships within the family. Many critics have pointed out that the relationships that Freud describes are neither inevitable nor universal. Granting this, it is all the more surprising that the feeling aspects of family relationships are so often almost exactly as Freud described them.

As to Freud's shortcomings in the field of developmental theory, we have already mentioned his slighting the developmental period between six or seven years of age and puberty. At the other extreme, although Freud referred from time to time to the significance of events occurring early in infancy, we believe that he erred in underestimating the intelligence and sensitivity of the extremely young infant. These characteristics, in conjunction with the extreme defenselessness and dependency of the human infant, create a potentiality for trauma and anxiety that too few psychotherapists recognize even today. This point of view has been brought out most ably by Melanie Klein (9), Ronald Fairbairn, and Harry Guntrip. The emphasis that they have placed on "pre-Oedipal" trauma (as contrasted with Freud's emphasis on trauma associated with the Oedipal conflict) has led to the development of a distinctive "British School" of psychoanalytic thinking.

Learning theory.   In spite of Freud's complete lack of formal training in experimental psychology and of any specific interest in learning theory, his descriptions of certain behavioral phenomena characteristic of learned behavior are so accurate and well defined that Dollard and Miller (10) have been able to "translate" most of Freud's psychoanalytic concepts into the constructs of Hull's *Principles of Behavior* (11). Since learning theory is a familiar frame of reference in general psychology, some of Freud's basic concepts, such as "transference," "resistance," "suppression," "repression," and "repetition compulsion," seem to gain clarity and usefulness by virtue of the translation.

Freud himself never explicitly defined the psychotherapeutic process as a process of learning, unlearning, or relearning. His formulations on psychotherapeutic technique might well have been considerably more extensive and definite if this had been the case. However, the efforts of such men as Dollard and Miller and Julian Rotter (12) have helped to rectify this situation, at least for those who find learning theory helpful to their understanding of the psychotherapeutic process.

Structural theory.   An entire book *The Unconscious before Freud* (13) has been devoted to delineating the various thinkers who antedated Freud in recognizing that many significant determinants of behavior were not part of the conscious or rational experience of an individual. Yet it still remained for Freud to explore and to describe some of the most significant characteristics of unconscious phenomena in a way that attracted the attention of psychologists.

It was Freud, for example, who suggested the vast disproportion between unconscious and conscious determinants of behavior with the overwhelming influence being attributed to unconscious determinants. It was also Freud who clearly described and, in a sense, documented the irrational principles governing unconscious activities. We refer here to the assumption that such concepts as "logic," "time," and "causality" exist only in relation to and as a part of conscious levels of functioning or what Freud sometimes referred to as "secondary processes." Freud further delineated some of the principal means for exploring and determining the nature of processes that are normally unconscious. For this purpose he used hypnosis and free association, and he analyzed dreams, humor, accidents, religion, folk-lore, myths, and artistic productions of various kinds.

Freud's other major contribution to the structural concepts of psychology was, of course, his division of the personality into id, ego, and superego aspects. Of these three aspects, ego theory is today so much a part of so many psychological fields and theories that it is often difficult to find the original Freudian nucleus. The reader who is interested in such detective work might try to separate Freudian from non-Freudian aspects of theory in the writings of such psychologists as H. A. Murray (14), Muzafer Sherif and Hadley Cantril (15), Gardner Murphy (16), and Kurt Lewin (17). It is interesting to speculate as to how much the development of personality theory and research would have been retarded and how much it would lack of its present formulations without Freud's contributions and stimulation.

As to Freud's ultimate influence in this field, Murphy states:

> It appears likely . . . that the various (theoretical) systems will be
> . . . reduced to a relatively orderly and uniform pattern in which the

primary role of the self, and of activities centered around it, will be placed in the central position which Freud, as early as 1913, suggested it might require (18, p. 347).

Freud's concept of a superego has been included in some form or other in every form of psychoanalytically derived psychotherapy, however much the dissenters may have differed with Freud on other points of theory. This uniformity of opinion among those who trace their intellectual descent from Freud makes it all the more surprising that problems of standards and values have long been neglected by psychologists. It seems quite inconceivable to us that either the process of human ontogenetic development or the problems that result from this process can be adequately conceptualized without being constantly aware that the whole training of the child is determined by standards and values. However, the neglect of this area is presently being redressed by the publications of Carl Rogers (19), Charlotte Buhler (20), and other psychologists in the field of psychotherapy.

The fate of Freud's construct of the id has been quite opposite to the wide acceptance of his ego and superego concepts, possibly because most of the important attributes of the id can be subsumed under the concepts of "primary process" and the unconscious. Indeed it is doubtful if Freud would have incorporated such a concept into his structural theory except for two problems that it helped to solve. First, Freud seemed to think that he needed a separate concept to describe the primordial self or self-state from which the ego and superego gradually emerged. Second, since Freud recognized that both ego and superego functions may occur as unconscious processes, he was loath to simply equate the id with the unconscious.

Looking at the situation from the perspective of modern psychology, we see very little of a primordial self, the functioning of which is determined by instinct. Rather we seen an individual who begins to adjust to the realities of his environment on the basis of "the pleasure princple" as soon as he is born. What is seen as being innately determined is only that general "style" of adjusting that is usually referred to as "temperament" (21). The superego develops as a direct function of the types of reinforcement provided by the person's social environment, that is, other persons. The developing individual's reaction to reality thus includes both a physical and a social reality from the beginning. It is the social environment, with its social values which determine the behavioral responses to be encouraged or discouraged in the child, that makes human adjustment quite a different process from the adjustment of feral animals.

With this understanding it is possible to dispense with the construct of an id, while still agreeing with Freud's awareness of constitutional or genetic factors that have much to do with the person's facility or difficulty in coping with a given environment. Nor do we need a "reality" principle as distinct from a "pleasure" principle if we simply recognize that social sanctions based on social values are every bit as real to the child as falling down and hurting his knee. The child will tend to do habitually those things that lead to a pleasant feeling within himself or to the reduction of the intensity of unpleasant feelings. Whether the feelings are produced by a physical reality or a social reality has no significance so far as this learning itself is concerned.

The psychotherapist often finds use for the concept of "ego strength" or of a more or less adequately functioning ego. Such terms, however, must be carefully defined, not just in terms of what the nature of the person's social environment actually is, but also in terms of what it might or should be so far as permitting a person the fullest use and enjoyment of his human potential is concerned. From this point of view, the psychotherapist may have a frame of reference that makes him as inevitably a critic of the society in which a person functions as he is a critic of how well a person is functioning in his social environment.

AN EVALUATION OF NEO-FREUDIAN THEORIES

General appraisal.   On the first page of *Sigmund Freud* Zilboorg makes the following statement:

> There are few, if any, among Freud's pupils or followers who made truly original contributions to that which has become known as psychoanalysis. With the exception of Karl Abraham, it is difficult to think of anyone whose contribution to psychoanalysis was not first suggested by Freud himself. There were, of course, Alfred Adler and Carl Jung, whose names occupy an illustrious place in the history of newer psychopathology. But both Adler and Jung are better known for the rift with Freud around 1911 than for any original contributions they made. This does not mean that Adler and Jung lacked originality, or that their contributions to psychology are negligible. It merely means that their influence on the development of modern psychology is really negligible as compared to that of Freud (3).

We find ourselves in basic accord with Zilboorg's evaluation of Freud's influence on modern psychology as opposed to the influence of those who disagreed with him while still maintaining a generally psychoanalytic frame of reference. There can be little question that psychoanalysis is basically Freud's own individual creation or that those who founded different schools of psychoanalysis generally agreed with Freudian theory on many more points than they disagreed with it.

There was, throughout Freud's lifetime, a strong tendency for those who began their therapeutic careers under Freud's guidance to set up their own special theories and/or techniques of psychotherapy. As a result of many such "divorces" over the years since 1911, there are far too many "schools" that differ from Freudian psychoanalysis in one respect or another to permit a comprehensive review or evaluation of them all here. In any event, excellent discussions of these schools are already available in books by Harper (22), Mullahy (23), Blum (24), Munroe (25) and Thompson (5). What interests us particularly are those theoretical deviations that, if they had been accepted by Freud or Freudian psychoanalysts, might have brought psychoanalytic theory closer to the mainstream of scientific psychology or might have created a more comprehensive and effective theory of psychotherapy.

The following review is highly selective, both as to which non-Freudian psychoanalytic theories are reviewed and as to the aspects of those theories selected which are actually discussed.

Otto Rank (26).   We consider Rank among the most underrated of the non-Freudian psychoanalysts. He remained for a long time within the Freudian fold and when the break did come, it came about partly because of a sincere desire on Rank's part to increase the effectiveness or efficiency of psychoanalytic therapy. Freud, probably rightly, had misgivings about the adequacy of Rank's therapeutic efforts, and on the basis of this, plus personal tension between the two men, Rank eventually established his own viewpoint.

Among psychologists the aspect of Rank's theory that has been most often mentioned is his concept of the "birth trauma" and its significance in determining "neurosis." Because this aspect of Rankian theory is so often rejected simply on the grounds of implausibility, very few psychologists or orthodox psychoanalysts have noted that the important theme of Rank's writing is the problem of dependency.

Rank, more than any other psychotherapist, calls attention to and accurately delineates the significance of the developing individual's struggle with his own desire for dependency. Each step toward independent functioning involves two extremely important social victories over the child's natural hedonistic inclinations. First, functioning independently requires the expenditure of more effort than does dependent functioning. Second, functioning independently involves (initially) more anxiety or less security than depending upon others. The person makes this adjustment successfully only when others are sufficiently reassuring, when they negatively reinforce dependent functioning, and/or when they adequately reward independent functioning.

Rank never states this premise quite this clearly or this completely; nevertheless we believe it is implicit in his theory and, to some extent, in the technique that he developed.

Alfred Adler (27).   Adler's name is, of course, automatically associated with the concept of the "inferiority complex." Adler's theory of compensation for inferiority became of general significance when it included two of Adler's later theoretical developments. The first of these was that every person *is* inferior (to older persons) at the beginning of his life and thus has feelings of inferiority that need to be "corrected" as competence replaces incompetence.

The second development was Adler's pointing out that the inferiority for which a person tries to compensate may just as well be "imaginary" as "real." In other words, and more generally, the significant determinants of a person's adjustment are not necessarily his real attributes as evaluated objectively by others, but rather his own evaluation of himself, which may be highly biased as compared with the opinions of others.

Carl Jung (28).   Freud, in his *History of the Psychoanalytic Movement,* clearly implies that Jung's rejection of Freud's sexual theory of motivation was attributable to Jung's desire for a quicker and easier acceptance of psychoanalytic theory. Freud was righteously indignant at what he considered Jung's pandering to popular prejudice. Shortly after their open disagreement on this issue, Jung left the inner circle of Freudian advocates in order to establish his own theoretical position.

From the perspective of an additional fifty years it becomes apparent that most of the schisms within psychoanalysis have stemmed from differences of opinion over the importance of sexuality as a source of adjustment difficulties in comparison with other sources and kinds of difficulty. Furthermore it is the Freudian insistence upon libido theory that is one of the stone walls separating psychoanalytic theory from psychological theory in general. In view of the changes in attitude toward sex (for most of which Freud was himself responsible) and in view of the universal disagreement with Freudian theory on this point, it becomes harder and harder to believe that everyone is out of step except Freud.

Jung made several contributions to psychological thinking. Among these were his concept of "complexes" (which Freud and Adler both borrowed and used also) and his concept of introversion and extraversion, which has long been a standby of personality theorists.

One of the major impediments to Jung's wider acceptance among psychologists of all theoretical colorings has been his clinging to his concept of a racial unconscious. On this point he and Freud were in agreement, although in Freud's interpretation, at least, this involved the acceptance of Lamarck's theory of the inheritance of acquired characteristics. Even when most liberally interpreted, the concept of a racial unconscious seems archaic and more than a little improbable to the modern psychologist.

Karen Horney (29, 30).   There is some reason for including Karen Horney in that class of Neo-Freudians which also contains Rank and Adler. We shall explain this classification since the basis for it may not be obvious.

Elsewhere in this book the reader will be introduced to certain developmental theories, including the concept of "developmental tasks." These might be defined as the major adjustments that must be progressively and adequately made during childhood and adolescence if a person is to function with maximum effectiveness as an adult. Coming to terms with dependency needs or desires (Rank) is one such developmental task and overcoming unwarranted self-evaluations of inadequacy (Adler) is another.

The contributions of Horney regarding the problems of dealing with hostility define still a third developmental task. One might say that the process of socialization is nothing if not frustrating. Others, specifically the child's social conditioners (usually and predominantly the parents) determine which responses will be permitted and/or rewarded and which will be punished, quite independently of what the affective consequences of these responses would otherwise be for the child. They also impose barriers between the child and many of his self-selected goals. Furthermore, the child, with his relative inadequacies, often finds himself unable to do what he sees others doing and would also like to do himself (such as ride a bicycle).

All of these situations may involve frustration. According to a series of researches done at Yale, the natural response to frustration is aggression (8). But, Horney points out, aggressive behavior on the child's part in our society is often responded to by punishing him. When this occurs, the impulse toward aggressive behavior soon comes to arouse anxiety. The problem of what to do about this anxiety and the inhibition that goes hand in hand with it is a major problem for social man and one which is seldom resolved adequately, according to Horney.

Melanie Klein (9).   Klein's conceptions of the sexual lives and experiences of very young children are so detailed and, to the uninitiated, so bizarre that it is almost necessary to read some one else's account of her work in order to appreciate a very significant aspect of her theory. Guntrip (31), although not the easiest writer in the world to read himself, nevertheless makes it clear that Klein was the first of the psychoanalytic group to insist upon the prime significance of "pre-Oedipal" trauma, that is, events causing overwhelming anxiety in the first three years of life. (Actually Freud himself made references from time to time about the possibilities and significance of such very early disturbances, but he did not focus the attention upon them that Klein did, nor could he reconcile himself completely with all aspects of her theory [2].)

It seems entirely reasonable to assume that the younger, the more helpless, and the more dependent the child is, the more readily and the more intensely he may be threatened. Such threats are particularly likely to be overlooked by adults, or regarded as insignificant, simply because most adults are not inclined to think of the infant's and child's almost complete helplessness and almost total dependence upon them. (We have noted in making psychological evaluations that parents are usually not able to give any sort of valid account of the origin of obvious and significant fears in their children.) More attention to very early trauma is entirely consistent with what is known from scientific studies about the child's very rapid development, especially in intelligence, in the first eighteen months of life. Those who do not have a special acquaintance with this stage of development will find Leonard Carmichael's *Manual of Child Psychology* (32) most enlightening.

Harry Stack Sullivan (33, 34).   Sullivan can be included among the psychoanalytic theorists because it is customary to do so and because it would be inappropriate to include him with theorists whose basic training has been in psychology. However, the major emphases of Sullivan's approach are upon aspects of psychotherapy that are readily identified with areas of psychological interest and research.

One of the distinctive aspects of Sullivan's approach to psychotherapy is his emphasis upon the importance of the relationship between therapist and patient. Freud's tendency was to keep the therapist's role as impersonal and as "nondirective" as possible. His rationale was that the irrational or transference aspects of the patient's reactions to the therapist could then be more readily detected and more easily interpreted. When Ferenczi suggested that the therapist should concern himself personally with the emotional needs of the patient, the difference between his viewpoint and Freud's led to a considerable estrangement between them (2). Sullivan, although not espousing exactly Ferenczi's viewpoints or techniques, has been explicit in considering in detail the effects of the relationship between patient and therapist on the psychotherapeutic process.

Along with this concern for the relationship of patient and therapist has gone a very considerable interest in and analysis of the communicative interaction between them. This duality of interest we see as being not only natural but inevitable, since in psychotherapy especially it is true that communication and relationship are virtually synonymous. It is, above all else, a communicative relationship, that is, a relationship that exists by virtue of communication and for the purpose of communicating, although the ultimate purpose is the improvement of the emotional lot of the patient.

Erich Fromm (35). Fromm is a nonmedical or lay psychoanalyst whose background of training is in the social sciences generally and in social psychology in particular. From this vantage point he has chosen to look at the society to which patients are supposed to adjust, as well as at the patient's problems in adjusting. In this respect he emphasizes a point of view that is implicit in much of Freud's own writings and has been previously emphasized by Rank, among others.

This look at the environment and at the standards and values current therein raises issues relating both to the psychotherapist's values and to the values that determine the objectives of the psychotherapeutic process. Freud apparently preferred to avoid such issues, except in specified areas of adjustment, such as sex and religion. Fromm points out that issues relating to values exist in many aspects of psychotherapy and cannot be avoided, therefore such issues are better dealt with explicitly rather than implicitly. Nor, says Fromm, can we afford to accept uncritically the values that are current in society.

Franz Alexander (36). Alexander is included among the neo-Freudians only with respect to his willingness to experiment with the therapeutic benefits of briefer contacts with persons seeking psychotherapeutic help. His variations on contact possibilities (short-term therapy, nonintensive therapy involving one or two contacts a week, the use of periods of "leave" from therapy, and so on) come in welcome contrast to the general tendency for psychoanalytic therapy to extend over longer periods of time without any compensatory reduction in frequency of contact.

The number of hours that Freud spent with a patient could originally be justified by Freud's need to learn more about unconscious phenomena and about the developmental process. Even so, many of Freud's

"disease" model of medicine is not only inappropriate when applied to problems of human adjustment, but is a significant hindrance to the development of effective psychotherapeutic techniques. We quote from the preface to his book:

> I became interested in writing this book approximately ten years ago when, having become established as a psychiatrist, I became increasingly impressed by the vague, capricious and generally unsatisfactory character of the widely used concept of mental illness and its corollaries, diagnosis, prognosis and treatment. It seemed to me that although the notion of mental illness made good *historical* sense— stemming as it does from the historical identity of medicine and psychiatry—it made no *rational* sense. Although mental illness might have been a useful concept in the nineteenth century, today it is scientifically worthless and socially harmful (41, p. ix).

In some respects Szasz may not go far enough in his criticism of the confusion involved in psychotherapeutic concepts. Not only is the concept of mental illness of questionable value, but the psychotherapist is often compelled to deal with one set of constructs in general psychology, other sets of constructs in dealing with the theory of psychopathology, still different constructs in the use of tests and projective devices, and another classificatory scheme when submitting a diagnosis. Yet he may have to resort to still another set of principles in determining how he will proceed in the psychotherapeutic process.

Concluding statement.   In concluding these all too brief comments we should like to make it clear again that our purpose has not been an unbiased or balanced survey of Neo-Freudian schools of thought. The reader who is interested in these points of view per se should by all means consult the various volumes referred to at the beginning of this section for more detailed and scholarly discussions of them. The points that have been selected for discussion here have been primarily those which have become emphasized in our thinking in ten years of intensive involvement with psychotherapy. More important, more characteristic, or more basic aspects of the work of each person discussed can readily be cited. The criterion that has determined this selection is nothing more scientifically respectable than what has proved useful or necessary in the process of conceptualizing the psychotherapeutic task. These are the concepts that will be referred to again in the chapters which follow, where there will be an attempt to show how they may be integrated with each other and with general psychological knowledge.

PSYCHOLOGICAL PSYCHOTHERAPIES

Introduction.   The list of persons trained in psychology who have become a part of the psychoanalytic movement and who have made significant contributions to psychoanalytic theory and technique is not inconsiderable. However, such of these as are relevant to our survey of psychotherapeutic theories have already been included in the preceding evaluations.

This section of the survey will be devoted to psychological approaches to psychotherapy in which the psychologist's emphasis is upon some theoretical or empirical formulation of a distinctly nonpsychoanalytic nature. In some instances the degree of rapprochement between the author's basic theoretical formulations and psychoanalysis is considerable, as is true of Dollard and Miller (10). In other instances, the psychologist is a firm opponent of the psychoanalytic approach to psychotherapy, as is Andrew Salter (41).

We shall state our own general evaluation in advance in order to explain our approach to this section of the chapter. It is our general conclusion that those psychological theorists who assiduously avoid any contamination of their approach with psychoanalytic concepts present us with theories which are conceptually "thin" and basically inadequate to the breadth of conceptualization which adequate psychotherapeutic practice requires. To put the matter on a more operational basis, we should balk at the task of attempting the comprehensive training of psychotherapists if the "rules of the game" prohibited us from utilizing concepts that originated in psychoanalysis.

This raises a delicate point concerning the implicit assumptions involved in psychological approaches to psychotherapy. Are we to assume that psychoanalytic concepts are included in a given approach unless specifically excluded or unless they are obviously incompatible with the writer's own concepts? Or are we to assume that psychoanalytic concepts are excluded unless specifically included? This is a matter about which we cannot always be sure, even concerning some theorists who are blatantly antipsychoanalytic in their explicit statements. It is certainly somewhat less than fair for a psychologist or any other theorist to blast psychoanalytic concepts in general and then to present a deviant point of view that is adequate as a basis for psychotherapeutic practice only if heavily bolstered by the very principles that the theorist has supposedly rejected. Unfortunately this type of two-facedness is not uncommon. Nor is it safe to assume the position that all psychologically trained theorists have produced theories or approaches to psychotherapy that are entirely consonant with good general principles of psychology.

What follows, therefore, will be much more a critique of theories than a review. On the positive side we shall try to recognize and point out ways in which psychological thinking has extended or improved the conceptual basis for psychotherapy. On the negative side, we shall be equally concerned to indicate where we believe the psychological approaches are restrictive or regressive so far as developing more adequate psychotherapeutic techniques is concerned.

Carl Rogers (43, 19).   The publication of Rogers' *Counseling and Psychotherapy* might be considered the beginning of modern psychological theories of psychotherapy. Certainly it impressed many upon its first appearance as a method of helping people which was based upon its own distinctive rationale and which thereby circumvented many of the practical restrictions of psychoanalytic therapy.

It was also soon apparent that this rationale was itself quite restricted and that nondirective therapy (the name under which Rogers' techniques first became widely known) was originally little more than a theory of psychotherapeutic communication. On the one hand, its use was limited to much the same kinds of persons with whom psychoanalysts could work, and on the other hand, it was not suitable for dealing with many of the kinds of difficulties which psychoanalysts considered treatable.

At a less tangible level there was something distinctly familiar about the "flavor" of the nondirective relationship as described and illustrated by Rogers. What was so reminiscent about it? Finally we realized that so far as one could tell from their respective accounts, the relationship aspect of the psychotherapeutic process was identical in Freudian and Rogerian procedures. The most obvious difference was in the nature of the communication from therapist to the person with whom he was working: Freud explicitly interpreted his patient's communications; Rogers did not.

Rogers, however, among all psychological theorists, best represents the experimental tradition in formulating hypotheses and subjecting them to experimental investigation. The clarity of his formulations has also permitted other investigators to do similar research quite independently of any theoretical affiliation with the Rogerian point of view. Both as a result of such research and as a result of the expansion of his own thinking, Rogers' theory as it stands today is a much more complete statement about the psychotherapeutic process than it was originally. Specifically, Rogers and his co-workers must be credited with significant contributions to thinking about the problem of communication in psychotherapy and about the problem of values. His value theory, in turn, relates both to the definition of the patient's role in psychotherapy and to the definition of psychotherapeutic goals.

Our present evaluation of Rogers' approach would be that all psychotherapy works (or should work) toward what we shall call a "Rogerian relationship." The essentials of such a relationship include maximum respect for the person as an individual and respect for his right to be the ultimate decider of his own destiny. They include acceptance of the person in terms of what he is rather than in terms of what the psychotherapist might want him to be. These essentials also include a role for the psychotherapist that is progressively less active and less directive as the patient establishes his own competence to direct the nature of his own adjustment.

We see many potential limitations to Rogers' theory as a general theory of psychotherapy (which, incidentally, Rogers has never alleged it to be). A truly general theory should provide a basis for conceptualizing and working with any and all types of functional maladjustments in persons of all ages, all educational levels, and all levels of intelligence. As valuable as Rogers' contributions have been, his theories and techniques as they have developed up to this point do not fit this definition of a general theory.

Frederick Thorne (44, 45).   Rogers' most trenchant and persistent critic outside of psychoanalytic circles has been Thorne, who has doctoral degrees in both medicine and psychology. Two points that Thorne makes are also characteristic of our own thinking. First, we agree with his criticisms of the limitations of the Rogerian approach. Second, he makes a good case for the most open-minded sort of eclecticism at this stage in the development of psychotherapy. Psychotherapy is not successful enough with a sufficiently heterogeneous group of persons and/or problems to warrant any premature closure of thinking on the subject.

Furthermore, it is difficult not to endorse his general thesis that the *responsibility* of the psychotherapist must be generally identical with that in all professional relationships involving "experts" on the one hand and those who come to them for assistance on the other. However, the extent or degree to which this responsibility includes specific "direction" of the patient is a matter to be determined by the patient's needs and best interests rather than a matter to be settled a priori by theoretical fiat.

As to our differences with Thorne, first, we distrust more explicitly than Thorne any sort of "cut-and-fit" eclecticism with respect to psychotherapeutic theory and technique. Our position is that while the psychotherapist may borrow as widely as he wishes in order to amass necessary concepts, he has certain responsibilities after he has completed his borrowing. He should, for example, develop an integration of his concepts that is self-consistent. He should attempt to develop a theoretical framework for his practice of psychotherapy that is not only self-consistent but is also general enough to be adequate for all psychotherapeutic situations. Furthermore, his theoretical framework should be sufficiently detailed (or have a definite potential for becoming detailed enough) to indicate both appropriate general strategies and specific therapeutic tactics in the psychotherapeutic situation.

Second, although we are fully in agreement with Thorne's emphasis upon efficiency in psychotherapy, we must agree with Rogers' reservations about the extent to which formal diagnostic procedures are an obstacle to the establishment of a therapeutic relationship and tend to give it shadings in which the psychotherapist's role becomes unduly identified with the role of the physician treating an organic disorder.

Dollard and Miller (10).   If the reader is aware that the intellectual environment of our graduate training was generally the same as that in which Dollard and Miller wrote *Personality and Psychotherapy*, he will not be surprised at any considerable overlap in viewpoints. As to the nature of that environment, it can best be summed up by a quotation from the preface to *Steps in Psychotherapy*: "The many imitators of the Institute [Institute of Human Relations, Yale University] have never reproduced its vital organs; its steady behavioral heart, its cultural lungs, its Freudian guts" (46, p. vii). The "steady behavioral heart" was supplied by the learning theory of Clark L. Hull, who was himself concerned with the question of what would be the appropriate "molar" level of postulates for an adequate theory of psychotherapy. (Hull, incidentally, concluded that the postulates of his own *Principles of Behavior* were too "molecular" for this purpose, that is, one should probably start with concepts that were more complex or general than simple habits.)

In spite of Hull's opinion on this matter, Dollard and Miller have succeeded in translating a large part of Freudian theory into the constructs of Hull's learning theory. While such a translation leaves Dollard and Miller at variance with Freud on some points, their efforts clearly indicate that most of psychoanalysis is indirectly relatable, via Hullian constructs, to a vast amount of experimental research and is, on many points, in agreement with the results of such research. This is an implication that has been largely ignored both by psychoanalysts and by experimental psychologists.

Because of the care that Dollard and Miller have shown in trying to represent Freudian psychoanalysis faithfully and accurately, it is possible to say that the limitations of their expressed position are very much the same as the limitations of psychoanalysis, with some minor and a few major exceptions. In their work to date Dollard and Miller have failed to realize fully many of the implications for psychotherapeutic technique that we see as inherent in any realization of the basically "learning" nature of the psychotherapeutic process.

Julian Rotter (12). Rotter is identified also with the learning theory approach to psychotherapy. However, his basic frame of reference, apart from learning theory, is that of clinical psychology generally rather than psychoanalysis specifically. In this more general frame of reference he considers such problems as communication (both within the psychotherapeutic process and about the psychotherapeutic process), the evaluation and description of personality, the nature of psychological therapy, and so on.

We consider one of Rotter's most valuable contributions to be his rather detailed analysis of motivation and reinforcement. These he examines from the viewpoint of learning theory, but also, and more importantly, from the viewpoint of psychotherapy. This results in conceptualizations that appear definitely more sophisticated and more appropriate to the task of psychotherapy than the comparable ideas of Dollard and Miller.

In spite of the value of certain aspects of Rotter's efforts to use the principles of learning in an understanding and formulation of the psychotherapeutic process, we believe that the possibilities of such an approach are, at present, far from exhausted. In fact we would say that no more than the most tentative of beginnings has been made in this direction. Those who might be tempted to follow this path could do worse than to consider Hull's advice, which was, in effect, "think bigger."

George Bach (47). Bach has consistently been one of the more exploratory and creative psychologists associated with group therapy. His work has stimulated much thinking about roles and relationships in the psychotherapeutic situation, and he has also been continuously aware of and concerned with affective interactions in psychotherapy at a much more complex level than the transference interpretations of most psychoanalysts.

In line with thinking for which Bach has been at least partially responsible, psychotherapists are now beginning to pay more attention to the rules governing relationships. Since there are certain analogies between such implicit rules and the rules of games, the rather unfortunate designation of "game theory" is often used to describe this area of interest.

Our own indebtedness to Bach includes a theory of motivation which differs sharply from Freud's theory of sublimation but which works together very well with Rotter's "expectancy" theory. Roughly stated, motivation for creative or other productive efforts is thought of as being determined by how well such efforts have been rewarded or reinforced in the person's previous experience. Bach believes that the productive person must be adequately rewarded (in terms of personal satisfactions) for his efforts if he is to sustain a favorable work attitude. This means that if such reinforcement does not occur spontaneously, the person who wants to remain creative or productive must see to his own rewards. This, in turn, dictates the importance of maintaining sufficient awareness of one's own real needs and desires. Depending upon what these are, one must then make the necessary efforts to establish the necessary preconditions for personal gratification, including the expenditure of time, money, and effort for this purpose.

Albert Ellis (48).   It would be difficult to ignore the influence of Albert Ellis on nonpsychoanalytic psychotherapy by virtue of the sheer bulk of his contributions, even if there were no more basic reasons to recommend him to the attention of the reader. Fortunately there are such reasons.

Ellis can be grouped with Fromm as a critic of conformity as the goal of psychotherapy. This, in turn, has not only opened the door to the consideration and definition of other objectives but has even served to force such consideration upon those who have become thoughtful about this matter.

Ellis is at least as staunch an advocate of an active and directive role for the psychotherapist as is Thorne. In certain respects he goes even further than Thorne in suggesting that effectiveness in therapy sometimes warrants a direct attack upon some of the patient's beliefs. In spite of this flexibility in considering and defining the psychotherapist's role, Ellis reaches much the same conclusion as the most orthodox psychoanalysts as to who are suitable "candidates" for psychotherapy. We would suggest that this preference represents an undue restriction in viewpoint and indicates a familiar predilection for patients with well-established intellectual orientations and communicative skills.

Ellis places much of his attention and concern on the significance of the symbolic cognitive responses that the patient makes implicitly. Ellis believes that what the patient thinks, believes, or tells himself about himself and his world has considerable significance in determining his behavior. We agree with Ellis that this is an aspect of the patient's functioning that most psychotherapists minimize to the detriment of their effectiveness in helping the patient.

Where Ellis most thoroughly parts company not only with psychoanalysis but also with much of experimental psychology is in his postulations concerning the relationship between cognitive processes and emotional response. Quite bluntly and insistently Ellis contends that what the patient feels depends upon what he thinks. This is certainly anti-thetical to the position assumed by all schools of psychoanalysis, since they maintain that one of Freud's principal contributions to psychology was to establish the extent to which human reactions occur quite inde-pendently of or even in direct contradiction to his thoughts and beliefs. Freud was also careful to establish the point that this is true not only of persons with problems but also for mankind in general.

Other psychological approaches.   We have attempted to review briefly and to evaluate in the foregoing paragraphs what we consider to be the most significant efforts of psychologists to form theories of psychotherapy upon bases distinctly different from the fundamental assumptions of psy-choanalytic theories. Our purpose has been primarily to orient the reader with respect to similarities and differences between these viewpoints and the ones which will be presented in the remainder of this book.

Through inadvertence we may have omitted some points of view that should have been included. However, some, such as Salter's (49) and Wolpe's (50), which center around learning theory, have not been discussed separately because of our opinion that they are more limited than (and can readily be subsumed under) general theories such as Dollard and Miller's and Rotter's.

We have ignored, except for Bach, perhaps more than we should have the contributions of group psychotherapy and psychodrama. Our impression, however, has been that with the exception noted most of the psychotherapists involved in group practice have been preoccupied with the problem of adapting the theories of individual psychotherapies to the situation of dealing with a group. This cannot be said of the development of psychodrama by Moreno, and the excuse for not devoting more time to his work is that it is somewhat peripheral to our central interests.

We shall mention now Wendell Johnson's (51) valuable services in helping to forge some of the final links between general semantics and an explicit theory of psychotherapy. We shall have an opportunity later in this book to express our appreciation also of Johnson's predecessors, the founder of the general semantics movement Alfred Korzybski and its most literate American representative S. I. Hayakawa.

Finally, we should like to acknowledge the contributions of Bram-mer and Shostrom (52) and Wolberg (53) in providing almost encyclo-pedic compilations of many diverse and specific aspects of psychotherapy in systematic and orderly treatises. These are excellent reference books and are recommended to all those who may experience feelings of distress because of any lack of documentation or specificity in this book.

SUMMARY

The introduction indicated that our purpose is to present an outline of psychotherapeutic theory and practice which is based upon principles of general psychology.

We then examined Freud's training and his development of psychoanalysis in order to show that psychoanalysis is based upon psychological principles which were—and which, to a considerable extent, remain—distinct and separate from principles of psychology based upon experimentation and scientific research. We also noted that Freud was possibly *not* primarily interested in psychoanalysis as a psychotherapy and that he was not notably sanguine regarding its therapeutic effectiveness.

In evaluating Freud's theories we reached the following conclusions. Of Freud's motivational theories only his pleasure principle can readily be fitted into general psychology. This principle appears to coincide with Throndike's "law of effect" and with reinforcement theory generally. We are in general agreement with Freud's developmental theory as far as it goes, but disagree regarding the reality of a sexual latency period. Also we accord considerably more importance to the "pre-Oedipal" years of early infancy. Freud was an excellent observer and reporter of learning processes and phenomena in the psychotherapeutic process, even though his use of his own distinctive nomenclature has tended to obscure this aspect of his work. As to Freud's structural theories of personality, we can agree with these except for his id concept, but find some need to redefine ego and superego.

Among those who parted from Freudian psychoanalysis before 1940, Adler, Rank, and Horney represent important additional aspects of development that pose a marked challenge to the individual's ability to adjust. These center around inferiority feelings, dependency needs, and problems of handling hostility, respectively. Jung was among the first, but by no means the last, to differ fundamentally with Freud on the sexual aspects of his motivational theory. Klein (and Anna Freud) extended psychotherapeutic techniques into the years of childhood and stressed the significance of very early emotional trauma. Reich indicated that the total "character structure" of the patient is his problem, so that it is impossible to deal with "the problem" as an isolated entity.

Among the later Neo-Freudians Fromm represents the social critic who discusses the "sick" aspects of society as well as the "sick" aspects of the individual's attempts to adjust to society. Franz Alexander has worked for greater efficiency and flexibility in psychotherapeutic techniques. Rosen has presented drastic new departures in means of communicating with and relating to the patient. Szasz has finally separated psychotherapy from the model presented by the medical treatment of organic conditions. Harry Stack Sullivan has presented a theoretical orientation that differs markedly from psychoanalytic thinking on certain points regarding both the therapeutic relationship and therapeutic communication, at least so far as emphasis is concerned.

In the field of psychological theories of psychotherapy, our basic identification is with the learning-theory–psychoanalytic orientation of Dollard and Miller. However, both their theory and their technique share most of the limitations of traditional psychoanalysis. Rotter's extension of the learning-theory viewpoint is, therefore, a welcome addition to the work of Dollard and Miller. We value especially his orientation toward motivation and reinforcement, but also his extension of clinical thinking into personality theory, communication theory, and so on.

On the directive–nondirective issue, we support the directive viewpoints of Albert Ellis and Frederick Thorne as being necessary for the widest possible application of psychotherapy. However, Rogers has done an excellent job of defining certain basic attitudes and values for the psychotherapist and of indicating the nature of the therapeutic interaction at a terminal stage. Beyond these points we have differences of opinion with all three members of this group. George Bach has made useful contributions to motivational theory and to transactional analysis.

Generally we have found psychological theories to lack both the theoretical scope and the flexibility in technique that we believe psychology has to offer to the field of psychotherapy.

SUGGESTIONS FOR FURTHER READING

The references which have been made in this chapter and which are listed below should provide the reader who has unlimited time or specialized interests with an adequate entree to the literature on psychotherapy. For the reader who does not have unlimited time in which to pursue this subject, the four books listed below should be considered first as supplementation to our own efforts.

Harper (22). An excellent and intelligent summary of Freudian, Neo-Freudian, and psychological theories of psychotherapy.

Thompson (5). Supplements Harper on Freudian and Neo-Freudian theories and gives a clear picture of the reasons for contemporary developments in psychoanalysis.

Dollard and Miller (10) *and Rotter* (12). Much of what we would otherwise have to say has already been said in these two books. We suggest that they be read either prior to or parallel with the remaining chapters of this book.

REFERENCES

*1. Puner, H. W. *Freud, his life and his mind.* New York: Dell Publishing Co., 1959.

*2. Jones, E. *The life and work of Sigmund Freud* (Abridged). New York: Doubleday, 1963. (Originally in three volumes, New York: Basic Books, 1953, 1955, 1957.)

*3. Zilboorg, G. *Sigmund Freud.* New York: Grove Press, 1960. (Scribner, 1951.)

4. Sears, R. R. Experimental studies of psychoanalytic phenomena. In Hunt, J. McV. (Ed.), *Personality and the behavior disorders.* New York: Ronald, 1944.

*5. Thompson, C. *Psychoanalysis: evolution and development.* New York: Grove Press, 1957. (Nelson, 1950.)

*6. Freud, S. *The origins of psychoanalysis.* New York: Doubleday, 1957. (Basic Books, 1954.)

7. Freud, S. *Collected papers.* New York: Basic Books, 1959. (These are available as of 1963 in a series of 10 Collier paperbacks.)

8. Dollard, J., Doob, L. W., Miller, N. E. and Sears, R. R. *Frustration and aggression.* New Haven, Conn.: Yale University Press, 1939.

*9. Klein, M. *The psychoanalysis of children.* New York: Evergreen, 1960. (London: Hogarth.)

10. Dollard, J., and Miller, N. E. *Personality and psychotherapy.* New York: McGraw-Hill, 1950.

11. Hull, C. L. *Principles of behavior.* New York: Appleton, 1943.

12. Rotter, J. *Social learning and clinical psychology.* Englewood Cliffs, N.J.: Prentice-Hall, 1954.

*13. Whyte, L. L. *The unconscious before Freud.* New York: Doubleday, 1962.

*14. Murray, H. A. *Explorations in personality.* New York: Science Editions, 1962. (New York: Oxford, 1938.)

15. Sherif, M., and Cantril, H. *The psychology of ego-involvements.* New York: Wiley, 1947.

16. Murphy, G. *Personality.* New York: Harper and Row, 1947.

17. Lewin, K. *A dynamic theory of personality.* New York: McGraw-Hill, 1945. (Also available in paperback.)

18. Murphy, G. *Historical introduction to modern psychology* (Rev. Ed.). New York: Harcourt, 1949.

19. Rogers, C. R. *On becoming a person.* Boston: Houghton Mifflin, 1961.

20. Buhler, C., *et al. Values in psychotherapy.* New York: Free Press, 1962.

21. Sheldon, W. H. *The varieties of temperament.* New York: Harper & Row, 1942.

*22. Harper, R. A. *Psychoanalysis and psychotherapy: 36 systems.* New York: Spectrum, 1959.

*23. Mullahy, P. *Oedipus: myth and complex.* New York: Evergreen, 1955. (Hermitage House, 1948).

24. Blum, G. S. *Psychoanalytic theories of personality.* New York: McGraw-Hill, 1953.

25. Munroe, R. L. *Schools of psychoanalytic thought.* New York: Holt, Rinehart and Winston, 1955.

26. Rank, O. *The trauma of birth.* New York: Harcourt, 1929.

27. Adler, A. *Understanding human nature.* Philadelphia: Chilton, 1927.

28. Jacobi, J. *The psychology of Jung.* New Haven Conn.: Yale University Press, 1943. (Also available in paperback.)

29. Horney, K. *The neurotic personality of our time.* New York: Norton, 1937.

30. Horney, K. *New ways in psychoanalysis.* New York: Norton. 1939.

31. Guntrip, H. *Personality structure and human interaction.* New York: International Universities Press, 1961.

32. Carmichael, L. *Manual of child psychology.* (2d ed.). New York: Wiley, 1954.

33. Sullivan, H. S. *The interpersonal theory of psychiatry.* New York: Norton, 1953.

34. Sullivan, H. S. *The psychiatric interview.* New York: Norton, 1954.

35. Fromm, E. *Man for himself.* New York: Holt, Rinehart and Winston, 1947.

36. Alexander, F. and French, T. E. *Psychoanalytic therapy.* New York: Ronald, 1946.

*37. Reich, W. *Character-analysis.* New York: Noonday, 1962.

*38. Rieff, P. *Freud: the mind of the moralist.* New York: Doubleday, 1961. (Viking, 1959.)

39. Freud, A. *The ego and the mechanisms of defense.* London: Hogarth, 1937.

40. Rosen, J. *Direct analysis.* New York: Grune & Stratton, 1953.

41. Szasz, T. S. *The myth of mental illness.* New York: Harper & Row, 1961.

*42. Salter, A. *The case against psychoanalysis.* New York: Citadel, 1963.

43. Rogers, C. R. *Counseling and psychotherapy*. Boston: Houghton Mifflin, 1942.

44. Thorne, F. *Principles of personality counseling*. Brandon, Vt.: Journal of Clinical Psychology, 1950.

45. Thorne, F. Directive and eclectic personality counseling. In McCrary, J. L., and Sheer, D. E., *Six approaches to psychotherapy*. New York: Holt, Rinehart and Winston, 1955.

46. Dollard, J., Auld, F., Jr., and White, A. M. *Steps in psychotherapy*. New York: Macmillan, 1953.

47. Bach, G. R. *Intensive group psychotherapy*. New York: Ronald, 1954.

48. Ellis, A. *Reason and emotion in psychotherapy*. New York: Lyle Stuart, 1962.

*49. Salter, A. *Conditioned reflex therapy*. New York: Capricorn, 1961.

50. Wolpe, J. *Psychotherapy by reciprocal inhibition*. Stanford, Calif.: Stanford University Press, 1958.

51. Johnson, W. *People in quandaries*. New York: Harper & Row, 1946.

52. Brammer, L. M., and Shostrom, E. L. *Therapeutic psychology*. Englewood Cliffs, N.J.: Prentice-Hall, 1960.

53. Wolberg, L. R. *The technique of psychotherapy*. New York: Grune & Stratton, 1954.

*Denotes paperback edition. In most instances paperback editions have been listed in preference to hard-bound in the interests of economy to the reader. Information regarding original editions is given in parentheses after such entries.

Chapter 2 | *Emotion: Theory*

GENERAL THEORETICAL ORIENTATION

The nature of psychotherapy. A basic objective of psychotheraphy is to change the habit structure of a person so that his behavior will result in more pleasant and fewer unpleasant experiences.

The means by which changes in habit structure are achieved is a communicative relationship between two or more persons. In order to effect the desired changes in the habit structure of the person seeking help, it is necessary to establish an *effective* communicative relationship. This means that we must permit the patient to communicate in any way that is possible for him, making due allowance for limitations related to age, intelligence, education, verbal facility, habitual inhibitions regarding communication, and the transient disruption of communicative skills due to intense emotional reactions. We must in turn communicate with the patient in terms and by means that are meaningful (convey our communicative intent or achieve our communicative purpose) to him.

A psychotherapeutic relationship can therefore be established with any person with whom it is possible to establish an effective communicative relationship. The limitations involved in any particular situation will be a joint function of the communicative limitations of the patient and the communicative limitations of the psychotherapist.

The communicative responses of the patient to the psychotherapist are primarily important as the means by which the psychotherapist becomes aware of the habit structure of the patient (and also aware of changes in habit structure as such changes occur). The communicative responses of the patient may therefore be defined as any behavior, verbal or otherwise, that has "meaning" for the psychotherapist in terms of elucidating the habit structure of the patient.

The changes in habit structure that may be produced involve the addition of new habits, the elimination of existing habits, and changes in the relationship or integration of existing habits. Four conditions are necessary for any of these changes to occur. First, an appropriate condition of motivation for the change must exist. Second, the patient must have cues or signals indicating the nature of the response to be learned and when the response should be made. Third, the patient must make the desired response himself. Fourth, the making of the response must be followed by more pleasant, or a lesser intensity of unpleasant, feelings.

The communicative means that the psychotherapist has available for creating these necessary conditions for learning may be conceived as generally or as broadly as desired, subject only to limitations of moral or ethical considerations. The use of chemical substances or physical energy (such as electricity) as means of communicating or establishing communication is limited by law to persons having competent medical qualifications.

The psychological means for motivating and reinforcing (rewarding) new responses in psychotherapy are the arousal of appropriate attitudes and feelings by means of communication. In this respect psychotherapy operates on the basis of the same principles that are applicable to both education and propaganda. Psychotherapy is distinguishable from education primarily in that the ultimate objective of education is the thinking and behavior of the person affected, whereas the ultimate objectives of psychotherapy are the feeling states that result from thinking and behavior. Psychotherapy is distinguished from propaganda in that the propagandist changes the thinking and behavior of others primarily for his own benefit, whereas the benefit of others is the prime objective of the psychotherapist, whose own "gain" is the fee that he receives for his services plus the satisfaction of performing his professional function adequately.

An evaluation of psychoanalytic objectives.   In order to clarify the relationship between psychotherapy in general and psychoanalysis, as the original and predominant professional form of psychotherapy, in particular, we should like to consider and evaluate three stated objectives of psychoanalytic therapy.

Freud's original conceptualization of the reasons for the beneficial effect of a psychotherapeutic relationship was that this relationship provided the patient with an opportunity for catharsis. Psychotherapeutic catharsis may be defined as the expression of feelings or the discharge of emotions through or during the process of communication. Catharsis may also result from the verbal expression or behavioral "acting out" of feelings when no other person is involved, but such solitary behavior is not included in our definition of psychotherapy.

Freud's theory of catharsis was based on the assumption that feelings or emotions could become "bound" to certain ideas. Unless these ideas were expressed in some way, the affect which was bound to them remained stored up within the individual and created further disturbance of feeling, thinking, and behavior.

The psychologist is unable to conceive of any mechanism or process by means of which feelings can be "stored." The psychotherapeutic patient is often or usually tense and unhappy. The psychologist assumes that his tension is the result of existing inhibitory habits that result in the suppression of motivated responses. The "unhappiness" may be partly associated with the unpleasant feeling aspects of tension states, but basically it is due to the fact that conflict or inhibition prevents the individual from satisfying significant needs.

"Catharsis" from this point of view is the result of changing the relative strengths of conflicting motives so that some response can be made. The ability to talk about matters associated with strong feelings and the ability to express the feelings themselves in the presence of another person is reassuring to the inhibited person. The acceptance of such verbalizations and emotional expressions by another person (the psychotherapist) may encourage the patient to express his own inner experiences, states, and feelings more fully to others outside the therapeutic situation. If this happens, and if such behavior on the patient's part improves his ability to satisfy his needs, then catharsis is "therapeutic." For some patients such a learning experience is necessary. It is seldom, if ever, sufficient in and of itself to guarantee a more satisfactory adjustment for the patient. It is usually most useful as part of a general program to improve the adequacy, accuracy, and appropriateness of the patient's communication with others.

Freud's further development of psychoanalysis led to lengthy reconstructions of the patient's developmental history with subsequent insight into the relationship between earlier experiences and the contemporary functioning of the patient. This development occurred primarily in the period between 1890 and 1900. During this period Freud undertook a self-analysis, using his dreams as a primary means of access to aspects of his own cognitive processes of which he was not normally or usually aware. The integration of this information with Freud's memory of past experiences and his knowledge of present desires, impulses, and behavior gave Freud new insights into the causal relationships between past experiences and present functioning.

It was these insights that formed the basis for Freud's psychoanalytic psychology. As to the therapeutic effect of such insights so far as patients are concerned, we surmise that knowing more about the principles governing his own functioning is of some (perhaps considerable) value to the patient in making decisions about future actions.

Such knowledge may also relieve the patient of some tendency to condemn himself for being as he is. Since such self-condemnation seldom serves any constructive purpose and may be closely associated with unpleasant feelings of depression and with low morale, this function of insight can usually be regarded as beneficial or therapeutic in an emotional sense.

The value of insight in altering subsequent adjustment depends upon the presence or absence of the conditions necessary for learning, such as adequate motivation, suitable reinforcement, and changes in the actual responses that the patient makes. From this point of view insight is primarily useful as a cue to which type of response might lead to more useful or gratifying results than have followed upon the patient's established habitual responses.

We can therefore regard insight as potentially useful, but as neither sufficient nor necessary to modifications of the patient's behavior in a psychotherapeutic situation. In such a situation, it is only *necessary* that the psychotherapist be adequately acquainted with cause-effect relationships in personality formation and reformation. In self-analysis such insight is, of course, a necessary but not a sufficient condition of behavioral reformation.

Freud's final formulation on psychotherapeutic technique stressed the importance of "working through the transference neurosis." This was based upon the assumption (with which, incidentally, psychologists are in agreement) that the patient transfers (the psychologist would say "generalizes") to the psychotherapeutic relationship responses that he has already learned in previous life experiences. In this sense the patient reacts to the therapist as if he were the same as other persons the patient has known. The "transference neurosis" described by Freud has certain characteristics in common with what both the layman and the social psychologist label as "prejudices." Like prejudices the transference neurosis involves certain expectations about what others are like and how they will react. The patient has certain attitudes toward the psychotherapist on the basis of these prejudgments, and he governs his own behavior in the psychotherapeutic relationship according to these attitudes and his expectancies concerning the therapist's response to his behavior. The neurotic aspect of the patient's behavior is that neither the attitudes nor the expectancies may correspond with or be justified by the actual behavior of the psychotherapist.

Working through the transference neurosis may therefore be generally equated with eliminating the patient's prejudices about the psychotherapist. This, of course, involves real changes in the patient's established habits of both thinking and feeling. If we could assume that the elimination of prejudices toward the psychotherapist left the patient free of prejudice in all relationships, then we could certainly expect that his reactions to others would gradually become more realistic. There are two problems here, however. The first is that the assumption involved is not only questionable but improbable in terms of learning theory. The second problem is that even if the assumption were correct, we would need to make a number of other assumptions in order to conclude that "working through the transference neurosis" is both a necessary *and* a sufficient condition for satisfactory psychotherapy. These other necessary assumptions may be summarized in the proposition that lack of transference responses is the only condition required for adequate or satisfactory adjustment. This proposition, however, hardly sounds reasonable.

Suggestions for a theory of psychotherapy.   We suggest that the basic formulations for psychotherapy must deal with the four concepts which we have already mentioned as critical for habit formation or habit reformation: motivation, cue, response, and reinforcement. If we adopt this frame of reference, we can then assign insight to the general category of cues determining the nature of response. The value of insight now becomes obvious: more accurate and detailed cues, more appropriate response. However, there still remain the problems of motivating response, getting the *patient* to make the appropriate response and providing (initially, at least) adequate reinforcement to ensure the continuation of the more appropriate response.

It is, of course, highly important for the psychotherapist to know in detail all aspects of the conditions and dynamics of development: genetics, maturation, the mores of the social environment, the social training methods and values of different social classes, and the nature of human beings of various ages and abilities as perceiving, integrating, and reacting organisms. Here the combined insights of psychoanalysis, psychology, sociology, and cultural anthropology are no more than adequate. *Some* of this information may be conveyed to the patient or some of his ideas about these matters may have to be changed as a part of the psychotherapeutic process.

The *most convenient* access to the patient's habit structure may be via verbal communication. However, the psychotherapist may for any of various reasons prefer to (or be forced to) resort to nonverbal means of communication. One may also for any of various reasons choose to bypass the patient's "conscious" experience altogether in either motivating, cueing, or reinforcing his behavior.

Such possibilities if utilized may pre-empt "control" of the course of psychotherapy from the patient and place it in the hands of the psychotherapist. It is therefore of extreme importance that the psychotherapist have no strong personal need to control others. There are two reasons for this requirement. First, the psychotherapist should respect the right of the patient to control his own behavior so long as he exerts such control without manifest danger to himself or to others. Second, one criterion of successful psychotherapy (for adults) is the ability of the patient to function satisfactorily without such external control or guidance. Therefore, at some point, he *must* be given an opportunity to decide upon his own goals and to determine his own course of action.

In the pages to follow we shall present an outline of a theoretical approach to psychotherapy that, we believe, is capable of encompassing all of the conceptions we consider necessary to effective psychotherapy. We shall not, in what is essentially an introduction or a conceptual framework, be able to present all the necessary concepts in detail. Rather, we have chosen the alternative of presenting the framework and certain key concepts, then of illustrating the use of these concepts in evaluating and dealing with problems of psychotherapy.

FEELINGS, EMOTIONS, AND MOTIVATION

Feelings and motivation.   The area of motivation is one in which there is much theoretical sound and fury among psychologists. Behaviorists, for example, go to great lengths to define motivation in objective, rather than subjective, terms. In Hull's *Principles of Behavior* "drive" is clearly defined as an intervening variable or theoretical construct. Only C_D, "the objectively observable phenomena determining the drive" (1, p. 383), can be specified.

Actually, the detailed study of "drives," such as hunger, lead to considerable complication in the concept. It would be simplest to define "primary drives," such as hunger, in terms of basic survival needs. If, however, a dog which has been without food for twenty-four hours is fed food that does not go into his stomach, but instead drops into a pan through an opening in the esophagus, the dog eats much as he would if the food were going into his stomach where it would "do him some good" in terms of his primary need for food. It seems rather obvious then that the dog's feeding behavior is probably controlled, at least in part, by sensory stimulation in the oral-lingual regions. Researches on thirst and other primary needs or drives lead us to roughly the same conclusion (2).

Now, if we do not mind being subjective for a moment, this finding should not be too surprising. We have all had the experience of sitting down to a large Thanksgiving dinner feeling ravenous for our first bite of turkey. However, the third helping of turkey is somehow not nearly so delicious as the first. We thereupon declare ourselves "full of turkey" and decline further servings. Yet, while we may be literally "full" far beyond the point of any legitimate survival need for food, we usually manage to pack in a piece of pumpkin pie with whipped cream on top of the turkey and refuse a second piece of pumpkin pie in order to try a sliver of the mince pie.

Why are we "hungry for" the pumpkin pie when we cannot eat any more turkey, and why do we enjoy the mince pie when we are sated with pumpkin pie? We lose our taste for one, yet enjoy the taste of the other. One is no longer pleasant to eat; the other still is. In other words, our behavior is controlled immediately and directly not by "survival needs" or "primary drives," but by the simple experience of less pleasant versus more pleasant.

Kurt Lewin (3) cut through many complex issues in motivation theory by illustrating that, for many practical purposes, motivation can be represented by valences (plus or minus, representing approach or avoidance impulses) and by vectors (arrows representing the directionality of these impulses with respect to environmental objects). This conceptualization seems quite adequate for the psychotherapist's purpose and has the added advantage of being easily integratable with other basic concepts that the psychotherapist needs and uses. We shall now proceed to a fuller exposition of this position.

Feelings and emotion.   Every student of psychology is familiar with Watson's description of three basic and innate patterns of emotional response in the newborn infant, namely: fear, rage, and love. The critics of Watson's conclusions tend to prefer the formulation of K. M. B. Bridges that the first emotion shown by the child is simply an undifferentiated excitement. Before the child is three months old, however, distress and excitement patterns are clearly distinguishable from each other, and a third pattern called delight can be distinguished from the other two. According to Bridges' schema, patterns representative of anger, fear, and disgust become differentiated from the distress pattern sometime between the third and sixth months of infancy.

Stratton presents a conceptualization of emotion generally that utilizes two dimensions of analysis, one dimension being defined in terms of "pleasant–unpleasant" and the other dimension being defined in terms of "differentiated–undifferentiated." (The significant aspect of this theory for our purpose is Stratton's ability to define our three reference emotions, anger, fear, and love, with respect to a pleasant–unpleasant continuum; the differentiated–undifferentiated dimension is incidental to our concern.) Stratton places *anger* in a neutral position with respect to "pleasantness–unpleasantness." He places *fear* on the "unpleasant" side of this continuum and *affection* on the "pleasant" side. (These three theories are conveniently summarized and evaluated by P. T. Young [4].)

Before we attempt to draw any conclusions of our own, we should also like to point out that psychoanalytic theorists have always been concerned with our same three reference emotions. Freud dealt with concepts quite similar to the three emotions of love, fear, and anger. Both his motivational theory of "sexuality" and his definition of "the pleasure principle" can be generally equated with "love" in the general sense in which the term is used here. In the "death instinct" of Freud's later writings we find a concept related to anger, and the Freudian correlate of fear would of course be "anxiety." Theodore Reik and Erich Fromm, among others, have dealt with the theme of love from Freudian or Neo-Freudian points of view. Horney has emphasized the problem of hostility or anger. Anxiety is a common concern of all psychotherapists, regardless of their theoretical differences.

Definitions.   Now, where are we? On the one hand, we seem to have three key or reference emotions, which we shall call love, fear, and anger. Whether all are present at birth or not, all are apparent very early in life. Together or separately these three emotions represent fundamental concepts (and, in a sense, fundamental problems) for any theory of psychotherapy, past, present, or future. So far as "motivation" is concerned, however, we have suggested that motivation is basically a two-way matter, involving only the distinction between unpleasant and pleasant feelings. How do we correlate three emotions with two feelings (pleasant–unpleasant), and how do we correlate both emotions and feelings with the valence-vector motivational theory of Lewin?

A solution to this dilemma is suggested by the Yale studies of frustration and aggression. The conclusion reached by these studies is that aggression in one form or another is the universal response to frustration (5). This enables us to integrate our motivational and emotional concepts by definition. We shall define "love" in terms of pleasant feelings and the impulse to approach some object in the environment. "Fear" is defined in terms of unpleasant feelings and the impulse to avoid. "Anger" is the emotion associated with the thwarting or blocking of movement toward or away from an object, and the correlated impulse would be to attack the source of frustration (or barrier, in Lewinian terminology).

Let us explain why we have gone to all this trouble to isolate three reference emotions, to relate these emotions by definition to feelings (pleasant–unpleasant), and to relate these feelings in turn to motivation. We have already stated our conviction that psychotherapy is essentially a learning process for the patient and that motivation (and reinforcement) are two of the conditions essential for learning. The motivational concerns and concepts of experimental psychology are much too complicated and unwieldy for the psychotherapist. The motives of the patient are seldom clearly manifest in the psychotherapeutic situation, nor are they subject to ready evocation by the psychotherapist. What the therapist soon comes to know much about are the emotions of the patient, his fears, his angers, and his desires. We have been attempting to show that these emotions always involve feelings (pleasant–unpleasant) which are also involved in motivation, and that emotions further fit the (Lewinian) definition of motivation by having valence and vector aspects or attributes.

In the section which follows we shall indicate that the feeling aspect of emotion will also serve the psychotherapist's needs for means of reinforcing or rewarding the patient's responses. We shall also discuss the intimate association between motivation and reinforcement.

Motivation and reinforcement.   Classical reinforcement theory as represented by Thorndike's "law of effect" and the more recent reinforcement theory of Hull (1) has been challenged by research, which seems to indicate that an "expectancy" factor is closely related to motivated behavior, even in animals. Some of the relevant research and a critical evaluation of the problem is presented by Hilgard (6). Rotter has found it desirable (or necessary) to include the construct of expectancy among the basic concepts that he uses in his approach to psychotherapy.

A quotation from Hilgard will help to clarify the problem for the reader who is not acquainted with this background.

> One of the earliest and most striking observations on reward-expectancy was that of Tinklepaugh (1928). In his experiment, food was placed under one of two containers while the monkey was looking. Later the monkey was permitted to choose between the containers, and showed skill in choosing correctly. The behavior which is pertinent here occurred when, after a banana had been hidden under one of the cups, the experimenter substituted a lettuce leaf (a less preferred food). The monkey rejected the lettuce leaf and engaged in definite searching behavior (6, p. 266).

In terms of the simplest and most straight-forward principles of motivation and reinforcement, this behavior is difficult to explain. The monkey was hungry (therefore, supposedly motivated). The lettuce was food which the monkey would normally eat and which would supposedly reduce his "hunger" motivation. Therefore, it should have been an adequate reinforcement for the monkey's response of finding the proper cup. In other words, according to behavioristic theories of motivation and reward, the monkey should have eaten the lettuce, instead of throwing it away and looking for the banana.

Our conclusion from this and other experiments of a similar nature, as well as our conclusion from clinical experience, is that it is impossible to define motivation per se. Rather, motivation can only be defined relative to a particular incentive or expected reward. In the experiment cited, the monkey reacts to a reduction in incentive as if he were not being rewarded, although he is presumably still hungry and the lettuce is edible.

Motivational theory.   Now let us see if we can put all of these considerations together into a theory of motivation that will fit the needs of the psychotherapist.

We believe that the problem of motivation-incentive can be handled adequately for purposes of psychotherapeutic theory and practice by assuming that a person tends to make those responses which, in his past experience, have been associated with a change from a less pleasant to a more pleasant affective state or experience. Conversely, a person tends to avoid making those responses which, in his past experience, have been associated with a change from a more pleasant to a less pleasant affective state or experience. He will not respond or "move" in any direction when there is no valence differential. We assume here that "valence" is determined by the person's innate affective reactions as modified by his life experience.

We agree with Rotter (7) and Lewin (3) that expectancy includes a definite element of subjective probability. What we mean by this is that what is critical in determining a person's behavior is his estimation of what the outcome will probably be. As Rotter indicates, this may be only loosely related to real or objective probability, as determined, for example, by scientific or experimental procedures. To illustrate: The psychotherapist may consider it rather probable that if his patient should ask a girl whom the patient knows and has discussed with the therapist for a date, the girl would accept. The patient may consider this highly *improbable*. However, the patient's estimate may be based on his own experience at an earlier time when he was less attractive and when the girls he asked were more rejecting than this girl seems to be. It is now up to the psychotherapist to help the patient to modify the probability element in his "expectancy" regarding acceptance or rejection.

We conclude on this point that motivation for a particular kind of behavior is based upon the person's anticipation of a certain increase in pleasant feelings or a certain decrease in unpleasant feelings *and that this anticipation also involves a probability factor*. In a complete formulation we must also include the fact that obtaining the incentive involves, at the least, some effort. It may also involve other possibilities of an increase in unpleasant feelings or a decrease in pleasant feelings for other reasons besides the effort involved. In the example of the man asking for a date, the probability or possibility of rejection (which would be unpleasant) is a significant counter-motivation that tends to inhibit the response of asking.

Finally, we must conclude that "reinforcement" can only be defined relative to expectancy. If a person experiences less of an increase in intensity of pleasant feeling than he expected to follow upon a given response, he may act as if "less than expected" is not a rewarding or positively reinforcing condition. Positive reinforcement, or reward, can only consist then of an increase in pleasant feelings which is equal to or greater than the increase that the person has expected.

Motivation and work attitude.   According to Gregory Zilboorg, when Freud was once asked what he considered the ultimate criterion of being normal, he answered: *"Arbeiten und lieben"*—to work and to love (8). Freud was a tremendously creative and productive person. Yet his own theory of motivation, productivity, and creativity leads to conclusions that every psychotherapist finds contradicted continuously in his work with patients.

Let us first of all consider Freud's theory of general work motivation or work attitude. His idea was that there was a general force or drive within the individual, libido, which was usually and normally associated with the search for sexual outlets and gratification. If, however, the individual would deny himself immediate and direct gratifications of the sexual impulse, some of this libido could be utilized for other purposes. Freud's most general conclusion was that the more desirable aspects of civilization itself were a product of (and a kind of monument to) suppressed sexuality.

Yet Freud's own account of the genesis of psychoanalytic theory states that on three different occasions men whom he highly respected told him that "neurosis" was caused by sexual frustration (9). The paradox which Freudian theory presents is this: how does one manage to get both hot soup and cold soup out of the same pot? In other words, how can lack of sexual gratification account for both neurosis and productivity or creativity? The answer which psychoanalytic psychology gives is that libido "properly" redirected can be used for constructive purposes. It is only libido which is improperly utilized that becomes converted into "symptomatic" behavior.

Unfortunately, this explanation does not really solve the problem. It would do well enough if we found that creative people were consistently abstemious and self-denying so far as pleasure and personal gratification is concerned, but this does not appear to be the case. It would do well enough if we found that people who were abstemious and self-denying were more likely to be productive and creative than those who were self-indulgent. This also does not seem to be the case. Our experience clearly indicates that persons who do not have adequate means of satisfying their needs for acceptance, love, affection, and sexual experience are usually, if not invariably, functioning at a productive level much below what we estimate their potential to be. Furthermore, as these same people become better able to satisfy these same needs, they become correspondingly more productive and efficient in the use of their abilities.

Freud was not a stupid man, and he was seldom completely wrong about any matter to which he devoted his attention. We would have to agree with the extreme position that his libido theory can be reduced to: namely, if a person were solely and completely oriented toward immediate sensory gratification, it is unlikely that he would produce any effort of social value. But no social individual could conceivably function in this manner; there are simply too many social barriers to such conduct in even the most primitive human societies. So we are all forced to forego a very considerable part of what would otherwise be innately determined means of obtaining gratification. What we want to explain is what specifically determines whether the time and energy thus "freed" from the search for primary hedonistic gratification will be used constructively or "neurotically." The following considerations may be crucial.

If a child's efforts to learn or to achieve are met with criticism, irritation, and/or punishment and lead generally to feelings of failure and inadequacy, what happens? He soon becomes discouraged, it is increasingly difficult to get him to study, and he "loses interest" in learning. By contrast, the child who is brought along slowly and carefully so that he usually "succeeds" in his learning efforts, who receives sympathetic attention and assistance from others when he needs it, and who is predominantly appreciated, praised, and rewarded for his efforts develops an interest in learning and manifests continuing motivation and effort.

All of this may seem obvious and reasonable enough, yet the *explanation* of such developments involve principles that are not a part of psychoanalytic psychology but are a part of modern learning theory. We start with the same assumption which Freud did, but which is not publicized as a part of his theory, namely, that the child at birth has certain innate survival needs, such as the need for food, the need for water, and the need for protection from injury. In Hullian learning theory these are called primary needs.

The infant, of course, is completely dependent upon others, usually the parents, for the fulfillment of these needs. The existence of the needs is "signalled" to the infant by unpleasant sensations, which innately lead to crying and other behavior indicating the child's distress. The satisfaction or fulfillment of these needs is accompanied by pleasant feelings. It is also usually accompanied by the presence of the person who is taking care of the child and whom the child sees, hears, feels, and so on, as these needs are being met and these pleasant sensations are occurring. This persistent association of pleasant feeling and awareness of the presence of others makes the presence of others a "rewarding" kind of experience also. After a few weeks the child will begin to indicate that he likes to be held or dislikes being alone, even when there are no primary needs to be satisfied. This desire simply to be with the parent may be called a learned, acquired, or secondary need. Still later the child may be motivated by a desire for the parents' acceptance, approval, or praise and feel rewarded when these are forthcoming.

In each instance the child is motivated by unpleasant feelings or the expectation (incentive) of more pleasant feelings. Initially, "feeling good" is only an aspect of some specific kind of sensory stimulation, such as the taste of food or the relief of dryness in the throat. Ultimately "feeling good" may be the result of getting a good grade in school, finishing an assigned task, or doing a favor for another person. This change comes about, however, not because the person is willing to forego gratification, but rather because he has learned to like such things as a result of their ultimate association with the gratification of primary needs.

Since such motives, incentives, and expectancies are the results of learning, they follow another basic principle of learning in that they tend innately to generalize or transfer to other situations besides the specific ones in which they were originally learned. In other words, the person who usually succeeds in obtaining what he wants, tends to develop a generalized expectancy of such gratification, and this in turn becomes an important component of his motivation for further efforts. Conversely, the person who "expects to fail" has his motivation to undertake new efforts undermined by this expectation of an unpleasant outcome.

Our general conclusion then is that productive and creative persons are those who have usually been rewarded for past efforts in terms of primary *or* secondary rewards or gratifications. Noncreative or nonproductive persons are those who have failed to receive adequate success, recognition, or other forms of personal gratification for their previous efforts. The only major qualification to this conclusion for practical purposes should be obvious, namely, that a person's productivity and creativity must be judged relative to his aptitude and training, that is, relative to his ability as of a given time.

FEELING AND PSYCHOTHERAPY

Emotion versus reason.   In any theoretical consideration of psychotherapy a basic issue is whether the primary focus of our concern shall be on how the person thinks or on how he feels. Our own position is this: while the psychotherapist has no access to the patient except via communication and the elicitation of symbolic cognitive responses, behavioral changes in the patient depend ultimately upon how the psychotherapist affects and changes the patient's characteristic attitudes and feelings. The reasons for this position can be illustrated by certain basic considerations that are related to neurology, learning theory, and clinical experience.

In a purely biological sense emotion is much more basic an aspect of life than is thinking. If we watch a one-celled organism reacting to its environment and to its own internal state, we note only a simple dichotomy of quiescence or activity (much the same basic distinction that can be observed in the newborn infant). The one-celled organism's activity is further divided into approach and avoidant behavior with respect to objects and substances in its external environment. Approach and avoidance are controlled by the relative chemical states of the organism's cellular material and the chemical nature of its environment. We have, in other words, behavior based upon direct chemical interaction between the organism and its environment, or what might be called in neurological terms, chemical mediation of response.

In more advanced, multicellular animals we find a primitive, ladder-like nervous system mediating the same and more complicated types of adjustment, both between the organism and its environment and among the cells of the animal itself. In still more advanced animals we find a central nervous system and, advancing beyond this, complex elaborations at one end of this central nervous system that constitute the brain. Yet we must note that control of function is not always vested in nor even mediated through the cerebral cortex of the brain, which seems to be the portion of the brain most directly concerned with conscious experience and voluntary control of behavior in man. Also, in man we find emotional responses being mediated through all three kinds of integrative systems, that is, chemical (the hormonal or endocrine system), ladder (the autonomic nervous system), and central (the spinal cord and the brain).

If we compare these elaborate and overlapping provisions for the mediation of emotional response with the relatively insignificant and recently evolved and vulnerable portions of the cerebral cortex that are associated with conscious experience, we have to conclude that so far as basic problems of survival and adjustment are concerned conscious experience may be regarded as useful but not necessary.

While on this neurological theme we note that much of the emotional response repertoire of the individual can be elicited without significant involvement of the higher centers of the brain. Could this be one of the reasons why so much that is of significance in determining behavior may be only scantily represented in conscious experience?

From the point of view of learning theory we find emotion much more significantly related to adaptive behavior than is thinking. We have already indicated that the feelings associated with emotion will serve quite adequately both to motivate and to reinforce responses. So far as thinking is concerned, however, we can only assign it a role as a portion of the internal stimuli that determine response. But the evocation of response is also determined by stimuli or "cues" provided by the external environment, so the best we can say is that thinking *may* be a part of the internal clues that, together with external clues, determine when and how the individual will respond. Organisms with none of the cerebral equipment upon which we assume thinking depends can nevertheless learn to adapt to their environment and to survive.

From the standpoint of clinical experience the psychotherapist is continuously confronted with people who have achieved a good level of "insight" into the reasons for their feelings and behavior without having been able to modify either their feelings or their behavior. These are the people who *know better* but who, for some mysterious reason, keep on behaving in ways that they know are detrimental to their own best interests. We assume quite routinely (and apparently quite correctly) that the "hidden persuaders" are, in fact, feelings. In this situation we confront directly the situation of the person who thinks correctly and accurately, but is helpless in the grip of well-established behavior patterns that no amount of thinking, in and of itself, will free him from.

The foregoing considerations should indicate why we have strong reservations concerning the general effectiveness of any psychotherapeutic approach that concerns itself primarily with how the patient thinks and only secondarily (if at all) with how he feels. True, the two are never totally unrelated. However, our own position would have to be one that regards feelings as the prime determinants of behavior and, therefore, the subject of primary concern in the psychotherapeutic process.

Dealing with emotion: expression.   Having declared this position, we now assume the obligation of indicating and evaluating what is known about how feelings can be changed and how motivated behavior can be modified.

When we review psychological experiments in eliminating conditioned fear responses (which we shall use for our example), we note that mere habituation is an extremely lengthy process and leads to results of doubtful reliability. The reduction of "anxiety" through repetition of the provoking stimulus situation without any further recurrence of a fear-provoking experience goes on and on, as does any "extinction" process. The subject reacts as if he were thinking, "Well, maybe not *this* time, but maybe next time that bad thing is going to happen again." We also note that even very infrequent reinforcements of the fear (by having the person become frightened again in the same kind of situation) will tend to prolong the extinction process almost indefinitely.

The psychotherapist is seldom in a position to so control or order the environment of his patient that such intermittent reinforcement of the original anxiety can be ruled out or avoided. If he is to have any real chance of success in reducing his patient's anxieties, he will be well advised to follow the paradigm of reconditioning rather than that of simple extinction. Reconditioning involves the association of a pleasant feeling with the situation that the patient is concerned about. The classical experiment in reconditioning fear responses involves bringing the feared object (such as a furry toy animal) into the general vicinity of the child when he is eating. If the procedure is properly handled, the association of the feared object with the pleasant experience of eating is an effective means of neutralizing the fear. It should be evident, however, that there is always the possibility of such a procedure creating unpleasant feelings associated with eating in the presence of the feared object.

Even this procedure of reconditioning through the association of a pleasant outcome with a previously feared situation is sufficiently complicated for the psychotherapist to resort to it usually only when no other strategy will adequately serve the psychotherapeutic purpose.

An alternative which is much more frequently employed is not to try to change the person's feelings so much as to change or redirect the response that he makes because of those feelings. For example, it is very difficult or impossible to avoid frustrations under conditions of social living and therefore (if we accept the frustration-aggression hypothesis) very difficult or impossible to protect the patient from feelings of anger and hostile impulses. Those who have been punished for acting aggressively in the past are inclined to inhibit direct expression of their feelings in behavior. For such persons the psychotherapist may be useful in encouraging the patient to be more expressive of his hostile feelings, while at the same time suggesting either innocuous or even constructive means of expressing these feelings.

To illustrate: one patient with whom we worked had a number of symptoms which all seemed to be related to strong frustrations in childhood, combined with a situation such that any direct expression of hostility on the patient's part was severely punished by others. In this situation we spent a good deal of time going over with the patient where he might now express his feelings without any reason for expecting the same amount of punishment that he had received for such behavior as a child. Another part of our work with the same person involved encouraging him in the study of law (in which he had a long-standing interest) on the basis that in this field of work our patient might find a constructive outlet for his latent aggressiveness, since it is perfectly permissible for a lawyer to "fight" for a client and against a legal adversary.

Dealing with emotions: discrimination.   Another common and reasonably practical strategy of the psychotherapist is to attempt to prevent the undue generalization of unpleasant feelings. (In psychoanalytic therapy the correlate process is referred to as "working through the transference.") From learning studies and learning theory we know that there is a natural and unavoidable tendency for a response learned in one situation to be evoked by any similar or equivalent situation. To illustrate: the adolescent who is basically concerned with fighting off the stultifying influence of dominating parents may generalize his "fighting" response to all representatives of authority, such as teachers, the police, adults in general, and a psychotherapist in particular. He does not bother to determine whether the attitude of these other persons is the same as his parents'. He automatically assumes that it is (or at least acts as if he does).

In the relatively simple situation of the learning laboratory we can deal with this tendency toward undue generalization by setting up conditions of "differential reinforcement." This involves creating a condition where the stimuli to which the response has been generalized become associated with pleasant, rather than unpleasant, feelings. In the psychotherapeutic situation, we may make a similar attempt at limiting the expanse of those situations that arouse a given response. In the example just given, we would try to encourage a different type of response from this type of adolescent by indicating by our general attitude and behavior that we shall not try to dominate and control him as his parents do. Our purpose is to let him know that not all relationships with adults are necessarily dominating and controlling ones and to indicate that perhaps he should evaluate each relationship on its own merit before deciding what his own response will be.

Controlling emotions.   The patient, the nonprofessional "adviser," and some few psychotherapists all seem to have considerable faith in *controlling* emotion as being the patient's best answer to his preponderance of unpleasant feelings. It therefore becomes appropriate for us to consider to what extent and in what respects such control is actually possible.

Two aspects of emotional response may be susceptible to some degree of "voluntary" control. The first is control over outward manifestations, such as facial expression, verbalization, and other aspects of overt behavior, for example, striking and running. Such control over outward manifestations is referred to in psychoanalytic theory as "suppression."

We might question the extent to which the term "voluntary" is applicable to such control as the individual exerts over the overt expression of feelings. Study of the child indicates that the newborn infant makes no attempt to control emotional behavior. The *capacity* for such control seems to develop gradually with age, probably as a function of subtle maturational changes in the central nervous system in general and the anterior portions of the cerebral cortex in particular. Such maturational changes almost certainly continue through the first six years of life, and it is quite possible that some such changes occur as late as the adolescent years.

This maturation may be considered a necessary but not a sufficient condition for the development of control over overt manifestations of emotion. The additional necessary component in the process is for the child to be somehow punished for such overt manifestations. The question of whether such control can be considered "voluntary" probably depends upon the frequency and intensity of such punishment and also upon the child's state of linguistic development at the time when the punishment occurs. If the punishment occurs *before* the child has adequate verbal means for representing the whole situation in his own thinking, then the emotional behavior may be effectively suppressed without the possibility of choice on the child's part. He has simply been conditioned or trained to inhibit that particular response and, in effect, has no recourse.

A similar situation prevails at later stages of development if the punishment occurs often enough and is sufficiently disturbing or traumatic to the person. Learning theory leads us to believe that under such conditions not only does the ultimate response become inhibited, but any conscious thoughts that may have preceded it may be inhibited also. We would then see the person responding, or failing to respond,

habitually or automatically, that is, without any specific awareness that he was "holding back" the response.

If, on the other hand, the person is still capable of thinking about what he might do, so that his eventual response is the outcome of deliberately considered and consciously evaluated expectancies as to the probable result of his behavior, this seems to us to fulfill any reasonable definition of "voluntary control." The only problem remaining is how any one other than the person himself can tell what the nature of his internal responses has been, a problem that becomes significant in determining intent, and therefore responsibility, in legal and some other situations.

The second aspect of emotional response that may be modified by experience is the conscious awareness that a particular feeling exists. How such modification occurs can best be explained by an extension of what we have already said concerning voluntary control of overt behavior. When a person is trained to inhibit or suppress a particular behavioral response at an early enough age, there may be no significant thought accompanying this learning process. In this case the child is "unaware" of any specific recognizable emotion simply because he does not have a verbal label for the emotion. He cannot say to himself, "I am angry," although he may be aware of feeling uncomfortable in some way that he cannot readily define. We could say under these circumstances that the inhibition of response is "unconscious," that is, the child does not know exactly what he is doing or why he is doing it (or not doing it). It would not be correct to call this lack of awareness "repression," because "repression" implies the retreat from consciousness of events of which the person has at some time been aware.

Repression does occur, of course, and is of considerable significance so far as a person's ability to direct his own adjustment is concerned. As we indicated in our discussion of "suppression," the stimulus-response complexes involved in emotional expression may be, and often are, accompanied by significant symbolic responses occurring within the individual. Such symbolic "input" may be crucial in continuing to elicit overt responses, as when the person chooses or decides to show outward manifestations of emotion even though he has been punished for so doing. Those thinking responses that tend to perpetuate the occurrence of overt responses, when such responses lead to punishment for the person, may then come under the influence of "retroactive inhibition." This means that the punishment tends to inhibit the thinking responses that have preceded the behavior, as well as inhibiting the behavior itself. When such thinking responses are so effectively inhibited that they seldom or never occur or are likely to occur only under special conditions (such as when dreaming or free-associating), then it is proper to say that

the response has been repressed and to consider this thinking response a part of what Freud called "the unconscious."

Relating all of this to the process of psychotherapy, we shall point out here (and expand later) the idea that a significant aspect of psychotherapy may be the restoring of appropriate thinking responses, which have been repressed or inhibited, to their former state. In this way we are not only involved with expanding the patient's awareness of inner experience; we may also be helpful in restoring a degree of voluntary control over behavior that has become automatic, habitual, or "unconsciously determined."

We have said that the idea of "control" over emotions seems to have some degree of applicability to overt expressions of emotion and to conscious awareness of emotion. We have also indicated in explaining our position that this control is by no means always "voluntary." The layman is not inclined to agree with this; rather, he is inclined to believe that he can "put things out of his mind" simply by resolving to do so. The experience of the psychotherapist leads him to a different conclusion. He can cite any number of instances in which patients have been unable to rid themselves of recurrent thoughts of the most disturbing and morbid nature. True enough, patients frequently "forget" things that they would rather not remember, but the process by which such repression occurs is much more complicated than it seems to the patient, and it is almost certainly not entirely under the patient's direct control.

The limits and limitations of control.   If we are willing to grant that control over emotional awareness and emotional behavior is possible, even in the limited sense and under the specific conditions given above, what significant aspects of emotion remain relatively uncontrolled and possibly uncontrollable under ordinary circumstances? We shall begin the answer to this question with another illustration.

This time our subject is suspected of a crime. We shall say the crime is murder, to make our illustration more dramatic. Furthermore, the suspect, realizing that his very life may depend upon his ability to control his emotions, may be assumed to be making every effort to exert such control. We now attach to appropriate parts of the subject's body a continuous recording sphygmomanometer which will indicate both pulse rate and blood pressure, a respirometer which will produce a detailed record of his breathing, and electrodes which are connected with a device to indicate changes in the electrical resistance of the skin. These various instruments will then, in most cases, indicate significant differences in physiological activity at times when even experienced investigators cannot detect any outward manifestation of emotion.

The point of this illustration is, of course, that emotions have

significant and diverse physiological aspects of response which seem to remain relatively unaffected by any effort on the part of a person to control them. In addition to changes in respiration, pulse, blood pressure, and electrical characteristics of the skin, many other kinds of physiological response may occur. The person involved may experience dryness of the throat. He may blush or turn pale as the blood supply to various parts of the body changes. He may experience loss of control over sphincter muscles, he may break into a sweat, and so on. At a still more concealed level numerous changes in the chemical and mechanical composition of the blood in particular and of the body cells in general may be taking place.

The relevance of such changes to psychotherapy rests upon the assumption that these changes are normally intended to be of relatively short duration, probably no more than a matter of minutes. During such a period, if the affected person is very active physically (and there is no further provocation), the various changes stop, and the body "automatically" returns to a normal state.

But suppose these conditions are not met. Suppose, for example, that the person inhibits any obvious, overt response. Our hypothesis is that when overt behavior is inhibited the duration of these abnormal or unusual conditions within the body may be considerably prolonged (10). As persons increase in age from infancy to adulthood, the intensity of their observable emotional responses tends generally to decrease, but the duration of their period of upset becomes correspondingly longer (11). If there are further provocations to emotion during this "recovery" period, then the effects of the new disturbance may summate with or be superimposed upon the remnants of the preceding disturbance. It is conceivable then that under certain circumstances a person might exist in an almost continual state of emotional upset, with the upset being manifested at this very basic physiological level even if it were not otherwise measurable.

What is the significance of all this to the psychotherapist? For one thing it indicates a potential danger arising from excessive emotional control over outward manifestations of emotion. Since the psychotherapist should also be aware of the dangers involved in the unrestrained "acting out" of feelings, especially of dangers arising from the social environment, he finds himself concerned with helping the patient to strike a balance between excessive inhibition and uncontrolled expression of emotion.

Another implication is that what the layman may consider "good" ways of dealing with emotion, suppression and repression, leave much to be desired from the psychotherapeutic point of view. By comparison, emotional retraining or reconditioning of the patient (while usually considerably more difficult) is in every sense a more thorough and satisfactory solution to emotional problems. If the psychotherapist must consider alternatives to these approaches, he should consider the modification of overt responses, either in the kind of behavior manifested or in the objective toward which it is directed, if such modifications permit the patient to express his emotions while minimizing the possibility of retaliation from other persons.

SUMMARY

The objective of psychotherapy is to change the habit structure of a person so that his behavior will result in more pleasant and fewer unpleasant experiences. The means by which this change is to be achieved is an effective communicative relationship between the person and the psychotherapist.

Freud suggested three specific objectives for psychotherapy: catharsis, the achievement of insight (especially into unconscious processes), and the working through of the transference neurosis. Although any or all of these experiences may occur in psychotherapy and have some therapeutic value, these objectives, singly or together, still leave the psychotherapeutic process inadequately defined and conceptualized.

We believe that any adequate conception of psychotherapy must begin with the assumption that it is a learning process. This implies that the psychotherapist must be concerned with *all* the conditions necessary for learning, unlearning, or relearning. These conditions are: motivation, cue, response, and reinforcement.

Motivation can be thought of as primarily a matter of feeling, that is, of pleasant or unpleasant subjective experience. At a behavioral level we need only concern ourselves with approach or avoidance tendencies, which (we assume) are innately associated with pleasant and unpleasant feelings. But we can also define "emotion" in the same way. We specify three reference emotions—love, fear, and anger (or their equivalents)— and specify further that anger is the result of frustrating the approach impulse associated with "love" or the avoidant impulse associated with fear. We suggest that the emotions of the patient be considered the most readily available "motives" for the learning that takes place in the psychotherapeutic situation.

We find it difficult to conceptualize motivation independently of the anticipation of a particular outcome of the motivated behavior. We suggest, therefore, that the terms be conjoined so that our operational concept is "motivation-incentive." The linkage between motivation and incentive is the "expectancy" of the motivated person. This expectancy involves an element of subjective probability as to whether the incentive condition will be obtained, and this probability factor may be different in the opinion of the patient than it is in the opinion of the psychotherapist. Only when the expectancy of the motivated person (in terms of more pleasant feelings) is met or exceeded can we expect to find an increasing tendency to make the response involved in obtaining the incentive.

So far as general motivation for productive effort is concerned, we are forced to reject Freud's theory of sublimation. We believe rather that work attitudes are created and conditioned primarily by the reactions of the person's "social conditioners" to the person's productive efforts.

When we apply this motivational theory to the psychotherapeutic task, we must reassert the predominant influence of emotion, both as a means of motivating and as a means of reinforcing the patient's learning efforts. Thinking (symbolic cognitive responses) comes into the picture as a possible part of the pattern of internal stimulation which, together with external stimulation, elicits a particular response.

Changing emotional responses can be difficult. The most basic changes involve either the extinction of emotional responses (which is tedious and not too practical) or reconditioning (which is more practical). The redirection of behavior to a different kind of response or the redirection of emotional behavior toward a different object are other practical techniques. Beyond this we may also be able to help the patient by preventing the undue generalization of emotional responses to inappropriate situations.

The layman tends to favor *controlling* emotions, that is, preventing their overt expression or avoiding subjective awareness of feelings. This can be accomplished, but usually only when other persons have consistently punished the person involved for expressing emotion. The person himself can control some voluntary expressions of feeling, provided he is adequately motivated to do so and provided the significant symbolic cognitive cues have not been lost through inhibition (assuming that they existed in the first place).

Suppressive and repressive training does *not* inhibit the physiological responses which are normally associated with emotions. Such responses can be readily neutralized (in terms of their effect on body chemistry, etc.) by appropriate *behavior* which helps to restore a condition of balance or homeostasis. Excessive suppression of such overt behavior leads to the prolongation of abnormal chemical and physiological states, which are both subjectively unpleasant and organically dangerous to the integrity of the cells and structures which are affected.

On the other hand, excessive or inappropriate expression of emotion may lead to significant "punishments" from the person's social environment. The psychotherapist can be helpful to the patient in reaching the most effective compromise between the conflicting needs of self and society.

SUGGESTIONS FOR FURTHER READING

The reader will find excellent summaries of the fields of emotion and motivation in Young's books (4) (12). Cannon (13) provides a theoretical approach which has become basic to much of modern thinking in both fields. His work has been further elaborated by Freeman (10). Jersild's article (14) will more than repay the reader's efforts with his thoughtful discussion of emotional development in children, which covers many topics of special interest to psychotherapists, including an evaluation of various methods of changing emotional responses. Rapaport (15) can be recommended as dealing with the subject of "emotions and memory" in depth.

The material in Dollard and Miller (16) which parallels this chapter will be found in Part II. The correlated chapters in Rotter (7) are Chapters V and VI.

REFERENCES

1. Hull, C. L. *Principles of behavior.* New York: Appleton, 1943.
*2. Birney, R. C. and Teevan, R. C. (Eds.) *Reinforcement.* Princeton, N.J.: Van Nostrand, 1961.
3. Lewin, K. *Principles of topological psychology.* New York: McGraw-Hill, 1936.
4. Young, P. T. *Emotion in man and animal.* New York: Wiley, 1943.
5. Dollard, J., Doob, L. W., Miller, N. E., and Sears, R. R. *Frustration and aggression.* New Haven, Conn.: Yale University Press, 1939.
6. Hilgard, E. R. *Theories of learning.* New York: Appleton, 1948.
7. Rotter, J. *Social learning and clinical psychology.* Englewood Cliffs, N.J.: Prentice-Hall, 1954.
*8. Zilboorg, G. *Sigmund Freud.* New York: Grove Press, 1960. (Scribner, 1951)
9. Freud, S. The history of the psychoanalytic movement. In Freud, S. *The basic writings of Sigmund Freud.* New York: Modern Library, 1938.

10. Freeman, G. L. *The energetics of human behavior.* Ithaca, N.Y.: Cornell University Press, 1948.

11. Hurlock, E. B. *Child development,* 2d ed. New York: McGraw-Hill, 1950.

12. Young, P. T. *Motivation of behavior.* New York: Wiley, 1936.

13. Cannon, W. B. *The wisdom of the body.* New York: Norton, 1939.

14. Jersild, A. T. Emotional development. In Carmichael, L. (Ed.) *Manual of child psychology,* 2d ed. New York: Wiley, 1954.

°15. Rapaport, D. *Emotions and memory.* New York: Science Editions, 1961.

16. Dollard, J. and Miller, N. E. *Personality and psychotherapy.* New York: McGraw-Hill, 1950.

° Paperback edition.

Chapter 3 | Cognitive Structure: Theory

THE NATURE OF COGNITIVE THEORY

Communication and cognitive theory. In considering the *psychodynamics of the patient* we have presumed a predominant position for emotion in the determination of behavior. However, in considering the *psychotherapeutic process* it is necessary to recognize that we are usually dealing with cognitive structure directly and are affecting emotions only indirectly or incidentally. This is because psychotherapy is primarily a communicative process in which the cognitive processes of the patient are most directly involved.

Definitions and assumptions. A "cognitive structure," as we shall use the term, is a system of knowledge and beliefs. The patient's knowledge and beliefs about himself constitute a cognitive structure, commonly referred to as "the self image." The patient's knowledge and beliefs about everything "outside" of himself constitutes a cognitive structure, as do his knowledge and beliefs about the relationships between himself and the outside world.

Our definition includes the supposition that within these major cognitive structures we can identify subordinate or more specific substructures focused on more particular or specific aspects of the self, the world, or the relationship between the two. Such substructures within the self image or self concept might center around the person's knowledge and/or beliefs regarding his intelligence, his health, or his sexual attractiveness. Substructures within the person's cognitive structure regarding the world might center around such matters as physical dangers, business opportunities, and the expectations of others. Cognitive substructures regarding the person's relation with the world might be focused on such matters as his status in the eyes of others, their acceptance of him, and those who feel rivalrous toward him.

No end would be served by trying to devise a definitive catalogue of the significant substructures in each of the three major cognitive structures. In any event the definition of "significant" substructure might very well change with our particular interest or orientation of the moment, and we could only arbitrarily define an "appropriate" level of specificity for such a catalogue. Our primary purpose is to make the assumption that such cognitive structures do exist, that cognitive structures can be changed, and that one of the objectives of psychotherapy is to effect such changes.

Why do we make the last of these three assumptions? It is because we continually note certain beliefs which patients have that we cannot accept as being "true" or "reasonable." Furthermore, we seem to find a correlation between what the patient believes and what he feels and/or between what the patient believes and what he does.

We are willing to concede immediately—in fact we insist upon the point—that what the patient believes more often depends upon what he feels than vice versa. This is, in fact, a major implication of our discussion of emotion. Here we only describe a certain *correlation* between feeling and belief, as well as between behavior and belief, which is of considerable interest to the psychotherapist.

The psychotherapist and reality.   Now we immediately run into a situation that is very awkward for the psychotherapist. When the psychotherapist concentrates his attention and psychotherapeutic efforts upon beliefs of the patient which he considers detrimental to the patient's emotional welfare, he must certainly consider the possibility that he may be "wrong."

"Client-centered" psychotherapists attempt to circumvent this difficulty by deliberately and designedly eschewing any attempt to pass judgment upon the beliefs of the patient or to change those beliefs. Rather they define their service to the patient as an "assistance" in changing his own beliefs and cognitive structures. But it is difficult to conceive how the psychotherapist can help a patient to change his cognitive structures if the therapist himself is completely open as to the direction that change should take. Indeed, we might ask why the psychotherapist attempts to help the patient change at all if the patient's own choice of direction could just as well add to his emotional difficulties as aid in resolving them. Such a position on the part of the psychotherapist would seem to suggest rather that either he has a strong faith in the inherent tendency of the patient to move in the "right" direction without directional guidance from the therapist or else that he is directing the patient in what he considers a "safe" and "useful" form of cognitive restructuring without intentionally doing so. We assume that the psychotherapist always has both a general intent to influence (or "assist") and also, whether he recognizes it or not, certain intentions as to the manner in which that influence will change the cognitive structure of the patient.

In other words, the only practical solution to the possibility of the psychotherapist's being "wrong" is for the therapist to accept his responsibility as an expert and to strive in his training for that adequacy of knowledge and that freedom from personal bias which will minimize the number of errors he will make. This, after all, is a problem that the psychotherapist shares with all other experts. For the person who realizes he is *not* an expert, the solution is simple: do not practice psychotherapy.

Cognitive structure as habit.   Let us return now to a further consideration of the nature of cognitive structure. A critical assumption which we make is that the "elements" of cognitive structure are, each and every one, "habits." The child starts life without significant cognitive elements. This does not deny to him a certain capacity for "awareness" or "consciousness" in terms of some sort of implicit response of the cerebral cortex to sensory stimulation. But when we speak of "cognitive elements" and "cognitive structure," we are essentially concerned with "meaning." In order to have meaning two factors are essential: first, we must have signs; second, the signs must be related to internal and external "events" and, eventually, to each other as well. When we speak of a cognitive element we are referring to a particular habit that has established an association between an internal or external event and a sign. When we speak of a cognitive structure we are referring to a habit, or perhaps a highly complex combination of habits, that establishes an association among signs or symbols. We must assume also that any and all principles which apply to learning in general also apply specifically to the formation of those associations we refer to as cognitive elements and cognitive structures. We must assume, for example (disregarding the more esoteric disagreements among professional learning theorists), that the formation of cognitive elements requires the existence of an appropriate stimulus complex, the elicitation of a response (in this instance, a "sign" response) in conjunction with this complex, and a suitable reinforcement of this conjunction through an appropriate affective consequence. Although Guthrie (1) has suggested that such associations may be established on the basis of a *single* effectively reinforced conjunction of stimulus complex and response, the usual experience is that *repeated* elicitations of the conjunction with appropriate reinforcement is required to assure that the response will be elicited *reliably* by the given stimulus complex or by stimulus complexes with a certain critical degree of perceptual similarity. It is this usual necessity for the *repeated* occurrence of a particular sequence of events that makes time an unavoidable ingredient in the creation and/or change of cognitive elements and cognitive structures.

The significance of time as a factor in psychotherapy becomes obvious when we consider the problem of changing cognitive structure. When we speak of "change" we necessarily imply that existing structures must be eliminated *and* new structures created. While it is considerably easier to *change* habits than to eliminate them, either process involves time.

A reasonable basis for evaluating the amount of time necessary for changes in simple habits to occur can only be acquired by extensive experience in conducting experiments in learning or by supervising the learning experiences of others. Obviously the layman (including the patient) usually does not have this knowledge. Often enough, and perhaps unfortunately, neither does the beginning psychotherapist. In any event, the conditions involved in changes in cognitive structure are much more complex than the conditions involved in changing simple habits. Consequently the psychotherapist relies to a very considerable degree on practical rules of thumb and his own cumulative experience with the more gross and obvious aspects of change in cognitive structure. It is primarily this difference in practical knowledge and clinical experience that accounts for the difference in viewpoint between professional and layman. Besides this, the layman is more likely to be influenced in his ideas about how long the process of cognitive change *ought* to take by his own strong wish that it not take very long. Most psychotherapists have probably begun their clinical experience with a similar emotional bias, if only because quick changes in the patient would testify to their own competence. If the experienced therapist thinks differently about the matter it is often only because he has had his nose rubbed in the error of his naive optimism.

The rigidity of cognitive structure.   The quality of resistance to change which is so obvious and significant an aspect of cognitive structures to the psychotherapist is often referred to in general psychology in terms of "rigidity." The person whose thinking can be changed only slowly and with the expenditure of considerable effort and time is spoken of as being "rigid," while the person who responds more readily is regarded as "flexible."

These terms are deceptively simple in relation to the complex and diversified phenomena they are used to describe. We are exposed to this complexity and heterogeniety as soon as we ask questions as to *why* a particular person might be more rigid (resistant to change) in his cognitive structuring than another person, or why the same individual may show varying degrees of rigidity in different aspects of his own cognitive structure. Some general ideas along these lines can be gained by regarding cognitive elements as habits and by regarding the associations between elements that create cognitive structure as being habits also.

We can then immediately suggest, as is true of learned behavior in general, that the greater the motivation involved in a particular learned cognitive association, the more difficult it will be to eliminate or alter that particular element or structure. Similarly we can postulate that the more frequently a particular association has been reinforced, the greater is the tendency toward the perpetuation of that particular habit. Also we can suggest that the greater the positive affect associated with need reduction in positive reinforcement and the greater the negative affect associated with negative reinforcement during each reinforcement trial in learning, the greater will be the resistance of the cognitive habit to change.

We are simply saying here that "rigidity" of cognitive habits is a function of motivation, frequency of reinforcement, and intensity of reinforcement—all very basic and well-accepted principles of learning in general psychology.

At a more hypothetical and less well established level we might suggest still other principles related to rigidity in cognitive structure. We might conjecture, for example, that when the simple habit constituting a single cognitive element is *joined* with other similar elements to form what we call a cognitive structure or substructure, the difficulty of changing any particular element might well be related to the number of other elements with which it is associated and how many of these other elements are in turn associated with each other. This takes us into the realm and concept of "integration" in cognitive structure, which we shall return to later on.

Cognitive structure and behavior.   The psychotherapist is concerned with cognitive structure primarily as it relates to feeling and behavior. We assume that cognitive elements and/or cognitive structures are in certain instances significant components of the total stimulus complex leading to a particular response. Indeed, if we account for the difference between sensation and perception as being due to the "addition" of cognitive elements to sensation to produce perception, we could assume a cognitive component in a very considerable part of human behavior. If, less radically, we simply assume that all *conscious* behavior must have a cognitive component or if we define "conscious" behavior as being that which has cognitive components in the stimulus complex that elicits the behavior, we can formulate other hypotheses regarding rigidity in cognitive structure. For example, we can suggest that the more a person likes the consequences of a particular kind of behavior, the more resistant he will be to attempts to change the cognitive components in the stimulus complex which customarily evokes that behavior. Put more plainly, if the patient enjoys behaving the way he does, he is resistant to any change of ideas that might tend to alter his behavior.

Many such hypotheses can be generated by further thinking along these lines. When we discuss psychotherapeutic strategy in relation to cognitive structure, we shall have more to say about the rigidity of cognitive structures under the heading of "evaluating resistance in patients" and again under therapeutic tactics when we talk about methods of dealing with resistance. Here we simply wish to point to certain obvious characteristics of the patient, such as age, intelligence, and education, and indicate how we might expect them to correlate with cognitive rigidity.

THE PROBLEM OF RIGIDITY

Age and rigidity.   Let us consider the matter of age first. Why should the psychotherapist in general expect to find greater cognitive rigidity in older than in younger patients? In the rather unlikely event of "all else being equal" we would explain this in terms of the likelihood of a given cognitive structure having existed longer and having been more frequently reinforced in the older person than in the younger. But in terms of our more basic formulation regarding the learned nature of cognitive components, we could also postulate that relatively new or recently acquired cognitive habits in an older person might be more readily changed than relatively old habits in a child. The same reasoning could also help to explain why, within the same person, some ideas are held on to more tenaciously than others. The basic considerations, overriding more apparent but superficial characteristics of the patient, would be those we have already referred to: intensity of motivation, frequency and intensity of reinforcement, the interassociation of cognitive components (how thoroughly one idea is integrated with or "reinforced" by others), and the desirability of associated responses to the patient in terms of their emotional consequences.

Education and rigidity.   These considerations still remain basic, although not always thoroughly decipherable in practice, when we consider the relation of education to rigidity of cognitive structure. Here we are considering education in its formal, or "school learning" sense. The interrelations between education and rigidity are likely to be many and complex. For example, we note that amount of education is positively correlated with intelligence. Yet in individual cases we often find very intelligent persons who are grossly undereducated, at least relative to their educative capacity. This immediately creates predictive difficulties, since intelligence may have its own relationships with rigidity irrespective of education.

Our general tendency is to believe, as is often assumed in the literature on psychotherapy, that (other things being equal) educated persons are generally more flexible in cognitive structure than uneducated ones. We might speculate that this could be attributed to the frequent disruption of existing cognitive structures "to make room for expansion" as successive stages of education are reached. Of course this assumes that these successive stages in education do *require* cognitive restructuring relative to what the person might previously have known, thought, or believed. Then the principle relevant to this particular hypothesis would be that the educated person is more flexible *because*—and only to the extent that and in the areas that—education has resulted in cognitive structures that are newer and less thoroughly reinforced.

Now we would have to begin to qualify our hypothesis to fit more specific situations. Other things being equal we would expect a recent college graduate to be less rigid in cognitive structure than a person who had graduated from college forty years earlier. Similarly, of two persons both twenty years out of college, we would expect that one who had continued his education by reading and other forms of exposure to intellectual stimulation to be more flexible than the one who had not done so.

We would also have to consider the nature of the cognitive elements and substructures that would be affected by various kinds of education. Can we assume that education in mathematics will affect the same cognitive structures as education in literature? Which would be more likely to lead to the reorganization of cognitive structures relevant to the objectives of psychotherapy?

We do not intend, because it is not that basic to our purpose, to be exhaustive in our examination of all the possible relationships between age and rigidity or between education and rigidity in cognitive structure. It is our purpose rather to illustrate that thinking of cognitive structure and cognitive rigidity in terms of learning and learning principles enables us to formulate more specific hypotheses than the gross proposition that rigidity increases with age or is negatively correlated with education. Also it is of considerably greater value to the psychotherapist when he attempts to understand why a young child is so resistant to cognitive restructuring or why a patient with a doctorate in physics is extremely rigid in his thinking about sexual behavior.

Anxiety and rigidity.   Certain other problems can be helpfully analyzed in terms of these same principles. For example, it is commonly observed by psychotherapists that rigidity of cognitive structure tends to increase as anxiety increases. A number of attempts have been made to verify this hypothesis experimentally, but with varying results. If we read the reports of these experiments, we find that often the investigators are attempting to correlate anxiety in general with cognitive rigidity in general. We do not believe that this is what the psychotherapist observes or means to communicate. Rather we believe that what is actually observed is that the patient is rigid in his thinking in these areas of cognitive structure that are associated with intense anxiety. Certainly this hypothesis, although more limited, is more reasonable. Also it would agree with studies of animal behavior. Here we note that in learned responses where the motivating state is (presumably) anxiety or fear, as in avoidance conditioning, and the learned response is an avoidant response, it is exceptionally difficult to get subjects to make the response that has previously been associated with punishment. Similarly, then, we would not expect a patient to give up easily those ideas (cognitive responses) that are a part of the stimulus complex associated more or less directly with anxiety reduction and/or the avoidance of punishment. As to general anxiety and general rigidity, we would certainly modify any hypothesis to indicate that rigidity should be greatest or most evident in cognitive areas directly associated with the feeling of anxiety and less rigid in areas of cognitive structure not as closely associated with the anxiety under consideration.

Incidentally, one might consider this an example of the point mentioned earlier, namely, the tendency of feeling to influence or even to control cognitive structure. Now we can say more specifically that the influence of feeling on cognition is exerted specifically through feeling serving as motivation and as reinforcement (sometimes also as a significant part of the stimulus complex) in the development, elimination, and change of cognitive habits.

Intelligence and rigidity.   As a final illustration of the usefulness of this frame of reference for dealing with problems related to cognitive rigidity, let us consider the role of intelligence in psychotherapy. Generally therapists prefer more intelligent to less intelligent persons as patients. Some psychotherapists have even made statements to the effect that a certain minimal level of intelligence (sometimes a rather high level is specified) is necessary before the chances of successful therapy justify the effort involved. Or put more simply, people below a certain level of intelligence are supposedly "not 'candidates' for psychotherapy." We would agree with this statement only when the level of intelligence is so low as to preclude the possibility of effective communication through any means reasonably available to (*not* just generally used by) the psychotherapist. Aside from problems in communication, we can only regard this position of some psychotherapists as being justified in their thinking by assumed negative correlation between intelligence and cognitive rigidity, that is, the less intelligent the patient, the greater is his cognitive rigidity.

Our point now is not to challenge this assumption; in fact, we are inclined to go still further and suggest that intelligence could be usefully (perhaps even operationally) defined in terms of facility in forming cognitive elements and structures and/or in terms of capacity for forming increasingly complex integrated cognitive structures.

But now to go back to the subject just discussed, we have previously agreed that *anxiety* is *also* associated with rigidity in the cognitive structures. If we encounter a certain degree of rigidity in cognitive structure are we to consider this rigidity as "due to" lack of intelligence or to anxiety?

For example, a child is brought in for evaluation. In an intelligence examination, such as the Wechsler Intelligence Scale for Children, we note that his functioning in certain tests is markedly lower than we would expect, considering his ability as manifested in other tests. If the discrepancy is greater than is expected on the basis of intertest correlations, we feel justified in assuming that he would test higher except for some "factor" that depresses his ability to function in certain tasks and not (or not so much) in others. Quite often we assume that this unknown factor is anxiety. (Incidentally, this example will also serve to illustrate our hypothesis that anxiety-rigidity relationships are apt to be relatively specific rather than completely general.) Please note that we would have been unable to make, or at least to justify, this assumption clinically without specific evidence and evidence that is dependent upon over-all performance on the test, not from the I.Q. scores alone. Note also that we are still dealing with a supported hypothesis, not a "proven fact," about the child in question. Note finally that we believe that there *are* many, many cases in which no such assumption can be justified.

THE ORGANIZATION OF COGNITIVE STRUCTURE

Integration.   We would like to direct attention now to the concept of "integration" in cognitive structure. As soon as we assume that two or more cognitive elements may become associated with each other, we may wish to consider certain matters that relate to the nature of such "relationships" between cognitive elements or between a cognitive element and a cognitive substructure or between cognitive substructures. The matter of such relationships may be dealt with under the general designation of "integration."

The relatedness or integration of cognitive structure is a subject of very considerable fascination for psychology in general. For example, we would agree with the often-stated hypothesis that new cognitive elements which are "congruent with" a pre-existing cognitive structure are more likely to be assimilated by or become associated with that structure than are cognitive elements which are "incongruent." We shall resist the temptation both to attempt to define "congruence" and to suggest still other hypotheses that are readily adaptable to the concept of "cognitive structure" in order to concentrate on matters of more direct concern to the psychotherapist.

What is the psychotherapist most likely to be concerned with pertaining to the integrative aspects of cognitive structures? We shall discuss three aspects with which he is likely to be concerned.

Lack of integration.   First of all, he will be concerned with *lack* of integration in cognitive structures. Such lack of integration may take many forms and occur at different levels. One example would be the isolated cognitive element or "idea" the patient holds on to although it is not logically consistent with other ideas he also "accepts." This sort of lack of integration is referred to clinically by the term "thinking in logic-tight compartments." At a more complex level, where major aspects of cognitive structure are almost entirely divorced from each other, we might see the development of multiple and dissociated personalities, as in Morton Prince's classical study (2) or the more recent and popular *Three Faces of Eve* (3).

Excessive integration.   The psychotherapist may also be concerned with an "excessive" degree of integration. Usually he is concerned with this when, as we indicated earlier, such excessive integration is associated with an undesirable degree of rigidity, as in the patient who "has figured everything out" and whose "mind is made up." The implication here is that logical relatedness may be different from (and therefore does not guarantee that a well-integrated cognitive structure corresponds accurately with) the "reality" of external events. In the simplest possible example, the cognitive structure may be consistently and logically related within itself, but this does not help the correspondence between cognition and reality if the basic assumptions upon which the integration rests are faulty.

Integration and the structure of reality.   Ultimately and always the psychotherapist *must* be concerned and *is* concerned with the relationship between cognitive structure and reality. There is no way of guaranteeing a correspondence between the two, as is evident because so often we note the discrepancy in our patients, if not in ourselves. A significant aspect of psychotherapeutic strategy is to improve this correspondence in the patient.

So, finally, the psychotherapist is concerned with integrations of cognitive structures that do not correspond with the structure of reality. Such deficiencies in correspondence may be classified under three headings. First, the patient may believe in something that does not exist in reality. The simplest example would be hallucination. Second, the patient may refuse to believe in or accept the idea of the existence of something that demonstrably to others *does* exist. This is often referred to clinically simply as "denial." Finally, the patient may accept reality only in a distorted way, so there are marked and significant discrepancies between his cognitive structure and the structure of events in reality. In such cases the psychotherapist may use descriptive terms such as "delusion" or "illusion" to refer to these discrepancies and to the fact that distortion is involved.

In general one may liken the matter of the correspondence between cognitive structure and reality to the relationship between a map and the area which the map represents (4). The psychotherapist asks himself: How adequate and how accurate is the patient's map of the world in which he lives? With this orientation we can then note the following kinds of inadequacies or inaccuracies. A portion of his map, corresponding to an area that he should or must know about, is blank. He does not know what to anticipate in this area, and he may therefore encounter (or he has already encountered) difficulty in this area. In another portion of his map he has a highway and a bridge, but there is no highway or bridge in the corresponding area of reality. Now he is in for difficulty when he does not expect to encounter any. Or, conversely, his map shows an untracked wilderness and an unbridged river, but in reality there is a fine highway leading to a good bridge. We expect the patient in such an instance to be more reluctant to traverse this area than the "real" circumstances warrant. Finally, the patient's map of an area may be distorted. It may indicate the distance between two points as being either five miles or fifty miles, when in fact the distance is twenty-five miles. In the first instance he will be overly optimistic to begin with, but is doomed to disappointment. In the latter instance he dreads the journey more than he "needs" to.

To relate these conditions to clinical problems, blank portions of the map would correspond with important areas of knowledge about which the patient is uninformed. In a later chapter some of these areas are discussed under the topic of *tabooed* topics of communication. Such lack of necessary information suggests that giving the patient information may be a legitimate and useful therapeutic procedure under certain circumstances.

Misinformation supplied by the patient's map of reality can be illustrated by the very common situation in which the patient underestimates his intelligence or attractiveness. This kind of underestimation causes him to consistently depreciate his chances of success in situations requiring the attributes in question with the subsequent probability that he will tend to avoid such situations or to approach them with undue anxiety.

A common example of distortion in cognitive structure as related to reality has already been discussed in terms of the patient's ideas about how long it should take for certain changes to occur as contrasted with how long they will actually take. Psychotherapists who work with children quickly learn that most parents expect the problems of their children to be "cleared up" in a few hours of consultation. It then becomes the psychotherapist's task to give them a more realistic conception of such matters based on his own more extensive experience with similar situations.

Cognitve structure and response.   In addition to being concerned with matters of internal consistency or relatedness in cognitive structures and the correspondence between cognitive structure and reality, the psychotherapist may also be concerned with the relationship between cognitive structure and certain aspects of response. The principal aspects that we want to mention briefly are emotion and overt behavior. In general, the psychotherapist notes that certain segments—certain substructures—of cognitive structure are associated with very strong or intense emotions. The clinical term suggested by Jung and often used to describe such an association of intense feelings with cognitive substructures is "complex" (5). An example would be intense feelings of inadequacy, inferiority, and/or unworthiness associated with a cognitive substructure usually referred to as the "self concept" or "self image." This would be the classical "inferiority complex," familiar from the writings of Alfred Adler (6).

Another example will slightly extend our thinking in this area. Let us consider the "controlled association" technique suggested by Jung for the detection of complexes. Here we introduce a communicative component. The investigator reads a list of words. The words, as perceived by the subject, are in turn associated by him with relevant cognitive structures that constitute the meanings of the word so far as he is concerned. If any of these cognitive structures is associated with and evokes a strong enough response, the investigator may be able to detect certain outward manifestations of emotion, which are the "complex indicators" he is looking for. In the concepts sometimes used in general semantics the cognitive structure associated with the stimulus word would constitute its "informative connotation" and the emotion would be its "affective connotation" (7). These matters will be taken up and amplified in the next chapter.

The conscious determinants of behavior.   There are numerous reasons why the psychotherapist may be interested in the relationships between cognitive structure and behavior. We shall only give two examples here and pursue the subject further in subsequent chapters.

Most obviously the psychotherapist is interested in this relationship because, in terms of the assumptions we have made, behavior can only be regarded as "conscious" when it is associated with a cognitive structure as at least a part of the eliciting stimulus complex. This leads the psychotherapist to certain practical concerns and questions. If a patient has been responding "unconsciously," can we introduce or create an association with cognitive components? If so, have we now made the response "conscious" in any significant way? Have we thereby increased the patient's capacity for "voluntary control" over the response?

Consider another possibility. We have a stimulus complex A, which includes a cognitive component a, and this stimulus component evokes response X. If now we can change the stimulus complex to A_1 by substituting a cognitive component a_1 for cognitive component a, will A_1 elicit another response, X_1? Translated into an example, suppose a man is pursuing a girl (response X) and a part of the situation (stimulus complex A) evoking this response is his assumption (cognitive component a) that she is "just like his mother." Suppose that communication in psychotherapy convinces him that this assumption is "wrong" (cognitive component a changed to a_1). In this new situation (stimulus complex A_1), will he still pursue her (response X) or will he decide to stop dating her (response X_1)?

We hope that this analysis does not seem too complicated or involved, because in actual practice the psychotherapist is quite often involved with the process of changing "cognitive component a to cognitive component a_1" with the purpose or intent of effecting some change in the patient's response.

Let us give an example of still another sort of modification in cognitive structure which the therapist may attempt. Suppose the patient has only been told that "sex is bad" and as a consequence he invariably avoids sexual behavior of any kind under any circumstances. If in the course of psychotherapy the patient acquires considerably more information about sex and the intricacies of our sexual mores (if, in other words, we "educate" him by adding additional cognitive elements to this area of cognitive structure), will he still behave as before? If not, how will he respond? Can we predict his behavior if we know what new cognitive components have been added? Or would we also need to know what emotions are associated with each new cognitive component (in other words, what attitudes were attached to each new unit of information)?

In this example we are modifying the original "situation" not so much by substituting a new "idea" or cognitive component for the preexisting one but rather by adding a number of new ideas *to* the old one. We might reasonably expect some modification of behavior under these new conditions. If so, we have changed the patient's behavior by giving him information. If we have also expressed certain attitudes, feelings, and beliefs in conveying this information (and in all probability we have, whether meaning to or not), we may also have created certain attitudes in the patient that are also of considerable importance in determining whether he will now behave differently.

Some psychotherapists speak rather disparagingly of "information giving" as a technique in psychotherapy. We are inclined to consider it of considerable value for reasons just indicated. We suspect that some prejudice about the value of information giving exists because it is not always clearly differentiated from "advice giving." But in advice giving we are attempting to elicit a specific behavior by telling the patient what *we* think *he* ought to do. This is considerably different from giving him information (with or without expressing our attitudes or otherwise attempting to influence his) and letting the patient determine his subsequent behavior.

THE PROBLEM OF CONSCIOUSNESS

Definitions and assumptions.   In this section we shall systematically review all of the concepts and assumptions that we consider essential to a theory of consciousness.

In classifying and defining responses we divide all responses into two classes: cognitive and noncognitive. For our purposes all noncognitive responses can be divided into two classes: physiological responses and behavioral responses.

We can divide cognitive responses into two classes: perceptual and nonperceptual. A cognitive response is defined as perceptual when the stimulus complex evoking the response consists exclusively or predominantly of neural impulses originating with the stimulation of sensory receptors. However, it is possible for a perceptual response to become associated through learning with other cognitive responses in such a way that these other cognitive responses become a sufficient stimulus to evoke the (originally) perceptual response. When a perceptual response is evoked by another cognitive response rather than by direct sensory stimulation, we must reclassify it as a "nonperceptual" response. Imagery, memory, dreaming, imagining, and thinking all involve such nonperceptual cognitive responses.

When we refer to a cognitive response that involves the words of a recognized language (or the symbols of a logical system, such as mathematics), we designate this special class of cognitive responses as "verbal" or "symbolic." "Vocal," on the other hand, refers to active speech in a behavioral sense. For example, "vocal expression" refers to manner of speaking, including such aspects as pitch, timbre, tempo, and loudness.

A stimulus complex which gives rise to a cognitive response constitutes a cognitive "element." The habitual association of cognitive responses with each other, so that one cognitive response may evoke another gives rise to cognitive "structures."

The nature of consciousness.   Where does "consciousness" come into the picture? According to the definitions and assumptions which we have made, "consciousness" is entirely dependent upon cognitive response. When the child is first born, only perceptual responses exist. Consciousness is therefore limited to the cognitive result of adequate (supraliminal) intensities of sensory stimulation. However, when two such perceptual responses occur closely related in time, and this occurrence is followed by pleasant feelings (is positively reinforced), then it may be possible for one perceptual response to evoke the other. We now have the beginning of cognitive structure and the possibility of a cognitive response (the one evoked) which is *not* the direct result of sensory stimulation. We believe that all of the higher mental processes, such as imagining, thinking, creating, and so forth are dependent upon this humble beginning and the development of increasingly complex cognitive structures as a result of learning.

It should be understood that consciousness is in no way essential to modifications of behavior. We assume that throughout life much and probably most of human behavior is evoked and modified without being influenced in any significant way by cognitive responses. In fact, some rather special modifications must take place before consciousness can have any influence on behavior. Since this matter has particular significance for psychotherapy, it will be pursued a little further.

Consider a simple sequence of events. An environmental "event" provides stimulation adequate to evoke a perceptual response, which in turn evokes a nonperceptual cognitive response (such as a verbal phrase), which has become associated with it. This phrase may in turn elicit a behavioral response. The person in whom all these responses were occurring might assume that the behavioral response occurred *because* he "thought of" the phrase.

From a more sophisticated point of view we can only assume that a thought occurred (the verbal phrase) *and then* the behavioral response occurred. The phrase may have been a necessary link in the chain of events to cause that particular behavior response to follow upon the original stimulation. This is different, however, from saying that the person's "awareness" of the phrase was *responsible* for his subsequent behavior.

This example may help to clarify why it is perfectly possible for a person to be aware of what he is going to do without necessarily having the ability to control or alter what he is going to do. The layman (and sometimes the psychotherapist) is inclined to make the error of assuming that when a person is aware of what he is doing, he should have no trouble in altering the final response if he *wants to*. The problem of "conscious" or "voluntary" control is, as we shall see, considerably more complicated than the psychologically naive person assumes.

This matter will be analyzed still further, because it lies close to the heart of psychotherapeutic efforts.

The development of cognitive structure.   Both physiological and behavioral responses may stimulate sensory receptors in such a way as to give rise to perceptual responses. We may then consider these perceptual responses as representing in conscious experience the behavioral or physiological responses that evoked them. Such perceptual responses (those which represent behavioral or physiological responses) may have affective qualities of pleasantness or unpleasantness. Examples would be: we usually "enjoy" the sensation of stretching our muscles after a period of inactivity; we usually find the dryness of the throat (a physiological response to "fear") unpleasant. Perceptual responses that originate with muscular activity readily become associated with other perceptual responses that immediately follow. Example: we bite an apple (a behavioral response that gives rise to a perceptual response that makes us aware we are biting); biting the apple releases juice which tastes pleasant; so we are aware of the biting and the taste, and the taste is pleasant. Our experience is: "I like eating apples because they taste good."

The conditioning of cognitive responses so that one cognitive response evokes another creates a simple kind of cognitive structure. To illustrate this process, suppose a child sees an apple, goes to it, picks it up, and takes a bite of it. The child may have gone to the apple and picked it up because he "liked" its color. He may have put it into his mouth because this is a typical response of children to objects they find attractive. However, the pleasant taste of the apple may have provided sufficient reinforcement so that all of the cognitive responses involved are now associated in such a way that each will evoke the other in the original sequence.

Whether or not such an association *has* been formed can be determined by observation of the child's subsequent behavior. If we later see him drooling when he sees an apple, we can be reasonably sure that the sight of the apple has evoked each of the original cognitive responses in turn, and the end result is the salivation (which originally occurred only as a response to the *taste* of the apple). In other words, the child now *anticipates*. We believe that this example and its explanation constitute a basic pattern for anticipation or expectancy.

Expectancy.   One thing which we now note as a general principle of psychology is that animals and infants are limited in their capacity to anticipate. If we show an apple to an infant (who has indicated that he "likes" apples and will always go to them when he sees them), and then put a screen in front of the apple and hold the infant still for awhile, he may or may not go toward the apple when he is released. A critical factor is the length of time he is restrained from moving toward the apple. If he is released almost immediately, he quite probably *will* go toward the apple. If he is restrained for an hour, he quite probably *will not* go toward the apple. If we were to speculate about why he probably will not go toward the apple after an hour's restraint, we would suggest that in the interval other perceptual responses have occurred and have led him off on other "cognitive chains" so that (as is commonly said) he "forgets about" the apple.

We note two things about the length of time that may intervene between perception of a goal-object, such as the apple, and overt response, assuming that our subject is able to respond correctly. First, the interval becomes longer as the age of the child increases. Second, age is not so critical a factor in the delayed responses of animals. Furthermore, animals cannot respond adaptively to anything like the period of delay that older human subjects can. While it is conceivable that both of these observations *could* be explained simply in terms of the ability of older humans to form longer cognitive chains, this explanation alone seems inadequate to explain the gross difference of time involved. We therefore assume that the existence and development of language as a specific kind of cognitive response is crucial in determining the superiority of human over animal subjects and of older human subjects over younger ones.

We must also assume that cognitive "maps" relating to future events and involving language are somehow more durable than those based on cognitive responses which do not involve words or language. If asked to suggest a probative basis for this assumption, we would point to the fact that a single word can stand for any number of specific "things" or "events." "Apple" stands for all apples, "screen" for all screens, and "behind" for all proximodistal relationships. Thus the cognitive map "apple behind screen" may have the advantage of many reinforcements establishing the meaning of "apple," "behind," "screen." In particular, the formula "x behind y" may have been heavily reinforced, since this is a common relationship in the experience of the infant or child. Remembering "where the apple is" simply involves the substitution of two specific verbal cognitive responses in this more general verbal formula.

The retreat from consciousness.   We have now dealt, at least briefly, with the establishment of cognitive responses as a part of conscious experience but independent of perception. Before going on to the matter of the control of behavior, we would like to indicate how some or all of these nonperceptual cognitive responses might drop out of the person's conscious experience.

First, we invite consideration of the observation that when learned responses are linked end-to-end in chain fashion, responses which are supposed to come later in the chain tend to move forward, cutting in front of or short-circuiting intermediate responses. If the shortened chain is reinforced as adequately as the longer chain, the intermediate links may be lost more or less permanently. But if these intermediate links have been cognitive responses, each with its own quality of consciousness or awareness, the learner would now be less aware of what he was doing than he would have been at an earlier stage in the learning process. Thus the experienced golfer, skater, or automobile driver is normally less aware of specific movements and adjustments than the neophyte. We are saying now that a person may become relatively unaware of "why" he is responding in a certain way or even of "how" he is responding due to the "short-circuiting" of cognitive responses that have proved unnecessary to the evocation of the final, functional response.

The other major way in which the conscious aspects of cognitive responses may be lost is in the specific instance where the final response is followed by unpleasant feelings. Such a sequence ("punishment" following response) tends to inhibit the responses that precede the punishment. Following familiar principles of learning, we assume that the response closest in sequence to the punishment is most inhibited. However, we assume that responses preceding the final one are inhibited also, the inhibition being less for those earlier in the sequence than for those closer to the final response. How much of the cognitive chain will be lost to such inhibitory tendencies depends upon the intensity and frequency with which unpleasant feelings follow upon the cognitive sequence.

We offer these two general conditions of learning as representing the equivalent of what the psychotherapist usually refers to as "repression." We note, however, that only the latter of the two examples corresponds with "repression" to the extent that "trauma" is considered a necessary precondition for the development of repression.

CONTROL, ADJUSTMENT, AND COMMUNICATION

The development of control.   Now we return to our hypothetical situation of the child and the apple. However, we shall change our experimental conditions. We replace the screen with a box which effectively encloses the apple and which will only be removed at our discretion. We also place in the child's view a *slice of apple,* which is considerably smaller than the whole apple under the box. The conditions of the experiment are that if the child eats the *slice* of apple, the box is not raised. If, however, he has not eaten the slice of apple in x minutes, the box will be raised, and the child will be allowed to eat the whole apple.

It is quite difficult to predict how any given child will respond to this experiment. The size of the available piece of apple relative to the size of the whole apple, the length of the period of delay, the hunger of the child, and the age of the child are all of some consequence. But so is the child's previous experience with delays or "promises" of this sort. If he has been fooled before by not getting the apple even when it was promised, we would expect him to have a stronger tendency to take the piece that is immediately and certainly available. Also, if the child has had no previous experience with situations where "it paid to wait," we would expect him to behave differently than if he had had such experience. On the other hand, if previous conditions had demanded a fifteen minute wait to get the whole apple, we might find him waiting fifteen minutes even if the apple is available after five minutes.

Here we are dealing with a situation which involves the matter of "control" over behavioral response. If the child cannot control his impulse to eat the slice of apple, he stands to lose the greater satisfaction of obtaining the whole apple. We might call this nonadaptive lack of control. If, on the other hand, he waits fifteen minutes for the whole apple when he need only have waited five, he has suffered ten minutes of deprivation without gaining any significant advantage. We might call this nonadaptive overcontrol.

With this simple example and formulation it may be possible to see how and under what conditions many of the adjustment problems of patients develop. To complete our consideration of feeling in relation to control, and of control in relation to adaptation and adjustment, we must add one more complication.

In our final example the conditions are these: the slice of apple is available to the child, but he is told it would be "bad" to eat it because his mother wants to use it in a salad. He is also told that his mother will go away for awhile. If the slice of apple is still there when his mother returns, she will give the child a "Good Boy" badge which he may wear for the rest of the day.

Our formulation would be the same as for our previous example. What has been changed is this: in the prior situation, "pleasant" and "unpleasant" referred to innately determined sensory qualities associated with "tasting" and "waiting to taste" respectively. In this last example, we are dealing with affective or feeling variables that depend upon specific kinds of learning, or what we sometimes refer to as "cultural conditioning." We have attempted to inhibit the child's tendency to eat the apple by describing such behavior as "bad." But this can only have an inhibiting effect if the word "bad" has, through prior experience, acquired the capacity to evoke unpleasant feelings. This presumes both a communicator who says "bad" and a reinforcer (who could be the same person) who sees to it that "bad" is associated with unpleasant feelings. Similarly, the "Good Boy" badge can only be a reward if having the badge has in some way been associated with pleasant feelings in prior experience.

Hedonism. In all of these examples and their extension into more complex situations we assume that behavior is hedonistically determined. In fact we assume that all behavior is hedonistically controlled or determined. But now it should be obvious that control problems, both those involving inadequate control and those involving excessive control, are complexly determined. When we consider the matter of cultural conditioning of feelings, we are well into the field of social values as distinguished from innately determined hedonism. We assume that this distinction between social and biological values exists only when behavior deemed necessary or desirable by a social group requires the individual to behave differently than he would if governed only by innately determined feelings.

Yet if we also assume that such innately directed behavior is at least generally oriented toward the survival of the individual, we must conclude that culturally directed behavior has a certain "antisurvival" or destructive potential for the individual from a strictly biological point of view. To offset this disadvantage, we note that social living tends to make certain conditions required for survival easier to obtain, such as adequate food, drink, shelter, and rest. At the same time, society, through individuals or institutions, stands ready to punish more or less severely and more or less surely those who fail to observe its rules and regulations.

The adjustment problem of each individual may then be regarded as that of obtaining as much pleasant experience as possible, considering both biologically and culturally determined values, while avoiding as much as possible either biologically determined or culturally determined unpleasant experiences. Such an adjustment includes the capacity to forego immediate gratification if by so doing the person involved stands to gain greater gratification at a later time.

Problems of adjustment.   We have already indicated that the sort of adjustment just mentioned requires the development of appropriate cognitive structures, that is, cognitive structures that enable the individual to anticipate accurately the probability of future events. However, the individual who relies only upon his own experience faces certain handicaps. First of all, he innately tends to overgeneralize the "lessons" learned from experience, so that he may apply them in situations where the outcome will be different from what he anticipates. Secondly, the person living in a complex society faces not only the problem of survival, but also the mastery of complex and culturally determined *means* of survival (for example, becoming a lawyer in order to earn a living). At the same time he must solve the problems of gaining socially determined rewards and avoiding socially determined punishments. In short, he has a lot to learn. Finally, he may have only a limited number of "tries" at certain major adjustments, such as obtaining an adequate education, achieving a successful marriage, establishing himself in a career, and functioning appropriately as a parent.

Ideally the person's "primary social conditioners" (parents, siblings, neighbors, teachers, friends, and others) would have these future social requirements clearly and accurately in mind when they superpose their own rewards and punishments upon the innately determined consequences of behavior. In the ideal situation not only would this be so, but the probability and intensity of reward or punishment would correlate perfectly with the probability and intensity of reward or punishment meted out by the secondary social conditioners of adult life.

Problems of communication.   We shall skip quickly past the errors conceivable in the situation outlined in order to add to them the problems involved in communication.

When it is considered necessary or desirable for the developing person to be prepared for conditions that he has not yet encountered, his "social conditioners" may undertake such preparation by communicating with him. In other words, they can tell him what might happen and what he "should" do in various situations and what may be the consequence of various kinds of behavior. But the knowledge of the social conditioner is never perfect, especially since conditions may change significantly between the time a person is trained and the time when he may use his training.

To all the problems of the accuracy of the conditioner's knowledge, we must also add the problems involved in the accurate use of language, since much of the person's training is verbal. We shall be primarily concerned with problems of communication in the next chapter, so we shall only preview a few of these problems here.

To list some of these: First, a given word may stand for a wide variety of "things" or "events" that may not have certain critical qualities in common, even though the common label leads us to believe that they are "all alike." Second, words have "affective connotation" (feeling-evoking capacities) which may predispose the communicant to a kind of response different from that intended by the communicator. (Tell a child that "only bad boys play hookey," and he may do it because what his parents consider bad boys happen to be the boys he likes.) Third, we mention the problem of accuracy, so far as the "informative" connotations of communications are concerned. Absolute accuracy in communication would require that a given word or sentence evoke the same cognitive responses in both communicator and communicant. This ideal is *not* likely to be achieved in reality, especially when there are gross differences in age, intelligence, education, or cultural background between the two persons involved.

If we compound errors in the social conditioner's information with his problems in communicating, and mix both of these with some measure of failure to achieve his intent, and finally add all of these errors to a person's own errors in learning from experience, then we begin to marvel that there is any accuracy at all in our subject's anticipations of future events. When we also consider that a great deal of learning may occur without cognitive representation, that cognitive elements can be lost from conscious experience in various ways and that cognitive structure can be changed through reinforcement without deliberate intent to do so, we should not be surprised that people have difficulty in adjusting. Nor do we consider it necessary to assume a special condition of "illness" to account for their confusion and for their distress.

SUMMARY

We have assumed a predominant position for emotion in the determination of behavior. However, our definition of psychotherapy as a *communicative relationship* assumes that we usually deal with cognitive structure more directly than we do with emotions. Quite frequently the psychotherapeutic process involves changing the cognitive structure of the patient as a means of achieving both behavioral and emotional objectives.

A *cognitive structure* is defined as a system of knowledge and beliefs. The total cognitive structure of a person can be thought of as composed of major substructures, such as knowledge and beliefs about the "self," about "others," and so on. An important aspect of psychotherapy has to do with the correction of cognitive structures when they fail to represent accurately the structure of "reality." The psychotherapist must, for all practical purposes, determine the nature of "reality" for the patient.

We regard habits as the basic elements in cognitive structure. The habits which constitute cognitive structure involve signs that have meaning primarily in terms of consistent association with certain types of perceptual response. Eventually, however, signs can be defined in terms of other signs. In either case, the development of meaning is synonymous with the development of habits, and changes in meaning involve changes in habits. Changes in cognitive structure are, therefore, governed by (or can most readily be understood in terms of) principles of learning.

The duration of psychotherapy is determined by the time required to change the habits involved in key or significant cognitive substructures. We define the characteristic of "rigidity" in cognitive structure in terms of the ease or difficulty of changing such significant cognitive habits. The basic determinants of rigidity are, therefore, the learning variables: degree of motivation, intensity of reinforcement, and frequency of reinforcement. However, we can also note or postulate certain general relationships between rigidity and patient variables or characteristics, such as age, education, intelligence, and anxiety level.

We have already noted that cognitive responses may become associated with each other in determining meaning. The relationships or relatedness of cognitive elements determines the "integration" of cognitive structures. Integrations or relationships may *not* exist in cognitive structure where such relationships do exist in reality, or a person may integrate certain cognitive elements (as in the development of superstition) when we doubt that similar relationships exist in reality. The general point is that the psychotherapist is concerned with the integration of cognitive elements in a given person as contrasted with integrations more generally accepted or integrations assumed to exist on a more objective basis, such as scientific investigation.

Certain cognitive substructures are associated with very intense feelings. Such substructures have been discussed in the psychoanalytic literature under the concept of "complex," such as Adler's "inferiority complex." These substructures tend to have an important influence on behavior because of the motivating effect of their affective component.

Since cognitive responses within the individual are a part of the total stimulus pattern determining what further responses he will make, such responses are closely associated with conscious control over behavior. The psychotherapist needs to know how any particular modification of cognitive structure may change a person's subsequent behavior.

Consciousness itself exists originally only as a perceptual response to sensory stimulation. Such perceptual responses may become conditioned so that one evokes another. This creates the possibility of conscious activities, such as remembering or thinking, which are relatively independent of immediate stimulation. However, we must be cautious about assuming that "awareness" of the cognitive responses which precede a response constitutes a necessary and sufficient condition for determining the nature of the response.

Such "control" over response is to some extent a function of anticipation or expectancy. However, expectancy determines behavior only via the anticipation of one or another outcome of behavior, and the significant aspect of "outcome" is its affective or hedonistic quality. This is determined originally only by innate biological or survival values.

As a result of social experience, the pleasant–unpleasant outcome of behavior may be altered by "social conditioners." Such social values, however, have an ultimate hedonistic basis also. The purpose of social conditioners may be to maximize the pleasant and to minimize the unpleasant experiences of the person being trained. However, the task involved is not a simple one, and serious errors in preparation may and do occur.

SUGGESTIONS FOR FURTHER READING

In Dollard and Miller (8), Chapters IX, XVIII, XX, and XXX are especially pertinent and should be helpful to the reader who lacks a detailed knowledge of learning theory.

REFERENCES

1. Guthrie, E. R. *The psychology of learning.* New York: Harper & Row, 1935.
2. Prince, M. *Clinical and experimental studies in personality.* Cambridge, Mass.: Sci-Art, 1929.
3. Thigpan, C. H., and Cleckley, H. M. *Three faces of Eve.* New York: McGraw-Hill, 1957. (Also available in paperback.)
4. Korzybski, A. *Science and sanity.* (2d ed.) Lancaster, Pa.: Science Press, 1941.
5. Jacobi, J. *The psychology of Jung.* New Haven, Conn.: Yale University Press, 1943.
*6. Way, L. *Adler's place in psychology.* New York: Collier, 1962.
7. Hayakawa, S. I. *Language in action.* New York: Harcourt, 1941.
8. Dollard, J., and Miller, N. E. *Personality and psychotherapy.* New York: McGraw-Hill, 1950.

* Paperback edition.

Chapter 4 | *Communication: Theory*

THE NATURE OF COMMUNICATION

Definitions. We shall begin our consideration of the theoretical aspects of communication relevant to psychotherapy by referring again to Jung's "controlled association" technique for the detection of complexes. To review briefly, this procedure involves the investigator's reading aloud a list of words and observing the subject for evidence of emotional response to each word. We shall now designate the investigator who says the words aloud as the "communicator" and the word as spoken the "communicative stimulus." We have suggested that if the communicative stimulus evokes a cognitive response from the subject, then we may say that the word "has meaning" for him.

If the word has meaning for the subject, we can then consider that a relatively simple form of communication has occurred. The investigator (communicator) has produced a stimulus that has evoked a meaning (cognitive response) in the subject. We note that the cognitive response may or may not serve to evoke an observable or measurable emotional response from the subject. If it does, it is quite possible that the subject may not be aware of this emotional response. He is almost certain not to be able to control certain physiological components, such as changes in blood pressure, pulse rate, respiration, and sweating, hence the investigative value of "lie detector" devices which measure just such physiological changes.

Nonsense and sense. Now suppose we use as our stimulus in controlled association a nonsense syllable spoken by the investigator. By definition, a nonsense syllable is a combination of letters, usually three letters with a vowel as the second letter, which has no meaning in the sense of having no established dictionary definition. "Zut" would be such a nonsense syllable. However, we note from experimental investigation that such nonsense syllables have different degrees of "association value" (1). This means that varying percentages of subjects will be able to give a word that the nonsense syllables makes them think of. Nonsense syllables may actually have a kind of meaning if they sound similar enough to words, because they may evoke the meaning of the word by stimulus generalization. So let us select a nonsense syllable that has zero association value.

If the communicator says this nonsense syllable aloud to the subject, will it evoke a cognitive response? No. We have ruled this out by our definition of "nonsense syllable" and by specifying that our stimulus word must have zero association value. Could we assign an arbitrary definition to such a syllable and teach it to our subject so that it would then have meaning (evoke a cognitive response) from him? Yes, as we shall explain when we discuss the development of language. All words are "nonsense" sounds to the child before he learns their meaning. If we developed a definition for the nonsense syllable in words which already had meaning for the subject and our subject learned it, this definition in words would then constitute the "meaning" of the nonsense syllable for our subject. The syllable would then evoke a cognitive response (the words in the definition) and have an "informative connotation." (2)

Sense and emotion.   Would the nonsense syllable have evoked an emotional response before it acquired a meaning? If we specify that our subject must never have heard the syllable before and if we control the problem of vocal expression by showing him the syllable printed on a card (rather than spoken), then we can be reasonably sure that the subject will *not* respond emotionally to the nonsense syllable. However, after he has learned our definition of the syllable, we can no longer be so sure. If words used in the definition arouse emotional responses (have affective connotation), then it is quite possible that presenting the syllable after its "meaning" has been learned *will* evoke an emotional response also. If so, then what was previously a nonsense syllable for our subject now has both "informative connotation" and "affective connotation" for him. The affective connotation has been acquired by a process known as "secondary conditioning" or, more generally, "higher order conditioning."

Why did we specify that our subject must never have heard the syllable before in predicting an outcome of "no emotional response" when the nonsense syllable was presented? We did this to guard against the possibility that the subject might have been *conditioned* in such a way as to evoke an emotional response. If fact we can do this ourselves if we wish. Let us perform the experiment (in imagination) of seating the subject in a chair with a seat which has been wired so that we can deliver a shock to the subject by pressing a button. Now we flash onto a screen a list of nonsense syllables, none of which has any "meaning" or association value for our subject. But each time the syllable "zut" is shown, we press the button and the subject receives a shock. If we also attach a lie detector to our subject, we will probably note that after a few such associations of the syllable with shock our subject is indicating all the physiological responses associated with emotion whenever "zut" is shown. We now have a "signal" ("zut") which we can assume arouses emotion even though the subject has never been given a formal definition for "zut." We could say that for this subject, at least, "zut" now has an affective connotation, although it has no "formal" (dictionary-type) informative connotation· We specify "formal" here, because actually "zut" now has a kind of informative connotation. Specifically it "means" to the subject: "I'm about to get shocked." In the same way, if one's car is stalled on a railroad track, the "signal" of an approaching train's whistle would have "affective connotation" and also "mean": "'Let's get out of here!'"

Vocal expression and meaning.   Why did we specify that the non-sense syllable should be presented visually when we originally tested our subject's emotional response to "zut" and presumably found none? As we indicated, the purpose of this specification is to control the element of vocal expression. If we had presented "zut" to our subject orally, but had deliberately said it in a harsh, "angry" manner, we might have evoked an emotional response. If this had happened, we would have concluded that it was the "vocal expression" (harsh, angry manner of saying the syllable) which evoked the emotional response, rather than the nonsense syllable. If manner of vocal expression arouses feelings it has "affective connotation." If the subject also interprets the expression as indicating the investigator is angry with him, then we would conclude that the vocal expression has "informal informative connotation." Here "informal informative connotation" is contrasted with "formal informative connotation."

Is our formulation concerning the affective and informative connotation of vocal expression applicable to "real life" situations? We believe it is. "Go to hell," can be a playful, even an affectionate, rejoinder or a challenge to combat, depending upon how it is said and the situation in which it is said. Which reminds us also to point out that communicative signals usually occur in a larger context of events in a particular situation or what we refer to as a "stimulus complex." Under these conditions the general situation as well as the vocal expression help to determine the meaning of the particular words spoken. Even if one's expression is intended to be playful, it is safer to tell a close friend to "go to hell" then to say the same words in the same way to a stranger or to an enemy. One might further insure against misinterpretation by smiling, thus adding further situational "cues."

A different example of the importance of situational cues is afforded by Lewis Carrol's poem "The Jabberwock" in *Through the Looking Glass*. " 'Twas brillig and the slithy toves did gyre and gimble in the wabe" has a kind of meaning for most persons on first reading, although most of these same people would probably be hard put to explain why.

Our reason for stressing the matter of vocal expression (and situation) as factors in communication will become apparent when we discuss the ontogenetic development of language. Briefly, our contention there will be that the developing child may learn the "meaning" of vocal expression (also facial expression and other situational aspects of communication) before he knows the literal definition or meaning of the words spoken to him.

Now we come to what we consider a very interesting question: Is a slap a form of communication?

"Behavior language."   There are certain things we can be reasonably sure of. First of all, we would expect the slap to stimulate pain receptors and thereby the sensation of pain in the person slapped. Pain is usually associated with negative emotional states, although under certain conditions it may not be or may have other kinds of emotional consequences (as in "masochism" where pain is associated with sexual arousal). However, assuming the more usual situation, we anticipate that the slap will also cause an unpleasant or negative feeling in the person slapped. In this sense we can say that the slap has an "affective connotation." We also note that it might be used as punishment (negative reinforcement) to discourage a child from doing something we do not want him to do, such as tearing up a book. Under these conditions the effect of the slap would be virtually identical, whether we were dealing with a puppy, a chimpanzee, or a child. In fact, it makes no difference whether the "punishment" is administered by a chimpanzee, a human being or a machine.

THE DEVELOPMENT OF COMMUNICATION

Verbalizing.   Suppose, however, that our "punisher" is some kind of verbalizing creature. Suppose further that the slap *is* accompanied by some form of verbalization from the punisher, and that words such as "stop" or "don't" are consistent components of what is being said while the child is being punished. After sufficient repetitions of this situation, we may note two things. The first, and more obvious, is that sometimes the child will respond to the word "don't" by inhibiting what he is doing or about to do. Secondly, and less obviously, the child is probably responding to the word "don't" with certain physiological changes which could be measured and which might be similar to (although probably of lesser magnitude than) the physiological changes accompanying a slap.

If we persist and continue to reinforce the inhibition of the unwanted behavior by slapping whenever the word "don't" alone fails to inhibit the response, we should eventually arrive at a point where saying the word alone *will* suffice consistently to inhibit the behavior. (We might add, as a practical note, that if "don't" alone fails to stop the child from doing what we do not want him to do, and we "make an exception" by not punishing him, it will take considerably more learning trials to accomplish this result.)

Reward and punishment.   Could this form of training be regarded as beneficial for the child? To answer this question, let us first consider the situation of punishment without accompanying verbalization. Here we note first that we have probably caused the child pain and also evoked an unpleasant feeling state. By so doing, we may have created a tendency for him to fear and therefore avoid the person who punishes him and perhaps even the situation in which he was punished. These particular consequences we would certainly consider "undesirable" in terms of the child's adjustment to his environment. On the other hand, if punishment prevents the child from running into the street where he may be killed, this might change our evaluation of its "desirability." Or suppose that our unpunished child behaves in a way which makes others want to avoid *him*. We would then have to weigh the undesirable consequences of punishment against the undesirable consequences of social rejection.

Of course children can also be "trained" through the use of positive reinforcement (reward). *If* the desired results, so far as modifying the child's behavior, can be and are being obtained in this way, there are obvious reasons for preferring the use of reward to the use of punishment. We also note in passing that punishment functions primarily to inhibit responses and is therefore of limited value when the subject is learning to make new responses, such as in learning to read or to perform other academic tasks.

We would regard the slap alone as fitting our general definition of "psychotherapeutic" only if the undesirable consequences avoided outweigh the undesirable consequences of the slap itself. Annie Sullivan, as portrayed in the play *The Miracle Worker*, was very "unkind" to Helen Keller in the initial stages of their relationship, but the consequences were highly "therapeutic" for Helen Keller.

The therapeutic potential of verbalizing.   Now let us consider whether
we have increased the "psychotherapeutic" value of the slap by introducing the verbal element "don't." In order to do this, we must continue our
analysis somewhat further.

All of our three hypothetical subjects, the puppy, the chimpanzee,
and the child, will respond in the same general manner if "don't" is said
while they are being slapped for misbehavior. If we are consistent and
persistent enough in our efforts, each will learn in time to react to "don't"
by inhibiting an incipient response. We can eliminate the slap unless
"don't" alone fails to suppress the response that we want to inhibit. We
might say that each of them now knows what "don't" means. But hearing
"don't" is certainly less painful and may well be less disturbing emotionally than being slapped. If this is the case, then the association of a communicative stimulus with the slap has increased the possibility that the
net result of our training will be "therapeutic," since we gain the same
result while imposing less of a burden of negative feeling upon the subject being trained.

Considering only the child now, we can make still further observations. Most parents have seen a young child approach a forbidden object
and either shake his head or say "no, no" aloud and then avoid the
object. The child can do something which the puppy and the chimpanzee
apparently cannot do, namely, react to his own impulses to touch the
forbidden object by making the same verbal response that the parent
might make if he were there. We shall examine the significance of this
phenomenon at a later point in this chapter. Here we shall ask whether
this presents any possibility of further increase in the "psychotherapeutic"
value of training.

Nonverbal communication.   Let us return to the situation of the slap
alone, and answer the question in a previous paragraph as to whether a
slap is a form of communication. If we assume that any stimulus which
has "informative connotation" is a "communicative stimulus," the question may be answered affirmatively. This reminds us that "communication" is not strictly a matter of words. In the first place the "communicator" who only slaps is not using words to convey meaning. In the
second place it is doubtful whether either the puppy or the chimpanzee
has any "word" responses as a part of its cognitive structure. The puppy,
the chimpanzee, and the child can all learn to respond to different tones
of voice or general patterns of vocal expression just as they learned to
respond to the slap, except that certain expressions may be "rewarding"
rather than "punishing." In the absence of verbal cognitive responses,
they would be forced to respond to vocal expression alone—in effect,
they would ignore *what* the person was saying and react only to non-

verbal cues. A "communicator" who is attempting to deceive usually concentrates his attention more fully on *what* he says than on *how* he says it. Is this the reason the layman often credits animals and children (and women?) with having a special faculty for knowing what a person is "*really like?*"

There are several conclusions of potential value to the psychotherapist that might be drawn here. Perhaps the simplest is that being honest with patients is the surest way to instill confidence. This is actually a corollary of the conclusion that the psychotherapist is likely to be "communicating" more about himself, his attitudes, feelings, and values than he intends and more than he realizes. Some interesting research has tended to substantiate this conclusion and to raise questions about whether the psychotherapist really has any chance at all of remaining a featureless mirror in which the patient sees only himself reflected or upon which the patient may draw whatever characteristics "transference" dictates (3). This immediately leads to many complex questions concerning the patient-psychotherapist relationship that we shall have to consider later.

Finally, we would suggest that the psychotherapist should make sure that he is devoting a sufficient amount of his own attention to the nonverbal cues that he may receive from the patient. There are so many of these that it is probably wise for the practicing psychotherapist to review a good summary of body changes in emotion from time to time to check up on cues that might be overlooked. For example, we once considerably altered our interpretation of what a patient was saying in an initial interview upon noting that, although her manner was quite calm, extensive perspiration stains were appearing in the axillary area. Since then we have made it a practice generally to shake hands both before and ofter an initial interview, partly for the purpose of noting amount of palmar sweating (which in any event is probably a more reliable index of tension than axillary moisture in these days of deodorants and anti-perspirants). We have also considered the use of GSR equipment as an adjunctive device during psychotherapeutic interviews.

At a more complex level of behavior we have generally found it safe to assume that a child patient has "accepted" us as soon as he asks if he may use our bathroom. Of course if he asks this immediately upon meeting us for the first time, we make quite a different interpretation.

The primacy of nonverbal communication.   Having delineated the basic principles involved in the development of meaning, we shall now turn our attention to more general aspects of the development of meaning and of language.

It *does* seem to be the case that each of us in the course of our development learns to respond first to nonverbal cues as communicative stimuli, such cues as gestures, facial expression, and tone of voice. This is not difficult to explain. The variety of expressions, whether gestural, facial, or vocal, that the child encounters is considerably less than the variety of words that he hears. Parents of average intelligence and education may have a "speaking" or active vocabulary of 5000 or more words which can be used in a tremendous number of meaningful combinations. Compared with this variety, the distinctly different patterns of emotional expression are relatively limited and relatively stereotyped. Any number of different things can be said in "an angry manner." The significance or meaning of the "angry manner" as a relatively constant aspect of the stimulus complex is readily learned also because it tends to be repeated much more frequently than most of the words which may be spoken.

A few words such as "bad," "no," "naughty," and "don't" may be used consistently enough to be learned relatively early. However, we believe that initially expression alone has meaning (as in the infant, who will smile back at us if we call him a dirty little thief in a smiling, friendly manner).

Expression–content balance.   Over the years this situation changes, with the listener or person being communicated to responding increasingly to meaning conveyed by verbal content. At the opposite extreme from the infant we might place the ancient professor whose leg can be pulled by students because he listens only to words and ignores the nuances of expression which convey irony, sarcasm, and so on.

We suggest that a variety of factors may be correlated with what we shall now call the "expression–content balance" in the listener. Among these may be age, intelligence, verbal level of environment, amount of education, and "emotional defensiveness." There is room for much speculation, and several doctoral theses could be written in this area alone. For example, consider the hypothesis that "expression–content balance" will tend more toward responding to "expression" in female than in male subjects when groups are equated for age, intelligence, and education. Such an hypothesis could be based on the assumption that the way in which girls are raised leads them generally to be less emotionally defensive than men. Our clinical experience would tend to support the assumption, but unfortunately case loads make poor samples from the experimental point of view.

One of the principal significances of these suggestions to the psychotherapist is that the same words said in the same way may very well mean different things to different patients depending upon the relative attention that they pay to expression and to content. We have long since become used to the fact that some patients show astounding sensitivity to the psychotherapist's state of health, degree of fatigue, and general mood. Other patients are quite oblivious to all except the most obvious clues. Some patients rather consistently misinterpret the therapist's feelings, which is not too surprising when we consider that research has shown considerable individual differences among persons in manner of expressing feeling but considerable consistency within the individual. What we assume is happening here is that the patient is interpreting the psychotherapist's behavior, expression, and so on in terms of what it would mean if he were someone else, such as a father, who expresses his feelings differently but in a way which the patient has learned to interpret.

Along these same lines again we raise the question of the extent to which the psychotherapist succeeds in protecting his anonymity (if he tries to do so) by the expedient of withholding information about himself. We sometimes find it necessary to explain to a patient "what is wrong" if this is the only way we can prevent the patient from misinterpreting the mood or the reason for the mood of the therapist. Of course, we also note the nature of the patient's misinterpretation, at least when we feel reasonably sure that it is the patient's error rather than self-deception on the part of the psychotherapist.

We might also conclude that the psychotherapist may well have to vary both content and manner of expression depending upon the age, intelligence, education, and so forth of the patient with whom he is dealing. Is this a significant reason why some psychotherapists are quite limited in the kinds of patient with whom they can work effectively? Could this be one of the reasons why attempts at psychotherapy were originally somewhat restricted in terms of patient selection with a marked preference shown for patients (adult, intelligent, educated) who could be counted on to be oriented toward "content" in the "expression–content balance" in communication?

GENERAL SEMANTICS AND ADJUSTMENT

Vocabulary and referents. There are certain points of interest in connection with the development of a vocabulary in the child. One of these is that nouns tend to dominate in the early stages of vocabulary development. The reasons for this are fairly obvious. We all remember the classic scene in which Tarzan says, "You Jane, me Tarzan," pointing to his mate and to himself in turn. This is an excellent example of early vocabulary building. At this stage, names (nouns) and the things they stand for are easily and readily associated both by the "teacher" and by the learner.

The importance of this particular facet of language development has been brought to our attention by those interested in general semantics. They point out that this initial experience in which all nouns refer to concrete "things" tends to create an expectation or assumption that *all* nouns refer to concrete things. Korzybski was among the first to suggest that we as adults often fail to distinguish between nouns with concrete referents and those with abstract referents. Some of the ways in which this failure effects human adjustment have been delineated by Korzybski (4) and some of his more verbal followers, including Stuart Chase (5), Hayakawa (2), and Wendell Johnson (6). In the remainder of this chapter we shall draw rather heavily on ideas that they have presented and clarified.

For example, they point out that if a man's goal in life is "to be successful," but the man himself does not specify in exact and concrete terms what he considers "being successful," he may live all his life without any feeling of satisfaction in achieving his goal simply because he does not "really" know what it is. The goals of patients are sometimes equally indefinite and/or abstract. In such cases, we may find that one of the things we shall want to do for the patient is to help him define his objectives in therapy and in life with greater clarity and concreteness. Needless to say, it is also helpful if the psychotherapist is equally definite in his own thinking regarding the case at hand.

Overgeneralization.   Another tendency which we note in the early verbal development of the child is his tendency to overgeneralize the applications of the nouns or names which he learns. This can be illustrated by the child's calling almost all four-footed animals "doggies" if "doggy" is one of the first words he learns to say and use. An even more embarrassing generalization is his tendency to call all men, including close family friends, "Daddy." In instances such as these, the child is taught when to use the word and when not to use it by "differential reinforcement." This simply means that the child is encouraged when he uses the word to refer to the correct "things" but is discouraged from using the word when a different class of "objects" is involved. Usually this process is combined with teaching the child the correct name of those "objects" which he misnames.

The problem here, according to the position presented by general semantics, is that this process of differential reinforcement and the resulting discrimination in naming is usually not carried far enough in the training of the child. Korzybski would, we presume, object violently to Gertrude Stein's proposition that "a rose is a rose is a rose." He might argue first of all that there are a large number of distinct varieties of roses. He would then point out that within any variety, no two roses are exactly alike. Finally, he woud indicate that a given rose is not the same from one day to the next.

This illustration may not bring out the significance of failing to make certain kinds of distinction, so let us use an example closer to the field of psychotherapy. Suppose a patient tells us that she cannot decide which of two men she loves more. Instead of plunging immediately into the problem as stated, we might wish to remind ourselves and the patient that the word "love" is used to describe a wide variety of emotional relationships, that each of these relationships is unique, and that the "same" relationship does not necessarily remain the "same" from day to day. In other words, we would want to know considerably more about each relationship: how it started, how long it has lasted, what kinds of interaction it has involved, what kinds of situation they have been in together, and so forth. We might ask for a much more detailed account also of how she has felt at various times about each man, the amount of conflict between them and the issues involved, other negative feelings (such as anxiety) which she may have felt, and, if possible, some further specifications as to the "kinds" of love or affection felt for each man. We might want to know whether it is similar to the feeling of a mother for a son, a sister for a brother, a daughter for a father, a friend for another friend, a younger person's "crush" on an older person with higher status. Does each or either involve intense feelings of infatuation, strong attraction to physical characteristics, admiration of intellectual qualities, and so on?

We might note in passing the peculiar generality of the word "love" itself. Experts in general semantics believe that terms tend to become more specific in meaning when distinctions in meaning and exact specification of referents is critical to adaptation or adjustment. A favorite example cited is that an Eskimo language may have several different words for snow depending upon whether it is or is not suitable for such vital functions as hunting, traveling, or house building. In this context we have always considered it interesting (and often very inconvenient) that in English we use the single word "love" to cover such a wide variety of positive feeling states, extending it even to include feelings toward objects, as in "I just love chocolate ice cream."

Time indexing.   While still on the subject of specificity of referents, we should note as a subject of special importance the matter of the time index or time specification whenever we are dealing with either persons or events. Usually in psychotherapy we find it necessary to discuss with the patient certain events and certain relationships with others in his past in order to understand various aspects of present behavior. Not infrequently we find that in the process of re-evoking cognitive components related to past events, the emotional responses which were originally associated with those events (and consequently with the correlated cognitive structures created at the time, which we now call "memories") are re-evoked also. Or, more accurately, we should say that recalling past events may still elicit emotional responses, the emotional response, if evoked, being very much a "here and now" event. We must keep in mind that the people and events of times past have reality in the present only in terms of evokable cognitive responses in our patient. The psychotherapist and the patient must both remain aware that "memories" represent what *was* true, not what *is* true, and that each bears (or should bear) a specific time "tag," such as July 4, 1957. This would tend to emphasize to the patient the unreality of hating "Father 1965" for an undeserved punishment administered by "Father 1952."

Another illustration of the importance of time indexing is the example of the patient who never seems to become emotionally involved in relationships and who keeps breaking off old relationships and starting new ones. We find that he believes himself to be cowardly, physically inept, socially unacceptable, and poor. This self-evaluation does not have much correspondence with reality as of 1965 but is a more accurate description of the patient as he was in 1960. The patient relates to others as if "myself 1960" is the "real me." He breaks off relationships before the other person can discover the "real me," and since he must always break them off, he cannot "afford" to become emotionally involved. If it is possible to get the patient to consider "myself today" as the "real me" and relegate "myself 1960" to the cognitive classification of "past events," we might reasonably expect some changes in his mode of relating to others.

Stereotyping.   We believe that the child's natural tendency to overgeneralize the applicability of nouns unless corrected is of considerable importance in accounting for what the social psychologist refers to as "social stereotypes" or simply "stereotypes" (7). Gertrude Stein's "a rose is a rose is a rose" implies the stereotype "all roses are alike." The swain who simply tells the florist to send his beloved "a dozen roses" is accepting such a stereotype. However if the girl "loves" red roses but "hates" yellow ones, he may be in trouble, depending upon which color the florist decides to send. The discriminating florist would help our young man "make a better adjustment to reality" and thus serve a "psychotherapeutic" function in his life by making inquiries as to the young lady's preference in roses.

The degree of generalization that is tolerable so far as *social* stereotypes are concerned depends upon how significant the persons stereotyped are to fulfilling basic needs of the "stereotyper." If we believe that "all Chinamen look alike," it might not make much difference in our lives unless we happen to be starving to death in a Chinese restaurant. In that event we had better start praying that we do not have a waiter who is convinced that "all Occidentals look alike." A generalization of probably much more significance would be a patient's saying (or acting as if) "You men are all alike." If her previous experiences with men have led to predominantly negative feelings, we may find such a patient avoiding men generally, even though such avoidance involves foregoing the satisfaction of a number of significant social and emotional needs. One "strategy" of the psychotherapist in such a case might be to attempt to create greater discrimination with respect to the classification "men."

The anticipation of reality.   Some part of each individual's confusion about which words have objective referents and which do not undoubtedly grows out of the fact that he is told about "things" before he encounters them in first-hand experience. Since none of these anticipated things or situations have concrete reality for the learner in terms of his own sensory experience, it is especially difficult for him to distinguish the "real" from the "unreal." If a child has never seen either the devil or Nikita Khrushchev, which one (if either) is he to consider real (or unreal)? Obviously so far as the world of the "not-yet-observed" is concerned, each individual is tremendously dependent upon the accuracy of *information received* for the accuracy of his cognitive "map" of that particular segment of "reality." This is true not only of the major aspect of objective *versus* abstract, but also with respect to each of the major defects of cognitive structure that we have mentioned previously: the cognitive map is blank where there is structure in the corresponding reality, the cognitive map shows structure where there is no corresponding structures in reality, and proportions of the cognitive map are distorted with respect to the corresponding structure in reality.

These anticipations of reality based upon verbal information supplied to the person by others, rather than upon direct sensory experience of the individual himself, obviously may form the basis for various sorts of opinions, attitudes, and judgments concerning those "things" about which the person is informed. Oversimplified conceptions of what the anticipated reality will be like is one source of "stereotypes," although we should note that stereotypes may also be based upon unwarranted generalization from limited experience with "real things."

Prejudice.   In the same way, attitudes that we might label as "prejudices" or prejudgments may be based either upon conceptions given to us by others or upon unwarranted generalizations from our own limited experience. When we speak of "attitudes" we are referring to the emotions or feelings attached to or aroused by certain components of cognitive structure. Since emotions bring us back to those aspects of "internal events" which both motivate and help to determine the direction and nature of behavior, we can see that what a person has been told about "reality" and which feelings are associated with the kinds of cognitive maps he has been given both may have considerable importance in determining how he behaves. We may also assume that when his behavior is influenced significantly by such "borrowed maps," the accuracy (adequacy) of his "adjustment" will depend to a proportionate extent upon the accuracy of the information that he has received. For example, at this point in history our survival may depend to a significant extent upon whether we do anything—and, if so, what we do—individually to protect ourselves from the effects of atomic bombing. Yet almost all of us are dependent for both motivation and direction on information supplied to us by others, since only a few hundred thousand at most have any idea of the effects of multimegaton bombs as a matter of direct experience.

The cognitive effects of prejudice.   We should like to note one further aspect of the individual's ability to "anticipate" on the basis of communication to him from others. This is that when a particular area of the cognitive field has been structured by such anticipation, we assume that it is no longer what we might call "equireceptive" to all further informational input. Rather we assume, all else being equal, that new cognitive components which have congruence with cognitive responses the individual has already made have a greater probability of remaining conscious than either cognitive responses which have never occurred before or cognitive responses that are incompatible with those which have previously been made. More freely translated, what we are saying is that we are more likely to believe something we have already heard than something we have never heard before or something which contradicts what we have heard before. Actually, experimental evidence suggests that we may even distort our first-hand perception of reality if it fails to conform with what we have previously been told. The same experiments suggest that our "memories" of experience are even more subject to distortion than is perception, and if we are called upon to make a "judgment," such as "good" or "bad," those judgments may be even more distorted (8). Such observations were made, in fact, long before there was any formal science of psychology and are probably the basis for prohibiting nonexpert witnesses from expressing an opinion while giving testimony in a court of law.

The applications of this principle to psychotherapy are many. Here we shall only mention that this characteristic of either rejecting (or accepting only with difficulty) comunications which are at variance with what the patient already "knows" or believes to be true is one of the most persistent problems which the psychotherapist faces. But before jumping to the conclusion that this is simply a form of "resistance" based upon a negative "transference," we should note carefully whether the patient is not equally "resistant" to accepting direct evidence which contradicts already existing beliefs. For example, we have listened to a patient, who is convinced that he is "stupid," make elaborate "excuses" to explain how he managed to get an "A" in a course ("the final was easy, the other students were dumb, the teacher gave me a break"), even though at other times he gives every indication of wanting to be "smart." The fact of the matter is that this patient is quite intelligent but concluded in childhood that he was stupid because he could not do things as well as an older brother could.

THE INFLUENCE OF OTHERS

Self-direction.   As soon as the child learns to use words, he also acquires the capacity to create verbal stimulus complexes for himself. Put more simply: first the child must be instructed, later he can instruct himself. (In computor terminology, the child can be programmed to program himself.) In certain situations whether the child responds one way or another depends upon the kinds of instructions he gives himself. These instructions may include the child's ideas about the outcomes or consequences of various courses of action, as when Red Skelton portraying "The Bad Widdle Kid" says: "If I dood dat, I get a whippin'." In this sense, the child may exert a considerable degree of control over his behavior. Note that he not only can instruct himself and anticipate (more or less accurately) the consequences of his behavior, but he also is capable of rewarding or punishing himself in terms of self-approval or self-disapproval after a particular kind of response.

Control.   What is crucial to our understanding of this phenomenon of "self-control" is that it begins as control by others. We strongly suspect that it basically mirrors in nature and effectiveness the nature and effectiveness of the original externally imposed controls. At least we note that patients who are excessively "self-controlled" regularly have parents who have successfully imposed a strong degree of control during the patient's childhood. Among the "unself-controlled" we find both those whose parents were lax and those who succeeded from time to time in evading or breeching the disciplinary walls that their parents attempted to maintain.

In psychoanalytic concepts we would say: "No tyrannical superego without tyrannical parents; no ineffectual superego without ineffectual parents."

Self-evaluation. The same "reflection of others" is noted in certain aspects of the child's self-evaluation. Originally the child is evaluated by others in verbal terms such as "good–bad," "ugly–pretty," "smart–stupid," and so forth. But as soon as he can also make this type of response, he may apply such "judgments" to himself as well as to others.

Initially the child seems to be quite suggestible in matters of self-judgment, especially when the opinion of the adult authority figure is *less* favorable than his own. We suspect that this is primarily due to the fact that judgment is a very complex function and that the child is often lacking in standards adequate for making any kind of independent evaluation, let alone an accurate one. We suppose the child rather soon learns from experience that it is "safer" to underestimate his abilities than to overestimate them, in the sense that the former protects him from "failure-experiences" while the latter subjects him to "failure-experiences." At any rate we note on empirical grounds the suggestibility of the child with respect to self-judgment, especially of a negative or depreciating nature.

This characteristic of the child is extremely unfortunate, since it often leaves his self-evaluation considerably at the mercy of his parents' judgment, and this may be defective for any one or more of a number of very common reasons. We note in passing that inaccuracies of parental (and other adult) opinion *may* lead the child to an exaggerated feeling of his own value, ability, or importance. Such exalted opinions, however, usually wear away on the stony soil of reality, especially that harsh reality which exists just outside the protected family circle. Those who do psychotherapy with children have many opportunities to see the child who is reacting in rather violent and strange ways to this "outside" reality, as represented, for example, by school.

We are more concerned with the parent who makes the child feel inadequate. This is rarely done intentionally, although sometimes it *is* done deliberately for hostile reasons. What we more commonly see is the parent who *wants* his child to be confident and believe in himself, yet manages to create feelings of inadequacy and inferiority.

Parental errors in evaluation. How does he do it? We shall go to the trouble of listing quite a few of the major and common problems which arise, because we consider "feelings" of inferiority and/or inadequacy to be a major problem in psychotherapy.

First of all, few parents understand and accept the concept of "maturational readiness" for learning. The typical parent believes that his child should be able to learn almost anything the parent wants to teach him at almost any age the parent decides to teach it to him. Few parents have any conception of how long it takes a child to learn a given task, ready or not. Few parents consider the importance of motivation (the child's, not theirs) as a factor in learning, and very few parents realize how very little motivation children have for learning the things their parents want them to learn. Finally, very few parents know anything of value about how to teach or instruct. What parents are most aware of is *how well they want* their child to perform and *when they want* their child to do it. Put them all together, they spell *trouble*. Trouble, because all of these conditions are highly conducive to creating a situation where the child first says: "I can't do it" and, eventually, "I can't do anything."

One error in teaching methods is especially deadly. It is the familiar statement: "You did that pretty well, but—" followed by a number of words of "constructive" criticism designed to indicate to the child just what he did wrong and how he could do it better. Whether it is called "constructive" or not, the net balance is usually one hundred or so words of criticism balanced against two words of faint praise. The net result is "negative reinforcement" which means negative feelings and, specifically, negative feelings about attempting to learn.

This is a subject which we cannot begin to exhaust in any reasonable compass. We shall only repeat that the child's self-evaluation mirrors closely the evaluation, direct or indirect, intentional or unintentional, which he receives from others.

Errors in self-evaluation.   Of course the child makes significant errors of his own. Most obviously, as Adler points out, the child *is* inferior and inadequate, compared to most adults. While adults have some basis for "making allowances" (although they seldom do so with a desirable degree of accuracy), the child has almost none. We are reminded of the child who, when complimented on a drawing as being exceptionally well done for a six-year-old, replied: "I don't want it to be 'ceptional well done for a six-year-old. I want it to be 'ceptional well done for *anybody!*"

What we wish to emphasize about self-evaluations of inferiority or inadequacy is that such self-given cognitive cues tend to evoke avoidant responses. The individual does not want to try, even if he actually *has* the ability to succeed, because he anticipates failure. Thus it is extremely difficult to "acquaint" him with the reality of his own competence. Also we can understand a little better why the student mentioned a few pages back makes a definite effort to "explain away" his academic success. He is afraid of being tempted into further efforts by a single "success," because the single success experience (or perhaps even a number of them) may not be sufficient to alter a heavily reinforced self-evaluation of inadequacy or to counterbalance the resulting fear of failure.

THE ADAPTIVE FUNCTIONS OF LANGUAGE

Anticipation.   Before concluding this chapter we should also consider the constructive uses of language and communication. In very general terms language is the means by which human experience is summarized, evaluated, and transmitted. It thus enables any literate person potentially to become the heir of all mankind's recorded experience. Although each person's initial contact with language is with behavioral and vocal communication, he establishes contact with a larger and more objective world as soon as he learns to read.

The most general advantage of language and communication is that it enables us to anticipate, to know about, "things" which we have not yet seen or may never see, but which may nevertheless effect our welfare very considerably. Many citizens of the United States live and die without ever knowing what their government is doing except indirectly by means of communication. Yet what the government does is dependent upon this knowledge through our communications back to officials of the government as correspondents and voters. At the other extreme, verbal instruction or a book of etiquette may help an inexperienced young man to enjoy himself more (or to suffer less) at his first formal dinner party than he would if he had to learn his "manners" on the basis of his own experience.

Reinforcement.   There are also more specific ways in which the use of language may help the individual to adjust. A very significant and important advantage of the use of language is as a "mediator" of reinforcement. The following description may help to clarify this concept. The impulse to do or not to do a certain thing is very closely tied in with what we expect to happen if we do or if we do *not* do it. Or, put another way, we are more likely to repeat responses which have led to pleasant consequences and less likely to repeat those which have had unpleasant consequences. However, we note in animals and very young children that what we have just said is true only with respect to consequences which follow almost immediately after the response, and the more immediate a given consequence, the greater its effect. But an older child *may* put his money in a piggy bank even though he hears the ice cream man's bell ringing outside his door. If questioned about this strange behavior, he may tell us that he is saving his money for a pair of roller skates. Now we must assume that the *anticipation* of having the roller skates (which is only possible through the use of language) provides enough satisfaction to motivate (and reinforce) the response of putting the money in the bank rather than obtaining immediate satisfaction by using the money to buy ice cream. In short, language greatly increases a person's capacity to orient his behavior in terms of more significant but delayed satisfactions rather than in terms of more immediate but lesser satisfactions.

Vicarious experience.   Consider another potential value of using language: it is the capacity to learn or to solve problems vicariously rather than through overt behavior, at a considerable saving in time and energy. For example: a group of Boy Scouts want to cross a mountain stream which is cold, swift, and of unknown depth. They consider fording the stream, but decide that this will be both uncomfortable and dangerous. Someone suggests building a bridge, but this is rejected as involving too much time and effort. Finally, someone suggests felling a tree. They look to see if there is a large enough tree in the proper position. Having found one, they finally consider the merits of felling the tree *versus* fording the stream. Some time will have been consumed in this process but with a potential net advantage in terms of energy saved and/or dangers avoided.

Mediated generalization.   As our last example we shall mention the value of language in "mediated" generalization. Here again the meaning of the term can be illustrated through a simple example. A person wants to go from Los Angeles to San Francisco so he considers various public means of transportation: airplane, boat, train, and bus. The term "public means of transportation," which applies to these various vehicles, makes them roughly equivalent for the general purpose of moving from Los Angeles to San Francisco, although they may have different values for more specific purposes such as saving time or money. In terms of *stimulus* generalization, a bus may resemble an automobile more than it does an airplane, but in terms of *mediated* generalization, bus and airplane belong together in the class "public transportation," which is appropriate to the person's needs, whereas automobile belongs in the class "private transportation," which is not.

However, we should note that the value of language in each of these instances depends upon the accuracy with which it anticipates reality. If the child saving money for roller skates is forced to buy clothing instead, he may wish he had used it to buy ice cream and will be less inclined to save money again. If the Boy Scouts decide to fell the tree, but find that it takes all day to do it, they may wish they had forded the stream or built a bridge. And if the traveler decides to take a boat to San Francisco, but finds that the boat runs only every other week and takes thirty-six hours to make the trip, he may have to change his plans. Ultimately the value of language in assisting a person to adjust depends entirely upon the *accuracy* with which it enables him to anticipate consequences.

SUMMARY

The psychotherapist should be an expert on the subject of communication and an expert in communicating. The earliest forms of communication are nonverbal. Moreover, nonverbal clues are more significant in both "sending" and "receiving" with some patients than with others. An awareness that the psychotherapist himself continually transmits nonverbal cues to the patient raises serious questions concerning the feasibility of the anonymous role which is recommended by both "classical" psychoanalysts and some "client-centered" psychotherapists. This question leads to another: specifically, in what manner shall the psychotherapist relate, if not anonymously?

Words as stimuli are capable of evoking both feelings and cognitive responses. Words which evoke feelings have affective connotation. Such words can be used to motivate and to reinforce other responses. Words which evoke cognitive responses have meaning in the usual sense of the term, or they can be said to have informative connotation. Many words, of course, have both informative and affective connotation.

Words which consistently accompany rewards or punishments may acquire punishing or rewarding properties. Eventually they can be used in controlling a person's behavior in lieu of primary rewards and punishments. Also, if appropriately trained, the child can take over some of these control functions himself and thereby function adequately without immediate supervision. We assume that he can do this when he is able to make the same verbal responses to himself that others have previously made to him.

While there are many advantages in the use of language, there are also certain difficulties or complications. For example, the child first learns words which stand for things. As a consequence, he may assume that words always stand for or represent some aspect of sensible reality, but this is not necessarily true. The word-user also tends innately to over-generalize the applicability of verbal labels and to assume that all things bearing the same label are identical. The principles of general semantics remind us, however, that the "same" person is not really the same if any appreciable period of time has elapsed between one identification and another. In order to be accurate in specification, all significant terms should be "time indexed."

One of the positive values of verbal communication is that it makes it possible to prepare a person for situations before he encounters them. Hand in hand with this goes the danger of inappropriate preparation, such as the development of social stereotypes and the predetermination of responses that may not result in optimal adjustment to the actual circumstances which will be encountered.

Actually, the process of communication puts every developing individual pretty much at the mercy of his social conditioners. They evaluate both the child himself and other persons for the child before he has any basis for independent evaluation. Parents are prone to several types of error in evaluating the child, and the child also makes errors in self-evaluation. Furthermore, the social conditioners may provide more or less adequate bases for self-direction and self-control. The psychotherapist is often involved with the task of correcting errors made by earlier social conditioners in these various efforts to prepare the child for later life.

Focusing on the potential *benefits* of language use, we have isolated and described four advantages of particular significance. Language is potentially valuable in enabling a person to use the experience of others in his own preparation for living and adjusting. A person can control and direct his own behavior in terms of verbal motives and reinforcements given to himself. Language provides an opportunity for vicarious rehearsal of behavior, which is economical compared with acting out the behavioral pattern itself. Finally, words often provide significant clues to the transfer of experience from one situation to another similar situation, when the similarity is based on a common classification and labeling rather than upon stimulus similarity.

SUGGESTIONS FOR FURTHER READING

Korzybski (4), Chase (5), and Hayakawa (2) are all appropriate sources for the reader with an interest in general semantics. Hayakawa will probably suit the needs and tastes of most readers better than the other two books cited. The application of general semantics to problems of adjustment is best brought out by Wendell Johnson (6).

For those whose interest is in the general problem of communication in psychotherapy, we recommend Ruesch (9) and Sullivan (10). Frank (11) deals with the rationale and techniques of persuasion as applied to psychotherapy. Tauber and Green (12) deal especially with nonverbal aspects of communication.

In Dollard and Miller (13), Parts III and IV are especially relevant. The most pertinent section of Rotter (14) is Chapter IX.

REFERENCES

1. Woodworth, R. S. *Experimental psychology.* New York: Holt, Rinehart and Winston, 1938.

2. Hayakawa, S. I. *Language in action.* New York: Harcourt, 1941.

*3. Marmor, J. A reevaluation of certain aspects of psychoanalytic theory and practice. In Salzman, L., and Masserman, J. *Modern concepts of psychoanalysis.* New York: Citadel, 1962.

4. Korzybski, A. *Science and sanity.* (2d ed.) Lancaster, Pa.: Science Press, 1941.

5. Chase, S. *The tyranny of words.* New York: Harcourt, 1938.

6. Johnson, W. *People in quandaries.* New York: Harper & Row, 1946.

*7. Lippmann, W. *Public opinion.* Baltimore: Pelican, 1946 (Macmillan, 1922).

8. Iscoe, I. *The effect of reward on objectivity: a study of children's sex choices.* (Doctoral thesis, University of California, Los Angeles, 1950–1951.)

9. Ruesch, J. *Therapeutic communication.* New York: Norton, 1961.

10. Sullivan, H. S. *The psychiatric interview.* New York: Norton, 1954.

*11. Frank, J. D. *Persuasion and healing.* New York: Schocken Books, 1963. (Johns Hopkins Press, 1961.)

12. Tauber, E. S., and Green, M. R. *Prelogical experience.* New York: Basic Books, 1959.

13. Dollard, J., and Miller, N. E. *Personality and psychotherapy.* New York: McGraw-Hill, 1950.

14. Rotter, J. *Social learning and clinical psychology.* Englewood Cliffs, N.J.: Prentice-Hall, 1954.

* Paperback edition.

Part Two | EVALUATION

Chapter 5	*Communication:*
	Evaluation
	of
	Problems

PROBLEMS OF CLASSIFICATION AND EVALUATION

Classifying.   From our point of view, traditional methods of classifying, explaining, and treating what have been called "mental" or "emotional" disorders leave much to be desired. Perhaps a few words of review on this matter would be in order before discussing alternative suggestions for evaluating and attempting to meet the needs of psychotherapeutic patients.

The first efforts made in modern times in the direction of understanding emotional difficulties and the behavior associated with them were similar to the first steps taken in establishing any science, namely, to classify. This led to the establishment of phenotypical categories (1). A major distinction was made, dividing patients into two broad categories: neurotic and psychotic. Then further distinctions were made dividing the psychotic group into the two categories of functional and organic psychoses—the functional psychoses into major subgroups such as schizophrenic, paranoid, and manic-depressive, and the schizophrenic into further categories, such as simple, catatonic, hebephrenic and paranoid. The difficulties in applying such categorical distinctions need not be gone into in detail. Suffice it to say that there were and are many such difficulties.

The limitations of classification.   The therapist's concern is that even when classification has been established there is no guarantee that phenotypical similarity or dissimilarity has anything to do with genotypical similarity or dissimilarity. It is true that if we find on empirical grounds a therapy that seems to "work" with one category of psychotics, we may also be inclined to try it on other psychotics to see if it "works" with them also. But this is pretty rough and crude empiricism. It reminds us of the man who decided to teach himself medicine. He successfully treated his first patient, a sick mule, by making it drink a pint of turpentine. Being an embryonic scientist, he started a notebook and under the heading, "Nostrums," placed the subheading, "Turpentine," and made an entry: "Cures sick mules." He tried the same remedy on his second patient, a carpenter, and the carpenter died. So he made another entry under "Turpentine": "Kills sick carpenters."

The limitations of phenotypical description and classification as a guide to suggesting etiology, treatment, and prognosis should be evident from three thousand years of medical practice. A superficial diagnosis of "hydrophobia" existed for hundreds of years without any further progress toward effective treatment or prevention. The same might be said for most of the major disorders and diseases of mankind, many of which still remain uncontrolled and essentially untreatable at present. Unfortunately, man, in his colossal ignorance, is all too often tempted to borrow a method or an approach to understanding which may have some value in one context and try to apply it in another (possibly quite irrelevant) one. The structural classification of plants and animals greatly increased our understanding of biology, but it has yet to be established whether the essentially "structural" classification of functional disorders has been more of a boon or a hinderance to the development of medicine.

The concept of mental illness.   From this point of view it is perhaps unfortunate that persons with impaired capacities to adjust to their environment were ever classified as "sick" or "mentally ill" in the first place. While this may be considered more enlightened than attributing their difficulties to their being possessed by devils, the concrete benefit to those in trouble are sometimes difficult to find.

Presently a great deal of effort is being devoted to "educating" the public to regard the drunk as an "alcoholic" and as "ill" rather than "bad." Even the thrill-slaying juvenile delinquent is supposed to be regarded as "sick," if not "sick, sick, sick." The rationale for this new approach is that efforts to reform these and other socially deviant groups through punitive measures have failed to produce progress in their treatment. We would respectfully point out that two hundred years of regarding psychotics as "ill" has produced remarkably little result in reducing the number of psychotics, and that educating the public to use the term "mental hospital" rather than "lunatic asylum" has not, after all, done much to reduce the number of persons who must be forcibly confined therein.

Theory and practice.   It is true that in the past eighty years there have been some interesting developments in the theoretical understanding of the maladjusted. If, however, we scan the writings of those whose theories have contributed most to this understanding, we find remarkably infrequent reference to concepts such as "illness," "sickness," and "disease." Instead, we find a completely different type of construct, which is more easily related to principles of psychology than to the techniques of medical practice. The drift away from the pathogenic point of view has recently been signalized by the publication of Szasz's book *The Myth of Mental Illness* (2). Various similar publications preceded this one; others, no doubt, will follow.

We are not particularly concerned with the rhetorical aspects of this controversy, with its overtones of professional jealousy and petty personal advantage. What we *are* concerned with and about is an archaic mode of conceptualizing behavioral and emotional maladjustment. At present the practice of psychotherapy involves a very awkward intellectual tangle. First, we have an ancient classificatory system of doubtful value. To the essentially rule-of-thumb procedures for classifying patients according to this scheme, we have added a fantastic plethora of diagnostic tests and other evaluative devices, most of which have principally presumptive or "face" validity. Meanwhile new theories of dynamics flourish on the left, and new suggestions for treatment flourish on the right, often not only ignoring each other, but also the diagnostic classifications and procedures in the middle.

The integration of theory and practice.   In the preceding four chapters we have attempted to set down, define, explain, and illustrate certain concepts and principles from the field of general psychology which we, at present, consider both necessary and sufficient for the psychotherapist. We have no particular prejudice as to whether these particular constructs are likely to prove better or worse than any number of alternative systematic approaches. We prefer to regard them, rather, as an "essay" (literally, an attempt) to state systematically what we have been forced to conceptualize in order to have any feeling of orientation in a field insufficiently ordered—or perhaps rather too impulsively disordered.

Specifically, we have attempted to consider the problems of patients in such a way that our ideas about what *might* be wrong direct our efforts to find out what *is* wrong in a particular case. Having decided what is wrong in a particular case, we should then find that our general strategy for the handling of that case is automatically defined and the specific techniques to be used rather clearly indicated.

Having presented in Part One our basic definitions and principles, we shall proceed to indicate how these may be applied to the evaluation and treatment of patients in this chapter and the ones to follow.

The psychotherapist's role.   By way of general introduction to the application of theory, we would like to make it clear that we consider the role of the psychotherapist to be essentially that of a "corrector" and/or "completer." He must do (or start on the way to being done) those things that are essential to his patient's adjustment. What has been done inadequately or incorrectly, he must try to correct. We can find no way to excuse him from the full responsibility for deciding what is wrong, what can be done, and what must be done to achieve the greatest possible benefit for the persons who come to consult him.

In this frame of reference we must also assume that the psychotherapist is initially always "directive" to a greater or lesser degree, and that this degree of directiveness should be determined by the needs of the patient rather than by the psychotherapist's wish to assume or eschew a position of control. We assume further that the direction of change in psychotherapy is always from greater toward lesser degrees of control of the patient by the psychotherapist. We believe that the ideal condition for the termination of a psychotherapeutic contact is for the therapist to "release" his patient with reasonable confidence that the patient will now do as well without his guidance as with it. We cannot hope to realize the goal of an "adjusted" patient, since he could only be adjusted to a static situation at a given moment in time. We *can* hope to realize the goal of an adequately "adjust*ing*" patient who will be able to cope with a dynamic world to the extent which his own innate capacities and the limitations of his environment make possible.

GENERAL CONSIDERATIONS IN
EVALUATING COMMUNICATION

The computer analogy.   If we analyze the communicative behavior of the patient, we note first of all that it has two distinct aspects: the individual communicates with others, and he also "communicates" with himself. When we say that he "communicates with himself," we mean that he is capable of making cognitive responses of a verbal nature which may then serve as stimuli to which he in turn responds with still other kinds of responses. As has been pointed out previously, the human being, once he learns to use language, is in part a "self-programming" system, although he also retains his capacity to be "programmed" by others. Furthermore, he reacts to a variety of "data," including verbal responses from himself and verbal responses from others.

We employ the analogy of the computer in this instance to emphasize the critical importance to the individual of accurate data input and adequate programming. So far as verbal data are concerned we

have tried to suggest the very great extent to which each person, especially in his formative years, is dependent upon others for his information
and for the accuracy of that information. Inaccuracy in data input, we
believe, should be regarded as one of the most significant sources of the
difficulties in adjustment leading to adverse emotional balances.

Lack of data.   Considering for the moment only defects in verbal
"data" available to the person, we would suggest the following as a
simple but useful framework for analyzing problems in this area. The
patient may lack data that he needs in order to make appropriate
responses. He may be ignorant of vital information (as noted especially
in the instances of the child, the mentally retarded, or the undereducated). This, in turn, can result in inadequate cognitive responses of a
verbal nature, which we have already assumed to be a major factor
in adequate and accurate "self-control." We note that essentially the
same problems confront the individual who has had such information
but who has inhibited (or "repressed") it as confront those who have
never received the information. However, we deal with a different
problem in psychotherapy depending on whether information has simply
not been received or whether it has been repressed. In the former instance we can proceed with a relatively straight-forward strategy of
"educating," subject to such limitations as (1) our ability as instructors,
(2) the motivation of the patient, (3) the patient's learning ability, (4)
our limited capacity to reinforce learning, and (5) the patient's "resistance" to learning when new data cannot readily be integrated with
information he already has. But when we attempt to re-elicit repressed
information we must add one tremendous difficulty to all of these,
namely that the repression has been motivated by anxiety and reinforced
by anxiety reduction. As indicated elsewhere, such "avoidant" responses
present a particular challenge to the psychotherapist.

Inaccurate data.   The patient may have inaccurate data. George Ade
put the problem succinctly when he observed that what a man didn't
know didn't hurt him as much as what he knew that wasn't so. The
problems listed above as challenging the psychotherapist when he
functions as "educator" all apply equally to the problem of "re-education," or more specifically, "corrective education." In such a situation
the psychotherapist *always* must contend with the patient's resistance
to learning. The patient has believed certain things to be true. When we
try to change his cognitive responses, we must somehow eliminate his
"mistaken" ideas and at the same time reinforce the new ideas so that
they are elicited as cognitive responses in the same situations which used
to elicit the old ones. This is often a tricky and laborious procedure in

itself. However, the problem is seldom as simple and straightforward as this. Cognitive responses usually exist in structures of interconnected cognitive responses. We are actually challenging the entire cognitive structure of which the "mistaken" idea is a part, if we attempt to change that idea. Often the patient realizes better than the psychotherapist does that if he accepts the therapist's information on one point, he will have to revise many cognitive responses that are associated with it in his own thinking. Furthermore, the revision of even one cognitive response, and especially the revision of a significant cognitive substructure, will usually involve further changes in behavioral and perhaps even physiological response.

To illustrate: a young woman patient is obviously unaware that her face is unusually beautiful. She regards herself as not particularly attractive. Her resistance to accepting the therapist's evaluation of her facial beauty can be partially attributed to the changes that she would have to make in her self-concept if she does accept his evaluation. In addition, she would then have "less excuse" for neglecting her appearance and would have to spend more time and money on clothes, make-up, coiffure, and so on. But having done this, she might still not gain acceptance (in her own opinion) because she is "too dumb, too naive, too scared"; so why try? In other words, the acceptance of this one idea involves many changes, involves her in much effort, yet only partially allays her anxiety about rejection. The psychotherapist obviously has a considerable job to do in *motivating* the patient to accept this idea, *presenting* it repeatedly, and *reinforcing* her acceptance of it. Furthermore he may not be able to succeed in this specific task unless he also is helpful in revising the whole appearance aspect of the self concept, provides or creates further motivation for making the necessary behavioral efforts, and deals successfully with her general anxiety regarding acceptance by others. And all of this he must be able to do primarily, if not solely, through communication.

In this small example we have provided, in capsule form, many of the challenges that psychotherapy offers to the therapist as a communicator. Let us return now to the communicative problems of the patient.

Communicative intentions.   In considering the "difficulties" in adjustment centering around language and communication, we must mention at least the basic problems of communication, per se. Most of our consideration on this point has centered around the individual as he is being communicated to, as he is learning to understand and use language, and as he communicates with others and within himself. Let us consider him now as a communicator attempting to convey certain internal events (wishes, thoughts, feelings, intentions, knowledge, instructions, and so on) to another by means of words, vocal expression, facial expression, gestures, and so on. To simplify matters we shall use the term "communicative intent" to refer to whatever it is the communicator wishes to accomplish by communicating and the term "communicative stimulus" to refer to whatever he does (such as speaking, gesturing, or hitting) to accomplish his purpose.

There are only three "intentions" of the communicator with which we need to concern ourselves. Basically, all a communicative stimulus can do is to evoke a response (or responses) in the communicant, and these responses can be classified in three categories: cognitive, emotional, and behavioral. Any or all of these responses may be evoked by a given communicative stimulus.

In considering the intent of the communicator, we are interested primarily in "success" or "failure" (or some intermediate evaluation) of communication. This can be defined in terms of the communicator's intent. We shall say that the communicator communicates successfully to the extent that he elicits from the communicant those responses that he intended to elicit.

Communication, in this sense, is obviously more broadly defined than if we confine ourselves to the question of whether a given word or group of words has the intended "meaning" (evokes the intended cognitive responses) in the communicant. This more limited problem is, in itself, extremely significant. Any psychotherapist must realize that even this limited aspect of communication cannot be assumed, and in certain cases definitely *must* not be assumed. For example, an adolescent patient uses the following terms "bitchin'," "cherry," "fairy," and "chop." A combination of inquiry and observation finally indicates that these words have the following meanings so far as the communicator (in this case, the patient) is concerned. "Bitchin'," adjective meaning "top-hole, first-rate, great." "Cherry," adjective meaning "perfect, the greatest." "Fairy," noun meaning "a sissy, but *not* specifically a homosexual." "Chop," noun, referring to "any event or remark that tends to lower a person's self-esteem." Also used as a verb, as in "I chopped her good." Since some of these words have changed not only their meaning but also their verbal classification (for example, "bitchin'" is used as an adjective rather than a verb), considerable communicative "failure" could have resulted if these new meanings had not been established as a *lingua franca* between therapist and patient. We would like also to point out that the question of *whose* definitions shall be used arises at least implicitly in every psychotherapeutic relationship and raises some interesting problems of technique. At any rate, the need for common definitions between therapist and patient should be obvious enough to require no further elaboration.

Communicative aspects of the psychotherapeutic relationship.   Now let us note, first of all, that the psychotherapist *must* communicate with his patient in order to establish a relationship. The relationship is undoubtedly important for many reasons. But the communicative interaction is also important in its own right. A signal part of its importance is that, first, it provides the psychotherapist with a means of evaluating how effectively the patient functions as a communicator. Secondly, it enables the therapist to evaluate the "intent" of the patient in a specific communicative interaction, namely the psychotherapeutic situation. Thirdly, it provides an opportunity for the therapist to assist the patient in becoming a more effective communicator. We shall try to indicate how evaluations along these lines (and others that relate to communication) might be made by indulging in some generalizations about different kinds of patients. In addition to illustrating *methods* of evaluation, the generalizations themselves may be of some value. However, it is well to keep in mind that these conclusions are based on the patients in a particular practice. Although they are tempered by psychological research and general principles, psychotherapists with other kinds of patients might disagree or draw other conclusions.

AGE AND COMMUNICATION

The young patient.   The most obvious variable which is correlated with how the patient functions as a communicator is age. The young patient lacks certain skills as a communicator for an obvious reason: lack of experience. But beyond this obvious consideration, there are other important ways in which he differs as a communicator from the adult. First of all, he is not primarily oriented toward the use of language as a means of conveying information for its own sake. If he is concerned about evoking cognitive responses in his communicant at all, it is usually as a means to the end of evoking some desired behavioral response from the other person. He depends less upon words and formal communicative methods and relies relatively more than the adult does upon "nonword" types of communication: gesture, facial expression, various kinds of emotional expression (crying, whining, smiling), pantomime, and so forth. His approach is primarily that of the propagandist or advertiser: he wants *action*. At the same time, his communicative means are crude and his intention is often all too obvious. This in itself is apt to evoke unpleasant feelings in adults, who in turn are inclined to punish the child for being too obvious in his demands or too blunt in his approach to topics about which adults normally maintain certain communicative taboos. The child, in other words, is a person in process of becoming inhibited about communication. He often approaches the matter of communicating with the psychotherapist with fairly recent experiences of being punished or criticized for "saying the wrong thing." *How much, what,* even *whether* he will communicate with the therapist will be strongly conditioned by such experiences. And how much he "opens up" with the psychotherapist obviously depends upon how the therapist reacts to what the child does choose to say. This is sometimes very apparent from observing the child. As he tells us something, he watches us most carefully to see how we will react.

This is a good place to emphasize that, in terms of the "expression–content" balance mentioned in Chapter 4, the child is strongly "expression" oriented. This is true in his own communicating, as indicated above: it is also true of his reaction to communication from others. He pays *less* attention to *what* we say than an adult does, and much *more* attention to *how* we say it. He is also much more attentive to and perceptive of other communicative aspects of the psychotherapist's behavior, such as facial expression and body movement. We believe this is why the child so often fails to be deceived by adult lying. The adult directs his deceptive effort toward the *words* he is using, but the child is "reading him" primarily in terms of other "clues." Since most children are used to being lied to by adults, the psychotherapist stands to gain considerably in his acceptance by the child simply by not indulging in this popular adult subterfuge.

The child's communicating, like his thinking, is oriented primarily toward the concrete rather than the abstract. He knows most about the tangible, sensible world and is only in process of developing generalizations and abstractions of a logical type. He may be unsure about the reality of ghosts or Santa Claus, but he is completely indifferent to Newton's Three Laws of Motion. He does not think in terms of cause-effect relationships except at a very primitive level. If you asked him *why* he has done something, you will seldom get a reasonable or useful answer. The reason is simple: he literally does not *know* why. Furthermore he doesn't even think in terms of "why," so the question is essentially meaningless to him in the first place.

As indicated earlier, the child uses language and communication generally with the intent of "getting action" from others. It is clearly and obviously to him a *means* to an end, rather than an end in itself. He may do a lot of talking in order to receive attention and response from others, when he wants attention and interaction, but in this situation *what* he is saying is secondary to his motives and is selected primarily in terms of its value for attracting attention. This, we believe, is why so much of the child's conversation seems silly, stupid, or "childish" to adults. The adults simply have failed to realize the child's frame of reference, which seems to be that *what* you are saying isn't too important as long as it serves its function of getting others to listen.

A direct corollary to this conclusion is that the child is usually much less interested in *what* an adult has to say than the adult is in saying it. He may have any number of reasons for wanting to talk; he seldom has much reason for wanting to listen. His tolerance for listening is consequently limited. In fact his tolerance for conversation, per se, is limited. He soon exhausts his own reasons for wanting to talk. He exhausts them even more readily if his communicative attempts "fall on deaf ears," because the adult is more concerned with what *he* wants to communicate to the child rather than with what the child is trying to communicate to him. For most children in most contacts with adults, conversation is a losing game in which he *does not* get what he wants and *does* get much that he *does not* want.

Every psychotherapist who has worked with children is aware of these problems in communicating with children, even if they have inadequately analyzed and realized the reasons for them. This is the reason, we believe, why "play techniques" quite naturally evolved as a solution to this general problem. The basic consideration here is that the child is interested in play and will accept a relationship which is play-oriented much more readily than he will accept a relationship which is conversation-oriented. And unless he finds a relationship with the psychotherapist acceptable, the therapist has no opportunity to affect his adjustment.

Some psychotherapists resolve this problem by offering the child a relationship on the child's terms and by depending upon the existence of the relationship to have some sort of therapeutic effect. This, we feel, is not enough. True, the relationship is a *sine qua non* of psychotherapy always. True, the relationship, if it involves mutual acceptance, may have direct emotional value for the patient and result in behavioral changes of a beneficial nature. But we must realize, beyond this, that the child has specific needs and problems in the *communicative area* of *functioning itself*, just as every patient has. We shall not attempt to specify exactly what these needs are and how they differ from the problems of older patients beyond what we have already indicated. When we come to the general and specific approaches to problems of remediation, we shall expect the reader to be able to make his own adaptations.

The adolescent patient.   On purely empirical grounds, which may be peculiar to the type of patient we see, we seem to find changes in the communicative aspects of patients' problems, and in the problems in relating communicatively to patients, that may begin around the twelfth

or thirteenth year and may extend through a considerable part of the adolescent period. As far as the communicative problems of these patients are
concerned, we can best summarize by saying that they are much like the
problems of adults, only more so. Three factors come increasingly into
focus as tending to differentiate the communicative problems of this
age group from those of younger patients. First, the older child's and
adolescent's world has expanded to include other adults (besides the
parents) as significant communicators—and reinforcers of communicative efforts. This has both its positive and negative aspects so far as
communicative skills are concerned. On the one hand, these other
adult communicators—notably teachers—may help to overcome limitations of the parents as communicative tutors. On the other hand, however, our faith in the teaching profession is not sufficiently blind to persuade us that this is *always* the case. We know that in some instances
teachers and other adults *create* problems in this area and may do so in
various ways. In any event, the child has to cope with an increasing
realization that not all persons think alike about the world and that the
"maps of reality" that he receives via communication from various people
do not all look alike. Furthermore he is confronted with the problem that
his efforts at communicating are judged by different standards and reacted to in various ways by different adult "authorities."

Also, as the child grows into older childhood and adolescence, he
communicates more with others of his own age and is affected more by
their communications to him and their reactions to his communication.
The standards of this peer group for evaluating communication, their
taboos regarding communication, and their accuracy as communicators
are all significantly different from those of the adult world. Here are
still other "maps of reality" with different portions filled in, left blank,
or distorted. Topics of conversation which may be *verboten* in the adult
world and evoke punishment from it may make one the center of attention
and respectful regard in the peer group. Even the vocabularies of the peer
and adult worlds are different. One must learn two languages, in effect,
and remember not to speak "teen-age" in the adult world or "adult" in
the teen-age world.

These are some of the basic reasons why the "twelve-to-sixteener"
is a different problem for the psychotherapist than is the younger or
older patient. He is, if anything, even more aware of and inhibited by
adult taboos regarding topics of communication than the child is. He is
also likely to be considerably more confused, both cognitively and communicatively. He is less dependent upon the adult world, and—perhaps
as a consequence—he is more aware of his own hostilities and differences. He is quite sensitive to the coercive authority of adults and
resents it. At the same time, he is almost certain to generalize or trans-

fer these feelings to the adult world in general and to the psychotherapist in particular.

The usual result is that the patient in this age bracket is inclined to be a communicative "clam." He, like the child, is usually "brought in" because of problems that the parents are more aware of and sensitive to than is the adolescent himself. Consequently his motivation to cooperate and to communicate may leave a great deal to be desired. Because the adolescent so often presents a special problem, we shall step out of sequence here to indicate how the problem of establishing communication with adolescents can be handled.

First of all, we must understand the peculiar or distinctive psychology of the adolescent, The child, as a completely dependent and largely inadequate person, is in a poor position to make independent evaluations or to espouse conclusions which bring him into significant conflict with his adult environment. The adolescent, as a person beginning to acquire some capacity for independent functioning, is more ready, willing, and able to develop his own ideas about matters. Due to a variety of factors, including lack of experience and being raised in a different environment than his parents have been (in a different era, at least), the adolescent may not be able to "see things" the way his parents do. The emergence of different values, standards, and viewpoints is actually a hopeful sign. On the one hand, it is indicative of having reached a certain degree of emotional security or self-confidence. On the other hand, it is indicative of the person's potential for individuality.

These aspects of adolescent "rebellion" are not always sufficiently appreciated in the adolescent's home and school environment. Instead, the adolescent may be subjected to increasing pressure to conform with parental demands, even those that might be outmoded or otherwise inappropriate to the general environment in which the adolescent functions. Psychotherapists usually see adolescents who have successfully resisted adult authority. Often the psychotherapist is appealed to as a kind of supereffective authority figure who can somehow enforce a conformity where others have failed.

The truth of the matter, of course, is that the psychotherapist has only such authority as the adolescent's desire for his approval may give him. Consequently, he can only influence the adolescent patient by establishing a "valuable" relationship. This can be done because the psychotherapist can supply two kinds of experience that the adolescent needs. First, he can offer the adolescent a genuine communicative relationship, which is to say that the psychotherapist can respect the adolescent as an individual and give the same aid, attention, and consideration to his attempts to communicate as he would to any other patient's. Second, he can offer the adolescent a relationship in which the adolescent finds support for values and adjustments that *are* pertinent to his immediate environment or valuable in the development of his own individuality.

This approach involves the psychotherapist in two types of communicative problems. In order to maintain his relationship with the parents, the psychotherapist must explain to them what he is doing and why, since in most cases he will not be doing what the parents have expected him to do. The fact of the matter is that the psychotherapist is not likely to be able to finish his work with the adolescent unless the parents are in agreement with his general objectives, although the therapist can seldom count upon their complete cooperation or complete understanding of his procedures.

The other communicative problem arises with the adolescent himself. It arises because all too often the type of relationship that the psychotherapist offers is unique in the adolescent's experience with adults. It is, first of all, difficult for the adolescent to understand *what* the rules of the psychotherapeutic relationship *are*, probably because of his lack of experience with this type of relationship. In addition, it is often difficult for the adolescent to accept or believe in what the psychotherapist communicates to him about their relationship.

The difficult initial stages of psychotherapy with adolescents are usually concerned with instilling this knowledge about and belief in the nature of the psychotherapeutic relationship. Once these objectives have been achieved, however, the adolescent often becomes a particularly responsive and rewarding person with whom to work.

The adult patient.   Beginning with the late teens we start to deal with problems of communication that are more significantly correlated with other variables than with age. We shall therefore turn our attention to these other variables. Before doing so, however, we want to pause long enough to point out that chronological age is only the roughest of guides to the actual developmental status of the patient. The adult patient may be, in fact, significantly less far along with respect to some of these problems and attitudes which affect communication than his literal age might lead us to expect. Furthermore, we have no right to, nor should we, expect of any patient a uniform level of maturity in different aspects or areas of functioning. The college professor who is a fluent communicator in front of his class may communicate with his wife like a seven-year-old talking to his mother and with the psychotherapist like a rebellious teenager talking to his high school principal. When resistances centering around communication arise in therapy, it is sometimes helpful to review some of the special communicative problems related to early and later childhood for clues as to why the patient is reacting the way he is.

OTHER VARIABLES THAT AFFECT COMMUNICATIONS

Intelligence.   We consider intelligence as one of the more significant patient variables correlated with communicative efficiency. To those acquainted with the intricacies of intelligence testing we hardly need to point out that for certain purposes "intelligence" and "verbal ability" come close to being synonymous. This is even more true in the measurement of very high levels of adult intelligence than it is for persons of all ages and all levels of ability. Without further analysis we might jump to the conclusion that the more intelligent person will be (other things remaining equal) the more effective communicator and less likely to have problems in this field than the less intelligent person. However, we would point out, first of all, that "verbal ability" and "communicative ability" are not exactly synonymous. In measuring or evaluating intelligence we are apt to rely on general standards of usage and fluency in our culture. But we have already suggested and will discuss in detail later certain cultural biases regarding matters that may be and/or are actually communicated about. Although the more intelligent person may have a somewhat greater capacity to overcome these culturally imposed limitations, other factors, such as education, are probably more decisive in this area. These areas of cultural neglect or taboo happen, quite naturally, to be intimately related to the kinds of communicative problem we are most likely to encounter in our patients, since cultural taboo and neglect are often responsible for significant "blank" areas in the cognitive structure. We *cannot assume* that our patients are immune to the general "black out" of communicative means in such areas on the basis of intelligence alone.

Although we agree in general with the supposition that the more intelligent patient is likely to be the more effective communicator, we would point to still other considerations in this area. Most psychotherapists are familiar with the term "intellectual defensiveness." It is used to refer to the tendency of a patient to deal with all matters brought up in psychotherapy in a strictly rational and objective manner. It may also refer to a patient's preference for dealing primarily with the cognitive and communicative aspects of his own adjustment rather than with feeling aspects. Some highly intelligent and highly educated patients seem almost literally incapable of realizing, analyzing, and communicating about their own feelings at the outset of therapy. Furthermore, they show considerable reluctance or resistance to "moving into" this area, both in psychotherapy and in their life outside the therapist's office. They are, in a sense, emotional illiterates, or perhaps more literally undereducated about matters relating to the emotions—their own or other people's. We might speculate that their generally superior adaptive and adjustive abilities enable them to "get by" with this type of avoidance more adroitly than can the person of average or inferior intelligence.

We do not want to leave this topic, however, without referring again to the matter of "expression–content" balance in communication. Here we shall suggest that a tendency which correlates positively with intelligence (as well as with age and education) is for "content" orientation to increase as these variables increase. We believe this to be true of the person both as a communicator and as a communicant. In other words, whether he is "sending" or "receiving," the more intelligent person pays more attention to "what" is being communicated and less attention to "how." In this way he may miss certain aspects of communication which are literally "there" for him to hear or see. To put it still another way, he may "get the words but not the music," or, to borrow a term from Theodore Reik, he may be a little deaf in his "third ear."

We want to emphasize this type of problem in communication for the reader's benefit in self-analysis and self-evaluation. Psychotherapists seem generally to "like" adult, intelligent, educated patients. In fact, some therapists will still solemnly assure the uninitiated that only persons who fall into that category are "really candidates for psychotherapy." We trust that most psychotherapists are sophisticated enough at this point to make the distinction between "easiest for us to work with" and "real candidates for psychotherapy." We would also point out how easy it is for the psychotherapist to indulge his own "prointellectual" and "prorational" biases with this type of patient. We get along so easily and understand each other so well when we stay away from those "nasty" uncomfortable emotional "jungles" and the subtler "feeling" aspects of communication.

Education.   Since intelligence and education are apt to be positively correlated to an appreciable degree and to have, in some respects, similar effects on communicative behavior and cognitive structure, we shall not say too much more about education as an independent patient variable. Of course it is necessary for the psychotherapist to note especially the particular communicative characteristics and problems of persons who have a considerable discrepancy between intelligence and education levels. On the positive side, we believe that distortions and omissions in cognitive structure tend generally to decrease as education increases. We have also suggested that education may "pay dividends" so far as increasing integration and flexibility of cognitive structure is concerned. On the other hand, these potential advantages of education are obviously dependent upon the *kind* of education to which the person is exposed. We might even conjecture that continuing education to high levels of specialization in increasingly restricted areas of specialization would eventually tend to reduce general communicative effectiveness. This is implied in the popular criticism of the academic scholar as a person who "knows more and more about less and less." It also goes along with the stereotype of the college professor as a man who "lives in an ivory tower" at least somewhat removed from the "world of reality."

At any rate we must recognize that our institutions of formal education are restricted and censored in terms of the taboos current in the culture in which they exist so far as what they are *permitted* to teach the student is concerned. Even less formal means of communication (books, newspapers, magazines, stage, movies, TV, comic books, and so forth) are subject to vigilant and militant censorship correlated with the prevailing mores of the culture in which they exist. Also, what is generally neglected in the parental preparation of the young for later life may be only slightly less (or, in some cases, even more) neglected in public than in private communication. We can summarize this problem by pointing out that there are certain significant lacunae (which we shall discuss later) in areas of communication that are actually quite critical in human social adjustment. We simply do not inform the young—or the older, for that matter—adequately or accurately enough to optimize their chances of satisfactory adjustment. Or, to put it more simply still, education is no safeguard against ignorance.

In certain other ways education may be conducive to the development of communication problems. The prevailing cultural mores determine not only what will and what will not be communicated about, but also what kinds of bias or distortion in informing others is acceptable or required. We feel that it hardly needs to be argued that students are rarely "educated" in the stricter meaning of that term (see Doob, *Propaganda and Public Opinion* [3]) in the first twelve grades of school. Rather they are indoctrinated with the prevailing values of their respective cultures, and the information they receive is "slanted" in accordance with these same values. We are not here arguing the desirability or general advisability of this procedure from various pragmatic points of view. We are simply asserting that this is what happens, and that, as a result, the developing individual is given "cognitive maps" that *are* knowingly and obviously distorted. This type of "education" is no safeguard against a certain kind of ignorance either. It is perhaps all the more dangerous because distortions in communication and cognitive structure tend to be less obvious than out-and-out "blanks" representing no advance information at all.

We would mention one further potential hazard of education, especially at the higher levels. In Chapter 4 we talked about the problems of distinguishing between communicative signs that have direct, obvious and concrete referents and those that do not. The general tendency is for "higher" education to deal more and more with abstractions several levels removed from concrete, sensible referents. Korzybski and others among the general semanticists and some important "schools" of modern philosophy have suggested that many terms in common use have no ultimate concrete referents at all. They also suggest (suggest? They insist upon!) the logical conclusion that some topics of general conversation and quite a few topics of "top level" intellectual concern are literally "nonsense" or simply "not sensible." We might then expect our more highly educated patients to be more prone to concerns about matters that are literally not "there" in concrete reality. In terms of our "cognitive map" analogy, we would say that such patients are more likely to be concerned about and to communicate regarding aspects of their cognitive maps that have structure where reality—at least in terms of what is perceptible—has no corresponding structure. This suggestion does not intend to imply that the relatively uneducated are immune to this type of error, but we suppose that they may be somewhat less susceptible simply through lesser degrees of exposure.

While we have taken pains to point out possible or probable qualifications to the general rule, we still believe that most generally education and communicative effectiveness are positively correlated. In this connection we would like to point up one important advantage of education that is specific to psychotherapeutic communication. At the beginning of this chapter we raised the question of "whose vocabulary shall constitute the basis for communication—the patient's or the psychotherapist's?" The literally or figuratively "multilingual" therapist who can speak the "lingo" of a heterogeneous clientele has obvious advantages over the psychotherapist who is essentially "monolingual." Sooner or later—and usually it needs to be fairly soon—the patient and the psychotherapist must be able to communicate with each other fairly effectively and accurately. However, even if the psychotherapist is able to adapt himself to the patient's communicative symbols and techniques, ultimately the patient will need to learn some of the therapist's vocabulary and concepts. This need arises simply because one of the patient's problems may be his lack of these same symbols and the concepts they represent. Or the patient may have such concepts but make very inadequate or inaccurate use of them in both "internal" and "external" communication. The more the patient is acquainted with and is able to use with accuracy those concepts that are more discussed in psychotherapy than in other kinds of "conversation," the less time and effort the therapist needs to devote to this specific kind of "educating" the patient. We believe this is what is usually meant when psychotherapists talk about "psychological sophistication" as a patient variable that correlates positively with "progress" in psychotherapy.

So far as the informative connotation of words is concerned, common meaning depends upon common referents. In fact we can extend this principle to affective connotation and to means of communication other than verbal. In other words, easy, effective, and accurate communication depends upon similarity of life experience between communicator and communicant, with the same words being used by both to refer to the same "things" and "events."

Cultural background.   An obvious conclusion which we can draw from this principle is that a person who now lives in an environment significantly different from the one in which he grew up may have adjustment problems that are attributable to communicative difficulties. Since the population of the United States is notably transient and mobile, problems of this sort are not uncommon in clinical practice. In addition, and even more generally, we can say that when a person with one kind of social experience attempts to communicate with persons of different background, problems in communication are likely to arise.

Without attempting to go into the problem in detail, we should like to mention some of the cultural shifts of relatively common occurrence and of potential significance in assessing communicative problems in the patient.

The general trend in population concentration in the United States has generally been from rural to urban and suburban areas. Significant shifts in areal distribution are still going on. On the West Coast, for example, we have had or are having a heavy influx from the New York and Chicago urban areas, a steady stream of immigration from the rural South, Midwest, and Southwest areas, and a considerable number of people coming directly to the area from foreign countries. We have large representations from various cultural groups, Jewish, Mexican, Negro, and Oriental. Religious groups whose backgrounds affect many aspects of adjustment, including communication, are represented by all varieties of Protestantism from Fundamentalists to Unitarians, Catholics, Mormons, Christian Scientists, and Jews. We also have patients who are more or less involved with Yoga, Science of Mind, Zen Buddhism, and other lesser known ideologies.

Differences in training experience, vocabulary, and/or communicative technique are apt to be fairly obvious in the instances we have mentioned up to this point. However, other kinds of differentiation of a subtler sort may be overlooked. A good example of subtler distinctions which can lead to communicative problems when communicator and communicant differ is that of age. Each generation has, to some extent, its own unique vocabulary and experiences. Adolescence, especially, is a time when slang fads create an almost continuously changing vocabulary, as we illustrated early in this chapter. We have found it desirable to do a certain amount of "homework" with publications such as *Mad*, *Playboy*, and *Seventeen*, and such current media as the comic strips to remain *au courant* with this group. But in a very real sense, grandfather does not "read" grandson too well, and daughter has trouble with mother. They literally "do not speak the same language." Our daughter knows more about the mathematics of space navigation than we do, but she has to be told what a crystal set is or a rumble seat, otherwise we are not "communicating."

Sex. We assert, without fear of successful contradiction, that male and female do not communicate about exactly the same things in exactly the same way. Women are not supposed to know or to be told certain things that men know and discuss freely among themselves; and *vice versa*. We even have the phrases "man-talk" and "woman-talk" to describe subjects supposedly of interest only to one sex or the other. In many social gatherings one of the hostess's main problems is to keep the men from bunching up to talk with each other while women form a separate conversational group of their own. So what happens when they try to talk with each other? One patient, a man, maintained a very active sex life with his wife, although they did not get along well in most respects. When this was commented upon, the patient's explanation was: "It's easier than talking with her."

Class. A considerable amount of hypocrisy exists about the matter of social "class" in the United States. While the psychologist and the sociologist are aware of many significant differences in social learning and social behavior that are "class conditioned," the layman usually prefers to ignore the reality of such social distinctions. For this reason he is very prone to puzzlement when he fails to understand (or to make himself understood by) persons of different socio-economic status. The owner of a business who has trouble communicating with his own employees, the matron who cannot understand why her servants "will not follow directions," and the customer who is irked by the "stupidity" of sales personnel may all be tripping over a communication barrier they cannot see because they will not admit that there is any "real" distinction between people of one socio-economic class and another. This distinction, like the others we have mentioned, goes beyond the matter of vocabulary to differentially "tint" many aspects of everyday life from attitudes on toilet training and drinking to sexual morals and behavior and to the kinds of books and magazines to be found in the home.

In fact, the astute psychotherapist can do an adequate and significant part of his evaluation of the patient through a few questions aimed at determining the socio-economic status of the parental home. We always ask adult patients (usually in the first interview) about their father's occupation, amount of parental education, the "kind of home" in which they grew up, and so on. A few questions along these lines are usually sufficient, along with incidental clues picked up, to give us a good idea of the social classification of the parental home. We thus acquire considerable general information about how the patients were raised, their attitudes toward many subjects, and at least a rough idea of their basic value system. All of this, of course, is tentative until verified by specific information from the particular patient involved, but our initial hypotheses based on such general grounds often require surprisingly little revision on the basis of much more extensive and intensive inquiry. Of course we ask similar questions regarding the person's present and personal situation and have other information at our disposal through place of residence, vocabulary, accent, appearance and social manner. We pay particular attention to comunicative problems when our evaluation indicates that the person now functions in a social *milieu* different from that in which he grew up.

Differences and difficulties.   This brings us back to our most general point in connection with evaluating communicative difficulties. We repeat: *look for problems in communication when the person functions in an unfamiliar social milieu.* And an obvious corollary is to expect and to be on the alert for communicative problems when the social environment of the psychotherapist differs from that of the patient. In both instances we would suggest that the greater the difference in social background (including *all* the aspects that we have mentioned), the more likely we are to find communicative problems and the more significant such problems will be in the adjustment of the individual.

SUMMARY

Our own practice in evaluating patients is to avoid the use of traditional classifications. We believe this approach to psychotherapy is outmoded and of questionable value. It tends to perpetuate the concept of maladjustment as an "illness," a concept which is also questionable. Furthermore, traditional classifications have *not* been closely coordinated with general scientific principles, with psychotherapeutic theory, with diagnostic procedures, or with psychotherapeutic techniques.

If we are to become more effective as psychotherapists, it would be helpful to have a theory of psychotherapy that is firmly related to general scientific principles on the one hand and to evaluative and therapeutic procedures on the other. This, of course, implies a common conceptual framework for processes of evaluation and of corrective efforts. In short, by the time we know what is wrong, we should also know what to do about it. A further consideration in the development of a theoretical approach to psychotherapy is that the same set of concepts and principles should be applicable to all types of patients and all types of problems.

In this chapter we have made some general suggestions concerning the communicative problems and limitations of various kinds of patient. We have noted the peculiar capacity of human beings to "program" their own responses by verbal means. The adequacy of their adjustment, however, depends both upon the nature of their training (whether directed by others or self-initiated) and upon the accuracy and adequacy of the data they receive. When a patient's information is inadequate, the psychotherapist can help by serving as an educator. When the patient's information is inaccurate, the problem is not so simple. One problem is that more accurate information disrupts cognitive structures in which the inaccurate information is a component. Another problem is that the acceptance of new ideas involves new adjustments to replace the adjustments predicated upon the incorrect ideas previously held.

One helpful function of the psychotherapeutic relationship is to increase the patient's skill as a communicator. We can help the patient improve his adjustment by encouraging more communication and by increasing the accuracy with which the patient achieves his communicative intentions.

The child patient differs from the adult patient in several ways. He is more inclined to use nonverbal means of communicating, and he is more oriented toward expression and less toward the verbal content of others' communication than is the adult patient. He communicates in order to evoke desired responses from others. He is not interested in conversation for its own sake. He is more or less aware of adult taboos concerning communication. The psychotherapist can help the child patient by being honest with the child, by relaxing cultural taboos, and by encouraging the development of better communication and more adequate verbal skills.

The adolescent patient is a potentially more skillful communicator than the child, but he has various reasons for being more inhibited in his communicating. Establishing an effective relationship with the adolescent depends upon helping the patient to differentiate the therapist's attitudes and values from those of other adults. Specifically, the psychotherapist must be ready and willing to support the adolescent in potentially constructive deviations from the conformity demanded by other adults.

With respect to other patient variables besides age, we expect communicative skills to increase as intelligence increases. However, there are various reasons for exceptions to this general expectation of which the psychotherapist must be aware. Two particular problems of the very bright adult are: first, the tendency toward exclusive "content" orientation; second, the tendency to use intellectualized concepts as a defense against greater awareness of emotional needs and pressures.

Education tends generally to produce greater communicative skill and flexibility, as well as increasing the amount of information upon which a person may predicate his own behavior. Unfortunately, much of the "education" that a person receives tends to produce a narrowing of perception and a predetermination of response. In terms of these effects, the training of the individual through high school better fits definitions of "propaganda" than of "education." Consequently, we cannot evaluate the effects on adjustment of varying amounts of education without evaluating the kind and quality of education involved.

Men and women do not communicate in the same way, and the psychotherapist must learn the nature of the differences between them before he can adapt his own communicative behavior to either sex with maximum effectiveness. Different characteristic modes of communication are also associated with different cultures and different classes.

The psychotherapist has two basic responsibilities to all these different kinds of patient. First, he must acquaint himself with their communicative limitations and peculiarities and adjust his own communicative behavior in such a way as to have the best possible communicative relationship with his patients. Second, he should use the psychotherapeutic relationship as a means of helping the patient to overcome his communicative limitations.

SUGGESTIONS FOR FURTHER READING

The reader should review the "Suggestions for Further Reading" for Chapter 4.

Our own library on psychotherapy with children includes references (4) through (12). We like Allen's book (4). Hamilton (7) has a chapter on the adolescent patient. Anna Freud (6), Melanie Klein (9), and Rambert (11) give three different views of the psychoanalytic approach to child psychotherapy. Rogers' book (12) serves the dual purpose of acquainting the reader with the state of child treatment just before

World War II and also of indicating the conceptual background for the development of Rogers' "client-centered" psychotherapy.

Georgene Seward (13) provides unique illustrations of the way in which cultural background becomes involved in psychotherapy.

In Dollard and Miller (14) Chapters I and II are most relevant. In Rotter (15), Chapter III will supplement the reader's knowledge of problems relating to psychotherapeutic theory.

REFERENCES

1. Brown, J. F. *Psychodynamics of abnormal behavior.* New York: McGraw-Hill, 1940.

2. Szasz, T. S. *The myth of mental illness.* New York: Harper & Row, 1961.

3. Doob, L. W. *Public opinion and propaganda.* New York: Holt, Rinehart and Winston, 1948.

4. Allen, F. H. *Psychotherapy with children.* New York: Norton, 1942.

5. Axline, V. M. *Play therapy.* Boston: Houghton Mifflin, 1947.

6. Freud, A. *The psycho-analytical treatment of children.* London: Imago, 1946.

7. Hamilton, G. *Psychotherapy in child guidance.* New York: Columbia University Press, 1947.

8. Jackson, L. and Todd, K. M. *Child treatment and the therapy of play.* New York: Ronald, 1950.

*9. Klein, M. *The psychoanalysis of children.* New York: Grove Press, 1960. (London: Hogarth.)

10. Pearson, H. J. *Emotional disorders of children.* New York: Norton, 1949.

11. Rambert, M. L. *Children in conflict.* New York: International Universities Press, 1949.

12. Rogers, C. R. *The clinical treatment of the problem child.* Boston: Houghton Mifflin, 1939.

13. Seward, G. *Psychotherapy and culture conflict.* New York: Ronald, 1956.

14. Dollard, J., and Miller, N. E. *Personality and psychotherapy.* New York: McGraw-Hill, 1950.

15. Rotter, J. *Social learning and clinical psychology.* Englewood Cliffs, N.J.: Prentice-Hall, 1954.

* Paperback edition.

| *Communication*
and Cognitive
Structure:
Evaluation
of Problems

COMMUNICATIVE TABOOS

Introduction.   Our second general principle, parallel with the one
that concludes Chapter 5, is to look for communicative problems and
"blank" areas in the cognitive structure of the patient in areas which are
socially taboo and/or socially neglected. Usually communicative areas
that are socially taboo are also neglected in child training and education,
as well as in general conversation. We would consider the subjects of sex,
feeling, self, religion, politics, and death as ones in which some degree of
taboo exists. Other areas, notably marriage, vocation, and parenthood,
are *neglected* or distorted in social communication although not necessarily taboo.

Sex.   When we speak of social taboos on communication about certain
subjects, we use the term in a relative rather than in an absolute sense.
For example, sex is a matter that is relatively more openly discussed today than it was in Freud's time. Information regarding sex is also available through various media of public communication. However, it cannot
be regarded as a perfectly "open" subject for communication. There is
little doubt but that sexual matters are the prime objectives of those
groups that maintain censorship over public media, including periodicals,
books, movies, and television programs, in the United States. In fact,
censorship is so vigilantly and universally maintained here that one is
hardly aware of it unless one visits other countries or relates it to the
peculiar lack of basic information which many patients manifest on the
subject of sex.

Besides public censorship there are various kinds of "taboos" that
relate to communication in interpersonal relationships. As indicated previously, there are some topics, including sex, which are more or less

taboo in "mixed company" so that husbands and wives must trade "dirty" jokes when they get home from a party if each is to know what went on in the other sex grouping. Some aspects of sex are not discussed "in front of the children" by adults (and, incidentally, not "in front of the adults" by children). When parents do talk about sex with their children, it is often in a hurried and inadequate way, partly due to embarrassment and partly due to their own lack of adequate and accurate information. There are even barriers to communication between certain class and professional groups, so that the "boys in the shop" are somewhat more "careful of their language" when the boss is around than when alone.

A particular peculiarity of our sexual mores and communicative taboos is that while sex may be discussed with children in a highly "hygienic" manner to explain how the species is reproduced, it is largely *verboten* to discuss it in terms of the relationship between two people or the feelings between them. If discussed at all, this very complex subject is usually dismissed with a parenthetical "of course you don't do this unless you love someone very much and are married to them."

Feelings.   This reticence about discussing feeling in relation to sex goes along with a general reluctance to converse freely about feeling in any context. The general bias in the United States is to deal with feeling by ignoring it. It is considered "not polite," at best, to be too open about feelings, whether it is a matter of talking about them or "displaying" emotion in front of others. These restrictions are more stringently applied against males than against females. The boy who cries in public, regardless of provocation, is fairly certain to be criticized as either a "cry-baby" or a "sissy." Public display of emotion is also considered both immature and unsophisticated among adults, with greater leeway still being permitted females than males. This differentiation in taboo may be responsible for the greater difficulty male patients seem to have in becoming aware of and communicating about their feelings.

However, a more general point is that a major problem that *both* sexes face in their adjustment is their lack of awareness of (and/or their difficulty in communicating about) feeling. It sometimes seems to be the "least kept track of" type of experience among all those the individual has. As indicated elsewhere, this is even reflected in the poverty of our vocabulary of terms relating to the feeling quality of cognitive responses. This ignorance of and reticence in communication is apparently attributable to and directly reflects social custom and usage. This ignorance may be directly related to lack of conscious awareness of feeling, which can be related in turn to the patient's feeling of "not knowing what's going on" inside himself and to his "control" problems.

Self.   It may, at first, seem strange to talk about there being communicative taboos that relate to the "self." The least amount of thought, however, will serve to indicate the reality of such taboos. For example, most parents are reluctant to give their complete positive evaluation of their own child in the child's hearing. In discussing the child's behavior or accomplishments with the child, parents seem almost naturally to underemphasize positive aspects and to concentrate on deficiencies in performance. Furthermore, if the child makes positive, accepting, or approving statements about himself, this is also more or less subtly discouraged. The parents' rationale seems to be that the child may "get a swelled head," be immodest, or think he has nothing more to learn.

On the other hand, parents may also be reluctant to let others know how "bad" the child has been at his worst and to protect his reputation even when the child has been grievously at fault.

Both biases, but especially the first, tend to make for a distorted self concept. As has already been pointed out, the child's self-evaluation is strongly dependent upon the evaluation made by others. Taboos or biases that alter the accuracy of communicative feedback about the self are almost certain to distort this self-evaluation in one way or another.

These biases against positive communicative feedback to the individual about himself do not stop with the person's childhood or adolescence. There is a general tendency toward distortion in this kind of communication regarding persons of all ages. The predominant tendency is to be quick to find fault and slow to praise. Only a minority of adults face the contrary problem of being more persistently praised than their actual performance and value warrant. Also, at any age, modesty regarding one's self is socially approved. But what is meant by "modesty" is "a conservative estimate of one's own assets and a disinclination to talk about them." There is also a social bias against talking about one's self, even when the matter of evaluation is not directly involved. Dale Carnegie wrote a best-selling book by advising people always to center their conversation on the other person. Fortunately, not *everyone* bought and read the book, so *some* people were (at least tacitly) granted the "privilege" of talking about themselves. In view of the more general taboo, this must have pleased them no end. No wonder the "listeners" won friends and influenced people.

These taboos against positive self-evaluation are carried to extremes at professional occupational levels. A physician, lawyer, or psychotherapist who publicly proclaimed his own competence in his profession would not only be frowned upon but might also be prosecuted for unethical practices, depending upon when and how he made his pronouncements. For example, *Ethical Standards of Psychologists*, issued by The American Psychological Association in 1953, states on page 27:

Principle 1.42–1. A psychologist, if he advertises or makes public announcement of his services, is obligated to describe his services with accuracy and dignity, adhering to professional rather than to commercial standards.

(1) Best practice requires that cards announcing individual clinical or industrial consulting practice should be limited to a simple statement of the name, highest relevant degree, certification or diplomate status, address, telephone number, office hours, and a brief explanation of the types of service rendered.

Further, on pages 27 and 28:

Public announcements of clinical services should be sent to professional persons only and not to prospective clients. Direct mail advertising, repeated press advertising, or radio announcements of clinical services are not acceptable procedures. Direct solicitation of clients is unethical" (1).

In other words, the psychologist is forbidden not only to tell prospective clients how good he may think he is; he is not even allowed to let them know directly that he exists or where to find him. Understand, we are not quarreling with these standards but rather cite them as an example of social taboos against positive self-evaluation.

This type of taboo is stressed for two reasons: First, it directs the attention of the psychotherapist to biases in the patient's communication when he talks about himself. It seems reasonable to assume that such biases are quite probable in talking about himself to other people and that similar biases in communication about "self" will operate in his communications with the therapist. The patient has been socially "conditioned" to observe certain taboos in discussing himself with others, so that his communication does not necessarily reflect accurately his own self-evaluation. Secondly, the patient's self-evaluation may be and usually is distorted by what others have said to him about himself, because these communications have themselves been distorted by socially conditioned reticences and taboos.

Religion.   As with the "self," it also may seem strange to talk about communicative taboos in relation to religion. However, here again we are simply suggesting that religion is a "loaded" subject about which people do not feel comfortable in expressing themselves freely. Communication about religion is heavily biased toward "conforming" public utterances, following the pattern of the "J-curve" familiar to social psychologists. Specifically, the social bias is toward "proreligious" public utterances. The person who expresses "antireligious" sentiments publicly may face strong social censure, some of which will probably come from those who privately are in agreement with the statements being made.

There are other communicative problems in this field. One of these is that parents are seldom clear in their own minds, either about their own religious beliefs or the religious beliefs of their faith (the two not necessarily being the same). Even those associates of the church who instruct the young are all too often poorly informed themselves and poorly trained (if trained at all) in instructing. The result is that we as a nation are woefully underinformed and misinformed about religion and religious issues. This is partly obscured by the fact that the majority of us are in some way affiliated with religious organizations and are actually involved in religious activities to some extent. The psychotherapist is in a better position than most, however, to realize how poor communication about religious matters is. He knows, at least, that few of his patients are able to give a coherent or integrated account of their own beliefs on religious matters.

Actually religion is a subject not often brought up nor thoroughly gone into on their own initiative by patients. Indeed, talking about religion under any circumstances is, to a degree, taboo in our society. The child who talks openly about his own religious feelings and beliefs is likely to be ridiculed by other children between the ages of six and twelve or thirteen. In the adolescent group, obvious and close church participation may cause a person to lose status with certain of his peers and may militate against his acceptance in certain groups. The minister and others closely associated with religious activities may be excluded from adult social groups and activities where they "wouldn't fit in." Conversation to and from such persons is usually subjected to a special kind of communicative taboo, also. We are reminded of the minister who had just topped his golf ball for the third time in a row on a downhill lie in the rough. Turning to the other members of the foursome he inquired: "Would you gentlemen consider it swearing if I called this inanimate object a bastard?"

Again, the point is that people are not adequately informed by others nor are they completely free to express their own thoughts and feelings about religion. As indicated previously, when communication is inadequate and/or censored to an appreciable extent as a function of either personal inadequacies or social taboos, one looks for problems in the patient's ability to communicate, and one suspects correlated distortions in cognitive structure.

Politics.   Censorship of communication regarding political matters and political beliefs should be mentioned here. While it may not have quite the same personal impact or significance as some of the other "problem" areas in communication, it sometimes has considerable importance for certain patients.

Traditionally, both formal (institutional) and informal (interpersonal) censorship have been applied to political information and opinions of the left or liberal persuasion. Strong public sentiment (mostly negative) on this issue goes back to the middle of the nineteenth century, at which time it was primarily associated with the issue of trade-unionism. In the early part of the twentieth century the I.W.W. and the Socialist Party carried the banner of the extreme left, to be succeeded by Communism in the 'thirties and up to the present. During this latter period the strength of social sanctions against avowed Communists, the degree of censorship regarding dissemination of Socialist and Communist doctrine, and the penalties imposed for expressing liberal political sentiments have varied considerably at different times. However, it seems safe to say that at no time has pro-extreme-liberal communication been as acceptable as that concerning less extreme political opinion. In fact, this observation can be extended to extremes of the right, or conservative, political position. From Theodore Roosevelt and his "trust-busting crusade" to the present general public attitude toward members of the John Birch Society, the conservative-capitalistic orientation has been in varying degrees "unpopular." A public school textbook that would take a position presenting either a fascist or the communist ideology in a favorable light would almost certainly never be generally accepted. What is considered the "ideal" textbook is as consistently apolitical as possible.

In contrast with this attitude as regards public instruction, private instruction of the young in political matters is almost sure to be one-sided. It is easier to believe that there are parents who do not discuss political philosophy with their children at all than it is to conceive of parents who present an unbiased account of all different shades of political thinking and then leave their children free to make their own choice. Most children, even as early as six years, know whether they are "Republicans" or "Democrats," if the question arises. The political "affiliation" of the child patient up to age seventeen is almost invariably the same as his parents (or the same as the parent primarily identified with, if the parents differ on this point). We consider this evidence of strong biases operating in political communications to the young from the parents.

Another aspect of social taboo in political communication, which politics shares with religion, is that the topic is often taboo in recreational social groups. "No discussions of politics or religion" is a fairly general rule, either explicit or implicit. Even more stringent taboos are frequently applied in business relationships where a difference of opinion in either of these areas might have economic consequences. An attitude of taboo also exists in more personal relationships, where open discussion usually occurs only if the persons involved are compatible in their political, and/or religious, opinions. Patients are often explicit in their curiosity about the psychotherapist's position and direct in their inquiries.

Death.   Finally "death" may be considered a topic of communication where the problems of neglect are enhanced by and, to some degree, determined by social taboos. The existence and importance of this area of communicative taboo is indicated by the frequency with which parents consult psychotherapists about how to "handle" the discussion of death with their children. This usually occurs only when a death directly affecting the child has just taken place. We interpret this as indicating that, except for this inescapable provocation, the subject of death is seldom dealt with between parent and child.

We cannot attribute this primarily to reticence on the child's part. The young child is naturally curious about dead animals and persons and wants to know "what has happened to them" and "why don't they move." To say "they are dead" tells the child nothing, except to give him a name for the nonmoving, nonnoise-making state. However, his further questions are apt to be discouraged or answered with vague and general statements. We remember our own daughter trying to make up for our deficiencies in this respect. Her cat, Doc, had died. Our answers to her questions must not have satisfied her, for several weeks later she looked very thoughtful as she watched smoke from a chimney gradually disappearing into a blue sky. She called our attention to this, and then added: "I guess something like that is what happened to Doc."

Children learn very early that direct references to the death of particular persons are strongly taboo. To say that a grandparent may die before too many years or that his parents will probably die before he does is considered "impolite" to say the least, however obvious the fact may be. Even to make such statements concerning a pet may be discouraged as being in bad taste. Perhaps the intensity of feeling elicited from others by such statements helps to account for the fact that children after a fairly young age will seldom voluntarily discuss their own death or their fears about dying.

This strongly suppressive social orientation is now carried over into adult years. This may, to some extent, reflect and be attributable to the shift from rural to urban living. The child on the farm was familiar with death in many forms, from the slaughtering of animals for food to the "family plot" in the burial ground adjacent to the church they attended. In the colonies, on the frontier, and in rural areas generally, visiting or nursing the ill, burying the dead, and consoling and helping the bereaved were a normal and significant part of social life. If nothing else, they provided a welcome break from daily routine and a justification for social gathering.

This is no longer the case. Except for those directly and unavoidably involved, deaths in urban areas are often regarded today as an imposition on the friends and acquaintances of the deceased. They are reluctant to interrupt their social and work arrangements on short notice (unless compensated), and their children are often not taken out of school for funerals and similar ceremonies. Cemeteries are not wanted adjacent to residential neighborhoods and a whole vocabulary of euphemisms has been developed to avoid such uncompromising four-letter words as "dead" and "bury."

The net result of all this avoidant behavior is that meaningful communication regarding death is extremely rare, not only among patients, but also among psychotherapists. Offhand we can think of only one psychologist, Herman Feifel, who lists as a research interest "meaning of time and old age and death," although we assume there must be others. However, the subject is very poorly represented by articles in scientific journals and by books on scientific lists. So we add "death" to the list of significant subjects that come under some degree of social taboo and that, therefore, are inadequately dealt with in communication.

NEGLECTED AREAS OF COMMUNICATION

So far we have discussed areas of communication (sex, feeling, self, religion, politics, and death) where social taboos may account for all or an appreciable part of customary deficiencies and/or distortions in communication. In the remaining three areas that will be discussed, namely marriage, vocation, and parenthood, the element of social taboo is less obvious. What is more apparent is simple, not to say willful, neglect of communication in areas of central importance to the adjustment of the individual.

Marriage.   Let us take as our first topic for consideration marriage. Sociological research assures us that the single most important factor in determining who marries whom is propinquity. In other words, people marry people who live close to them. According to one report, the average distance separating the residences of those who marry is something on the order of six or eight blocks. Such research leaves a lot unsaid but implied about the relatively "chance" nature of such matings. At least we believe it does unless one is willing to assume that "marriages are made in heaven" and that heaven conveniently arranges matters so that the "chosen two" will have minimum difficulty in locating each other.

Actually there is something to be said for propinquity as a factor in marital choice. Sociologists who study the distribution of population in urban and suburban areas assure us that while the city as a whole may be markedly heterogeneous in the social characteristics of its inhabitants, local areas or neighborhoods achieve a remarkable degree of homogeneity when population distribution is not changing too rapidly. Socio-economic status is a major aspect of this homogeneity, but other important considerations are race, national origin, and religion. Those who marry others from the same or adjacent neighborhoods are likely to have important "background" characteristics in common, although there are always exceptions, as exemplified by "Abie's Irish Rose." To the extent that propinquity means similarity of interests, values, and customs, we may consider it conducive to marital adjustment, whether or not this is consciously realized and/or communicated about.

Unfortunately, other critical aspects of marital choice and marital adjustment do *not* arrange themselves so conveniently. Often the divergent value and control systems within otherwise (superficially) homogeneous families lead to markedly divergent kinds of individual. The example usually cited to illustrate this point is the lower east-side neighborhood of New York City in the first quarter of the twentieth century that simultaneously spawned Murder, Inc., and some of our more famous entertainers, artists, and professional people. When this degree of divergence is possible, marked individual variation from the general culture can be assumed. Therefore the attraction that propinquity turns into marital pairings is no guarantee of compatibility in individual personalities.

Actually it would be better for marital happiness if each individual making a choice were aware of the research that has already been done showing which aspects of compatibility and incompatibility are correlated with marital harmony and discord. There are enough problems that arise when the initial choice has been "good" from a predictive point of view to discourage all except the most ardent from making a choice that has the statistical odds strongly stacked against it. But instead of informing the young to this effect or motivating them to seek relevant information in their formative years, our culture through both private and public media encourages the opposite. We applaud the romanticizing of marital choice, which simply means "emotional determination," and boo the "arranged" or practical choice. We are intrigued by the marriage of opposites, such as the heiress and the garage mechanic or the boss's son and the girl who works in his father's store. These are well-known and hard-used ploys of popular fiction and other mass entertainment media.

We can only believe that their popularity is attributable to minds suit-ably prepared for basically unsuited lovers.

And, of course, such stories always end with the statement or impli-cation that "they lived happily ever after." As a matter of fact, incompati-bility and unhappiness are more literally "built in" to the marital state than increasing compatibility and happiness even when the initial choice is well made. First of all, as soon as the marriage vows are said, what has been a voluntary relationship that lasts only to the extent that it is mutu-ally rewarding becomes a situation where both parties to the marriage are "locked in." Secondly, the focus of the relationship becomes the bread-and-butter business of daily living, rather than the dessert of recre-ation. Thirdly, in this bread-and-butter existence all sorts of transferences (emotional, expectancies, and others) from the original family and home situation can and do occur. Fourthly, emotional gratification, which is a prime reason for the premarital association, is relegated to a relatively insignificant role among the wide variety of needs that the marriage must attempt to gratify for each individual. Fifthly, compared with the "occupational" similarities of the premarital pairing (for example, both are students, both are working—often on the same job or at least in the same industry), the jobs and/or occupational roles of the married couple become usually increasingly divergent. Even if the wife continues to work her job opportunities are usually markedly different from those of the husband. If the wife stays at home, then occupational roles definitely will differ to a marked degree. Sixthly, the wife's and the husband's self- or ego-evaluation then center in different situations, so that their value systems necessarily differ. These, and perhaps other, aspects of the mari-tal relationship are what we refer to when we speak of "built-in" in-compatibility factors. To us it is obvious that the problem of maintaining a degree of compatibility in marriage is much more challenging than that of making an appropriate choice in the first place. Our experience with patients suggests an appalling ignorance of the information gen-erally and readily available about marriage, although marriage is by all odds the number one concern of single patients of marriageable age, and also the number one or two problem of married patients. We could put the matter still more succinctly: the single blame their unhappiness on being unmarried, and the married blame their unhappiness on being married. Of course this reminds us of an addition to our list of built-in incompatibility factors in marriage: Husband and wife find a natural scapegoat and/or a perfect screen for the projection of their own short-comings in the marital partner and the marital state.

An awareness of these problems in marriage does not actually re-quire formal courses in psychology or sociology. The information is reasonably available to anyone who has been married for a few years:

certainly to all parents by the time their own children might profit by communication in this area. Yet it is the custom in most families *not* to talk about marital problems and difficulties either in front of the children or *with* the children. This gives the children a splendid opportunity to do their own learning from experience, although there are heavy penalties for making the wrong marital choice and/or for failing to work out adequately the many challenges of the marital state. Why do parents fail to prepare and train their children for such a supposedly significant aspect of their total life experience? It is difficult to find an answer. All we know is that communicative failure is rife on this subject, so that it is one of the cognitive areas the psychotherapist is well-advised to investigate thoroughly in *his* communication with the patient.

Perhaps a major cause of communicative failure in areas that are not literally socially taboo is the ego-involvement of the parents (as prime preparatory communicators) with the areas of marriage, vocation, and parenthood. If people are generally reluctant to face and acknowledge their own errors and inadequacies, we can imagine how much more difficult it is to talk about such matters with others and how especially difficult it is to do so with one's own children. There is a natural reluctance to "tarnish" the parental image for the child beyond the haze that accumulates from the child's first-hand experience. Parents may rationalize their reluctance as being "for the child's good," but this rationalization is difficult to maintain if they have any awareness of how detrimental to "the child's good" inaccurate or inadequate communication about these critical life adjustments can be. We suspect that these particular restrictions on communication serve the purpose of protecting the parents' egos better than they serve the purpose of protecting the child's welfare.

Vocation.   The matter of ego-involvement arises again in considering communication about vocation, because it appears to be such an important factor in parental "guidance" of their children on this subject. Here we are concerned with two different kinds of ego-involvement. First, parents and other adults have a vested ego-interest in their own occupations. Their status depends to a considerable extent upon the status that their work has in the eyes of the general social community, as well as upon their own particular position in that kind of work. This creates a bias in favor of evaluating one's own work as having special significance or value, even when this may not be apparent to those outside the field. Thus the butcher sees butchering as more vital to the welfare and happiness of the community than the nonbutcher, and the psychotherapist is more aware of his value to mankind than is the nonpsychotherapist.

Second, parents (and others to a lesser extent) are ego-interested in the outcome of their children's vocational choices in the sense that "superior" choices and achievements are regarded as enhancing the status of the parents while "inferior" choices and/or achievements are regarded as detrimental to the status of those involved in the child's upbringing. We include persons besides the parents, for this is an area of adjustment where teachers, preachers, other adult friends, peers, and even siblings stand to gain or lose status depending upon the extent to which they identify with the person involved. It is not just a matter of "my son, the doctor," but also a matter of "my ex-student, the professor" and "my brother, the car-thief."

Since formal education is now so great a part of vocational preparation, the pressure upon the individual to achieve begins early and continues long. Two generations or so ago less than half of the students graduating from the eighth grade were given an opportunity to finish high school. The rest were started on vocations at about the fourteenth to sixteenth year, and the "choice" was limited to which employers (including the parents) might be willing to give them room, board, and pocket money in exchange for the dubious value of their services.

This situation is grossly changed now where legal requirements, if nothing else, usually keep youngsters in school until sixteen or older. Much more commonly, these days the adolescent is not only *told* that he will go to high school and told that he *shall* get good grades, but more than half of high school graduates are strongly "encouraged" to go on for more schooling with the top status jobs as the only limit as far as the parents are concerned. Despite what they might *not* be aware of regarding vocational choice and their offsprings' aptitudes, interests, and abilities, almost all parents *are* aware of the principle "the more, the better." Of course "better" is defined in terms of higher status and, to a considerable extent, greater income. This we consider the principal reason why parents are so prone to deprive the world of great carburetor mechanics in order to turn out mediocre brain surgeons.

Of course, in this one area, more than in perhaps any other that we have mentioned or shall mention, the adult communicators-with-the-young can plead simple ignorance as an excuse for failure, even when they can also be found guilty of aggravated self-interest. After all, the parents know more about their own work than any other, and their advice *pro* and *con* is at least based on knowledge, however biased it may be by their own ego-involvement. Beyond the area of personal parental knowledge (expanded perhaps by the personal knowledge of friends, acquaintances, and "leading citizens") lies a vast and heterogeneous domain covering about 20,000 distinct job titles and descriptions. Aside from the decision as to whether father wants son or mother wants daughter to follow in his own footsteps or choose a different route, it is difficult to give specific guidance.

The problem is further complicated by the fact that most adults have only vague and probably biased ideas about the job-related characteristics of the person they are supposed to be guiding. These include, besides intelligence, a number of specific aptitudes (all of which are probably determined to a considerable extent by inheritance), interests, values, and special motivations. We cannot completely blame the nonexpert in this field for failure to do a satisfactory job. In fact, society itself is not really at fault since the whole problem is a relatively new one in many respects.

Our purpose, therefore, in this discussion is not so much to point the finger of responsibility as it is simply to indicate that this is a "neglected" communicative area, and that a part of what is not neglected may be significantly biased. Again it behooves the psychotherapist to examine this field on his own initiative if by any chance it is not thrust upon his attention by the patient.

Parenthood.   The last of the neglected communicative subjects to be considered here is parenthood. Parenthood is a significant area of communication because, as is true of marriage and occupation, errors are not readily correctable, and a person's "success" or "failure" as a parent is of considerable consequence to both his ego and his happiness. Yet, as is also true of these other areas, the amount and accuracy of preparation that most persons receive through communication is usually far short of what they need to function with maximum effectiveness in the parental role.

Deficiencies in communication in this field cannot be attributed primarily to the indifference of the communicators, although occasionally a parent (usually the father) does seem relatively indifferent to his parental role and responsibility. Just as often, however, and perhaps more often among middle-class families, we find the parent or parents who go to the other extreme and seem to be making a complete career out of raising one or two children. Such parents usually have read all the "standard" and "popular" books about children, gone to numerous lectures, consulted assiduously with their children's teachers and principals, and still manage, somehow or other, to be making a mess of the parental role.

Psychotherapists themselves must take some of the responsibility for the misinformation conveyed to parents via both public and private communication. The dangers of inhibition and repression as potential foundations for maladjustment have been so much stressed that many psychotherapists in the recent past and some still at present have rebounded to a position of encouraging extreme permissiveness in the raising of children. The result of a generation or two of such an orientation is now being seen and felt heavily in clinical practice. We would estimate that at least 75 per cent of the children and adolescents referred to us (from predominantly middle-class families) could be adequately diagnosed by the simple designation "control problem." If we broadened the diagnostic category to include "problems in learning motivation," the percentage would rise close to 90 per cent. In these cases the "problems in learning motivation" can be described by such terms as: "daydreams," "can't concentrate," "refused to do assigned work," or "won't follow instructions."

Let us examine the type of parental "errors" responsible for such complaints. First, parents have been cautioned by "authorities" against the dangers of *excessively* inhibiting their children. Since most parents were more frustrated than they considered necessary as children, the general idea of not being as "mean" to their own children as their parents were to them has considerable built-in appeal. On the other hand, parents who were handled permissively when children themselves are not likely to attribute their own characterological or personality deficiencies to such "spoiling." So the "let's give the kids a break" idea appeals to almost everyone and "makes sense."

Unfortunately, parents are not very often communicative with their own children about the job of being a parent, nor are they inclined (for ego reasons) to discuss their mistakes as parents with their own children even when they are capable of realizing and analyzing such mistakes. When these children, in turn, become amateur parents, they often lack really adequate verbal preparation. Having nothing better to fall back on, there is a strong tendency to rely uncritically upon the *example* set by their own parents, unless they have strong negative feelings about this example. Even in this instance, however, they are frequently bound by parental example, since so often they proceed by doing just the opposite of what their parents did with them. In neither situation is there likely to be much critical sifting of the wheat from the chaff of parental example, and (as indicated above) the parents who have set the example are unlikely to be helpful in such a winnowing.

So let us say that there may be enough "communication" of a particular kind (largely example) to enable people when they become parents to function in the parental role. However, how "good" ("reasonable," "realistic," "valid") the communication may be is open to serious question. We believe that few parents are capable of evaluating their shortcomings as parents objectively, and we doubt that those who can are inclined to use the results of their own analysis to help their own children to be better parents. Regrettably even "authorities" have, in our opinion, been fallible when consulted because of an undue bias in favor of permissiveness.

Another major failure of communication to parents and prospective parents centers around the subject of what is and what is not innately determined about the child's behavior. Individuals as parents are prone to make both the error of assuming certain characteristics to be inherent when they are not and the error of ignoring innate limitations when such limitations actually exist.

To deal with the first of these errors, the most common error of this nature is to attribute specific "bad habits" to heredity. We have heard heredity blamed for almost every symptomatic act from nail biting to bad temper and lack of learning motivation. The parents' assumptions are simple and straightforward: "We know it is inherited because we used to do it and now he's doing it." Apparently it never occurs to parents spontaneously to believe that their child has their "problems" because they are making the same mistakes with their children that their parents made with them.

Paradoxically, parents (partly through ignorance and partly because of ego-involvement) are loath to accept other aspects of the children's limitations as being genetically determined. If they do not like the child's physique or temperament (perhaps because it so closely resembles their own), then all the authority of all the research that has been done on this subject may not be enough to convince them that the child has inherited his physique and/or temperament from them. On the other hand, they may also ignore or refuse to believe that their own child does not have the same desirable attributes, such as intelligence and various specific aptitudes, that they themselves have. It is quite apparent that most parents have only the simplest and vaguest notions of how heredity actually functions in determining these characteristics. No one (including some psychologists when they are functioning as parents) seems to have heard of Galton's principle of "regression toward the mean." And apparently no one informs parents about maturational stages in development. Gesell's books and other books on the subject that have achieved some popular distribution have apparently not been sufficient to overcome parents' personal biases on such matters.

The result is that parents waste much money, time, energy, and concern in attempting to change traits that we have good reason to believe are not very changeable. In the process they not only frustrate themselves but impose unwarranted feelings of frustration and failure on their children. So far as intelligence and specific aptitudes are concerned, the child's ability to develop is all too often appraised only in terms of what the parents themselves have been able to achieve or (worse yet) what they would like to see the child accomplish for their own ego gratification. As to *when* or *how soon* a child should be able to do certain things (roller skate, ride a bike, read, write, spell, do arithmetic, and so on), this is especially likely to be decided in terms of parental desire rather than by the maturational "readiness" of the child.

The net result of considerable ignorance in this area of communication in conjunction with the ego needs of the parents is that many children consider themselves "failures" at the age of seven, eight, or nine years. Their natural tendency toward feelings of inferiority and inadequacy has been heavily reinforced by their inability to measure up to the unreasonable and unrealistic expectations of their parents. They have already "failed" so many times in attempts to learn that they avoid learning situations whenever and however they can. Yet so often these "failures" are synthetic, manufactured entirely out of erroneous ideas that the parents have as to how soon and how quickly their children should be able to learn whatever the parents want them to learn.

Such errors make a considerable contribution to the "problems in learning motivation" referred to above. Some such problems exist only in the parents' minds as their explanation of why their child is not "doing better" in school. In such cases we find the expected correspondence between intelligence and grades achieved and have to "communicate" to the parents our conclusion that the child's problem is not lack of motivation but lack of aptitude.

Most of the rest of the learning problems grow out of still another aspect of parental ignorance, which may sound paradoxical in terms of what we have already said about the contemporary bias favoring permissiveness in raising children. Yet we so continually encounter this paradox that we have to believe in its reality. Let us make our position clear on this point before going further. First, experience (both personal and professional, and both practical and theoretical) has convinced us that so far as general behavior is concerned it is advisable to establish control habits at an early age and to give the child progressively more freedom as he matures. We envisage the parental control function as an inverted cone, in which close early supervision and control provides the necessary "safety factor" that permits the parent to progressively widen limits as the child becomes more mature and competent. In the second place, we consider punishment an effective means of *inhibiting* undersirable behavior, and its effectiveness as an inhibitor makes it the control method of choice for that particular purpose (always assuming that rewards will be used simultaneously to reinforce desirable behavior). However, in our own minds we are quite clear and un-equivocal on the point that punishment is only desirable when our objective is inhibited or avoidant behavior. This makes it completely unsuitable as a reinforcement when the child is attempting to learn *to do* something, such as learning to read or write. For such positive types of learning, *learning to do rather than not to do,* punishment is not only inappropriate but creates a strong impulse on the child's part to avoid learning situations. If he cannot avoid learning *situations* literally because of compulsory school attendance laws or similar adult coercion, he can avoid really attempting to learn. He may also "escape" by day-dreaming, "goofing off," forgetting assignments, and lying about whether he has done his work. On the other hand, if learning is encouraged by appropriate rewards, we are not only reinforcing the child's attempts to do something constructive, but we are also helping to create positive attitudes (pleasant feelings) that are associated with learning, school, lessons, teacher, and so on. From such experiences eventually grow the "interest in learning" that parents are so anxious to see develop.

Now to our paradox. Many times the very same parents who are smitten with the kissing bug of permissiveness where their child's gen-eral behavior is concerned become punitive tyrants when their child is trying to learn to do something, such as read or write. Their expecta-tions are unreasonable, their demands are excessive, and their approach is primarily critical (which means "punitive," however "constructively" phrased the criticism may be). We attribute this predominantly negative reinforcement of the child's attempts to learn partly to ignorance, partly to excessive ego-involvement, and partly to lack of skill, understanding, and patience as instructors. We feel that a considerable part of the difficulty that individuals have as parents trying to raise children could be alleviated by more adequate and more accurate information about the task.

OTHER COMMUNICATIVE PROBLEMS

We, ourselves, have done a lot of communicating about the matter of evaluating patients' deficiencies or distortions in communicating or in being communicated to. In the preceding chapter we have talked about which persons are most likely to have difficulty in communicating. In this chapter we have discussed *areas* of communication where errors are most likely to occur in the preparation of the individual for adult life. Even so, we are a long way from having exhausted the subject. In the remaining pages of this chapter we shall suggest, rather than explore definitively, some additional aspects of evaluating the patient's communicative behavior.

Vocabulary.   It is not a simple matter to determine either the extent or the nature of the patient's problems in communicating. Actually, there are several aspects to this communicative behavior that we must differentiate. We may consider the patient as he communicates with himself. But what he "knows" and "says" to himself may or may not be the same as what he communicates to others. For example, each person has a "passive" vocabulary of words he understands that is considerably larger than the "active" vocabulary he uses when talking to others. In between the two is his "written" or "correspondence" vocabulary, which may be either larger or smaller than his "active" vocabulary when speaking and may include different words.

Social inhibition.   The patient's effectiveness as a communicator may depend to a considerable extent upon his ability to adapt his vocabulary, syntax, and general mode of expression to the person with whom he is communicating. What he will or will not communicate depends upon the age, sex, education, occupation, and other characteristics of the person being communicated with (including the psychotherapist). Across these considerations runs another determinant that has to do with the degree of familiarity with the other person, the nature of the relationship between communicator and communicant, and the communicator's evaluation of "how much further" what he says will be communicated to others. We know from research, as well as from practical experience, that there are varying degrees of correspondence between communication about behavior and the nature of the behavior which is communicated about. For example, people tend to be more "conforming" (with respect to social standards) in their speech than in their behavior. So it is not always easy to judge what the person is *capable* of communicating by what he actually *chooses* to communicate to others, including the psychotherapist.

Social expectancy.   What the patient is capable of communicating is not necessarily a fixed and definite amount. In this connection we must attempt to differentiate several possible situations. The simplest is that in which the individual has never received certain kinds of information. This varies only to the extent that the person *acquires* information. Then we have what might be called "neglected" areas of communication in the sense that the patient is not normally asked for nor does he customarily volunteer some of the information he has. If the psychotherapist "waits for" communication in these areas, he may have a long wait, although the patient is not necessarily reluctant to discuss these matters if asked to do so. We have also encountered the opposite problem of having patients volunteer information they believed we would be particularly interested in but for which we could find very little "use."

Suppression and repression.   Next we come to the problem of distinguishing between suppression and repression, as well as distinguishing either of these from the other reasons for "noncommunication." We use the term "suppression" to refer to the voluntary withholding of information of which the communicator is "aware." In other words, we assume that the communicator makes cognitive responses corresponding to the information which we want, but he will not make the corresponding behavioral (communicative) responses. We further assume that the communicative response is withheld or inhibited because such response in the past has been followed by some kind of "punishment" or negative reinforcement. Finally, we assume that the inhibitory habit is generalized or "transferred" to the therapeutic situation.

We differentiate "suppression" from "repression" by assuming that in the latter instance, the punishment which has followed a communicative (behavioral) response has been intense enough and/or has been repeated often enough to create an inhibitory habit "cutting off" the cognitive response which normally preceded the behavioral response. If this happened, then the patient is no longer "aware" of the information desired, although he has "known about" it previously.

Loss of awareness.   In order to be comprehensive, at least in survey, we shall also review two further conditions that may account for a patient's lack of "awareness" and/or "unwillingness" to communicate about matters he has been aware of in the past. First, we refer to the process of "short-circuiting" by which links in a cognitive chain that are no longer "necessary" to the evocation of response are dropped out (see pp. 77–78). For example, the man with a beard is not necessarily aware of whether he sleeps with it over or under the covers, although he has not been "punished" for talking about the matter. Secondly, we mention again the possibility that links in a cognitive chain (or more complex cognitive substructure) may "fall out" of the chain by becoming more strongly linked to other behavioral responses. For example, if we are assigned a new telephone number, eventually we "forget" the old one. In both of these situations we assume that the problem in re-establishing "awareness" and/or communication is significantly different than in the other types of "noncommunication" previously described.

Methods of dealing with these and some of the other problems in communication that we have described will be discussed in our chapters on communication strategy and technique.

Evaluating communication and cognitive structure.   Our purpose in presenting these aspects of communicative behavior is to suggest some of the complexities involved in evaluating cognitive structure by means of the patient's communicative responses. Only repression and loss of awareness which is a function of habit formation represent deficiencies in the symbolic cognitive responses of the patient. The other conditions are peculiar to communicative behavior and represent the extent to which this communicative behavior may fail to represent adequately the actual cognitive structure of the person.

The technical problem for the psychotherapist is to determine whether noncommunication does or does not represent deficiencies in cognitive structure. Closely correlated with this problem is the consideration that errors in the patient's cognitive structure cannot be evaluated until communication occurs. This returns us to the problem of Chapter 5: the matter of the patient's communicative skill. The psychotherapist must ultimately decide whether an apparent error in cognitive structure actually does represent such an error or whether the apparent error is a function of the patient's inadequate communicative skills.

IMPLICATIONS FOR PSYCHOTHERAPY

The importance of communicative skills.   At the risk of unduly laboring points that may be obvious, we want to make clear what we consider to be the importance of these last two chapters.

Until quite recently there has been a tendency for psychotherapists to underestimate the significance of communicative skills in determining the patient's problems in adjusting to his environment. Such an underestimation may be attributed, at least in part, to psychoanalytic techniques, which involve a deliberate attempt to go beyond the limits of normal communication by the use of dream material and by insistence upon "the rule" of free association.

These special communicative techniques play a very important part in expanding the "awareness" of the patient about the nature of his inner experience and the pattern of his behavioral responses. Therefore, we have no quarrel with such techniques per se; in fact, we consider their use essential in any effort to effect the greatest possible efficiency in adjustment. However, interest in the usual communicative processes and in the patient's communicative skill can be traced largely to the work of Rogers (2) and Korzybski (3). Apparently, this interest has still not sufficiently penetrated the conceptualizations of many psychotherapists.

Why have we placed so much emphasis on this subject in a book devoted to fundamentals of psychotherapy? This emphasis is not difficult to defend if the reader will grant certain assumptions, which we shall now make explicit.

Our first assumption is that man's greatest potential for satisfying emotional experience involves interaction with other persons. At the top, as the most satisfying emotional experience, we would place the emotion of love.

Our second assumption is that "interaction with others" is synonymous with "relating," and that both terms are essentially synonymous with "communicating." In order for these equivalences to make sense and to be acceptable, we must consider "communicating" in its broadest sense, which includes both nonverbal and verbal means of expression and involuntary, as well as voluntary, communications. In this broader sense, for example, sexual intercourse would be regarded as a communicative act, and as a communicative act that may have any of several different "meanings."

We can further support the reasonableness of our second assumption by pointing out that the only means of contact between the inner experience of one person and the inner experience of another is via some act of communication. If we are willing to grant this, then the basic identity of "relating" and "communicating" is difficult to question.

It should now be obvious why a person's skill in communicating (his success in achieving his communicative intent) is so critical to his adjustment to others and to his own achievement of emotional satisfaction. When his intent is to influence the behavior of others, his skill as a communicator determines his degree of success. When his intent is to inform others about himself, the accuracy of his portrayal will be a joint function of the accuracy of his self-knowledge and the effectiveness of his communicative techniques. We can perhaps simplify the point by saying that a person cannot relate any more effectively than he can communicate.

Psychotherapy and communicative skills.   Chapter 5 dealt with persons who may have communicative difficulties, especially when they are dealing with those who are different from themselves. We believe that the psychotherapist is in the best possible situation to note the limitations in his patients' communicative skills. How these limitations adversely affect the patient's relations with others, and thereby limit his opportunities for emotional gratification, may not be immediately obvious. However, such consequences should not be too difficult to infer, especially since some of these will be manifested in the psycho-therapeutic relationship itself.

The most practical implication of these observations for the psycho-therapist is that he can perform a significant service for the patient by helping to increase the patient's skill as a communicator. In fact, this is one of the patient's problems the therapist can deal with most di-rectly, since communicating is a response that the patient actually makes in therapy and that the therapist can evaluate, motivate, reinforce, and direct. In view of the basic relationship between communicating and relating, we can only conclude that the general neglect of this problem in psychotherapy has been a matter of oversight rather than a duly considered exclusion.

The importance of adequate information.   The tabooed or neglected areas of communication, which we have stressed in this chapter, are areas where patients are most liable to be underinformed or misin-formed. In our introduction to Chapter 5 we compared the person with a computer, which is programmed and then given data to process. The actual habits of the person can be compared with the "program" of the computer: they determine *how* data will be processed. However, in the human example, the adequacy of the programming is limited by the adequacy and accuracy of the information available to the "pro-grammers" (the person's social conditioners). This programming may be, and usually is, further distorted by emotional biases affecting the programmers.

Obviously we cannot afford to assume the adequacy of the patient's data processing programs, so far as ensuring his optimal adjustment to his environment is concerned. Returning to psychotherapeutic terminol-ogy, we may find defects in his methods of drawing inferences, arriving at conclusions, evaluating, and performing other "operations" upon the information he acquires.

Beyond these problems, we may find that the patient lacks informa-tion or has misinformation regarding some of the most basic and signifi-cant functions he is supposed to perform. In terms of our analogy, he lacks data to process, or the data he has is inaccurate.

Psychotherapy and education.   We stress these points because the fascination of psychoanalytic procedures and theories has tended to obscure some rather obvious aspects of the psychotherapeutic situation. Again, as we pointed out a few paragraphs ago, our concern is not with disparaging the objectives or techniques of psychoanalysis. Rather our concern is with psychotherapeutic efforts that are disparaged or neglected by some because of their exclusive preoccupation with psychoanalytic concepts. Thus, education, re-education, information-giving, and attempts to correct the thinking processes of patients have all been disparaged by some psychotherapists as "superficial," as "merely supportive," or simply as "not psychotherapeutic—in the 'true' sense of the word."

These are attitudes and evaluations with which we strongly disagree. Since the great bulk of the developing individual's preparation for future adjustments is verbally mediated, we can think of nothing more critical to this adjustment than the accuracy and adequacy of the advanced information that he receives and the effectiveness with which he uses it in determining his own responses. Rather than assuming that this is a superficial problem, the psychotherapist is apt to find that there is more of a job to be done in supplementing or correcting prior efforts to prepare the patient than the therapist can conveniently handle.

For example, the industrial psychologist knows that a person who is too intelligent for the job he is holding finds it difficult to maintain high morale in that position. Yet this may be the highest level job for which he has adequate training. This lack of preparation, in turn, may be due to underestimations of the person's intelligence in childhood, underestimation of the value of or need for advanced education, and so forth. Quite frequently in our experience we encounter persons thus inadequately prepared. We have been unable to conceive of any reasonable adjustive alternative other than the person's returning to school and becoming further educated.

In more specific areas of inadequate or erroneous information, such as the ones we have reviewed in this chapter, is there really any alternative to supplying more adequate or more accurate information? We do not know of any. The only question concerns the most economical means of supplying the necessary information. For example, it is difficult to justify using therapeutic time to convey information unless it is not readily available in appropriate form in public media or unless the psychotherapist has reason to suspect that the patient may have emotional resistances that will have to be dealt with as a part of the educative endeavor. It may be entirely necessary for the psychotherapist to create an appropriate motivation for learning, and he may also be responsible for directing the patient to appropriate sources. These, however, are matters of "how to" help the patient, not matters of "whether to." We see little basis for disagreement on this latter point.

One final observation before we leave this subject. We would like to suggest that one of the reasons why the educative needs of the patient have tended to be ignored is that it requires a considerable degree of attentiveness to determine what the patient does *not* know. It is our hope that by reminding psychotherapists of communicative areas that are often neglected in the person's training, they may become more sensitive to this issue and more adequate in detecting and in dealing with it. We have also tried to establish the validity of such evaluations and corrective efforts as both a legitimate and a necessary part of psychotherapeutic procedure.

SUMMARY

Our purpose in this chapter is to review areas of information that are inadequately or inaccurately represented in cognitive structure because of social taboos regarding communication or because of deficiencies in the preparation of a person's social conditioners. Under tabooed subjects, we list "sex," "feelings," "self," "religion," "politics," and "death." Areas where information is often inadequate or distorted, although not specifically tabooed, are "occupation," "marriage," and "parenthood."

Although sex is more openly discussed now than formerly, it continues to be a prime target of public censors. Furthermore, many aspects of social taboo remain. Sex "education" usually does *not* include a discussion of the complex relationships between sexuality and emotion.

There are today many subtle taboos about the expression of feelings. Much of the childhood training, especially of boys, encourages the suppression and even the repression of feelings. A considerable ignorance of subjective experience in this area is only one of the unfortunate results of such inhibitory training.

Although each person is very much dependent upon the evaluations of others to form a basis for self-evaluation, there is a definite bias in this kind of communication to the child. The net effect of this bias is to underemphasize the positive attributes of the person, while not infrequently concealing also some real and significant deficiencies. Modesty in self-evaluation and self-description is encouraged, even at the expense of being unrealistic in these respects.

The open discussion of religious attitudes, values, and points of view is subtly discouraged at most ages, partly because it is a subject that few persons can now discuss comfortably, partly because it is capable of producing social friction. Real ignorance in this area is commonly concealed behind a "front" of superficial conformity, which is often more apparent at a verbal than at a behavioral level of response.

Political convictions and beliefs are often matters settled by family tradition or reactive rebellion. "Proper" political beliefs are rigidly defined. Both institutional and informal censorship deprive most persons of the opportunity to make a thoughtful choice among various ideologies.

The increasing urbanization of our population helps to make death an unfamiliar and disturbing topic of communication. Although taboos are often handled as matters of politeness or good taste, the effect of such suppression is much the same as if stronger injunctions were involved. Basically, most persons are left without adequate attitudes for dealing with the subject on either a social or personal basis.

Occupation, marriage, and parenthood involve highly significant and complex adjustments that provide only limited opportunities to learn from experience. Since these are complex adjustments, the knowledge we now have about them is mostly a matter for professional training and for communication by "secondary" social conditioners who are more or less expert. However, the knowledge we have is not always made available to those who need it most, when they need it most. The more complete and effective utilization of professional resources for this purpose would, of course, constitute an important mental hygiene measure.

When we consider the preparation of individuals in these three areas of adjustment by their primary social conditioners (usually parents), we are especially impressed by two prime sources of distortion and error. The first of these is deliberate or unconscious communicative suppression relative to the totality of the parents' knowledge of a given area of adjustment. Parents do not necessarily tell their children all the parents know about marriage, occupation, or parenthood. Rather, the parental tendency is to communicate only what they believe the child "should" know. The parental effort is often limited to the inculcation of standards or ideals. This may leave the person being trained relatively unprepared to deal with the other realities of these various adjustments.

Secondly, we are impressed by the extent to which poor preparation is determined by the parents' ego-involvements and by their own ego needs. This is dramatically obvious in the areas of education and occupation, where the child is often (and illogically) expected to "come up to" or to "make up for" the achievement level of his parents. In the areas of marriage and parenthood, the ego needs of the parents are reflected in the suppression of information or the substitution of misinformation to the developing individual because such misrepresentation covers up the deficiencies of the parents.

Although we are primarily concerned in this chapter with delineating significant cognitive areas where patients may lack information or have defective information, we have also pointed out that the determination of such deficiencies is by no means a simple matter. The gist of this problem is that it is not always easy to distinguish between what the person does not know and what he may know but does not choose to communicate. Furthermore, when the psychotherapist does evaluate the patient's communications, he is faced with the further problem of distinguishing between defective knowledege and defective communication.

What the person "knows" and his skill in using this knowledge in the determination of his own behavior determine the effectiveness of his conscious efforts to adjust to his environment. While these are by no means the only determinants of his behavior, we believe that many psychotherapists have become unduly preoccupied with "unconscious" determinants to the virtual exclusion of obvious problems of considerable significance. The obvious question is why either aspect of the person's adjusting should be ignored for the sake of the other.

The question becomes even more pointed when we consider psychotherapeutic neglect of the obvious issue of the patient's communicative skills. We are unable to conceive of "relating to others" in any concrete way other than through communicative behavior. We conclude, therefore, that the patient's skill or effectiveness in such behavior has much to do (if it is not synonymous) with his effectiveness in relating. The psychotherapeutic situation is ideally suited for the evaluation of communicative deficiencies and for the improvement of communicative skills.

SUGGESTIONS FOR FURTHER READING

We recommend to the reader Ruesch's excellent book (4). For those who must be selective, we suggest the reading of the initial chapters and Chapter 24. Sullivan (5) is also a good reference at this point, particularly Chapters 1, 6, and 10.

Carl Rogers (6) has some interesting observations on the therapeutic potentials of education in Chapters 13, 14, and 15. He deals with problems of family life in Chapter 16 and discusses disruption of communication in Chapter 17. Albert Ellis (7) discusses marital problems and sexual adjustment in Chapters 11, 12, and 13 of his book.

In Dollard and Miller (8), we suggest the reading of Chapters XVIII, XIX, XX, and XXVII. Rotter (9) has a few pertinent comments on pp. 217–221.

REFERENCES

1. *Ethical standards of psychologists.* Washington, D.C.: American Psychological Association, 1953.
2. Rogers, C. R. *Counseling and psychotherapy.* Boston: Houghton Mifflin, 1942.

3. Korzybski, A. *Science and sanity* (2d ed.). Lancaster, Pa.: Science Press, 1941.

4. Ruesch, J. *Therapeutic communication.* New York: Norton, 1961.

5. Sullivan, H. S. *The psychiatric interview.* New York: Norton, 1954.

6. Rogers, C. R. *On becoming a person.* Boston: Houghton Mifflin, 1961.

7. Ellis, A. *Reason and emotion in psychotherapy.* New York: Lyle Stuart, 1962.

8. Dollard, J., and Miller, N. E. *Personality and psychotherapy.* New York: McGraw-Hill, 1950.

9. Rotter, J. *Social learning and clinical psychology.* Englewood Cliffs, N.J.: Prentice-Hall, 1954.

Chapter 7 | *Cognitive Structure: Evaluation of Problems*

DISTORTIONS IN THE SELF CONCEPT

The "reality" of cognitive structure.   In considering the evaluation of problems that relate to cognitive structure, it is important to note a particular point. In our theoretical discussion of cognitive structure we have called it the patient's "map" of reality. This it is from the point of view of an outsider, specifically, the psychotherapist. From the patient's point of view, however, what we consider the "map" is what he considers "reality"—the "thing" itself. The "world" in which he lives and upon which he postulates his behavior is the "world" in his head. It requires a certain degree of intelligence, education, and sophistication even to question intellectually whether "what I believe" is or is not exactly the same as "what is true."

Of course the psychotherapist is not sure of "what is true" either. But we expect him to have the ability to detect major and significant distortions between any particular individual's personal conceptions and what a reasonable consensus of fairly objective observers might be about the same matter. In this he is aided by an advantage that we all have in considering the problems of others: the mote in *his* eye is more apparent than the beam in our own. However, clinical experience has taught us that the psychotherapist may either exaggerate or ignore defects in the cognitive structure of the patient which parallel defects in his own cognitive structure. Therefore we expect him to examine thoroughly, not just once but continuously, the validity of his own conception of reality and the emotional pressures that might tend to distort it. The third major safeguard that the psychotherapist can offer the patient in evaluating the patient's cognitive structure is to be aware of the most common and characteristic distortions in people's concepts of reality.

Communicating about the self.   It is probably apparent from preceding chapters that we routinely look for and expect to find distortions in the self concept. By "self concept" we mean that significant group of cognitive responses which have to do with the self, in terms of both description and evaluation. We assume, incidentally, that not all of these cognitive responses related to the self are necessarily associated with behavioral (communicative) responses. In others words, the patient may "know" certain things about himself that he is, initially at least, *unable* to tell us. In addition, the patient may "know" certain things about himself that he is *unwilling* to tell us. The various reasons for these barriers in communication have been summarized at the end of the preceding chapter. In any event we cannot afford to assume that what the patient *is* able and willing to tell us represents a complete and accurate representation of his cognitive substructure relating to the self. As indicated in Chapter 6, a common bias, created and reinforced by social conditioning, is to be modest and reticent with respect to positive self-appraisal. Yet we also know that if we make negative appraisals of the patient or assert that he makes negative evaluations of himself, he is often vehement in his denial that he possesses or believes himself to possess "bad" characteristics. Thus we face the paradox of modesty, real or false, on the one hand and what is commonly referred to as "ego-defensiveness" on the other. Both tend to distort, but in opposite directions, the nature of the patient's communication about himself.

Negative self-evaluation.   We have already suggested in several places in the preceding material that the predominant bias in the self-evaluation of the patient population is to consider the self as having fewer "good" qualities and more "bad" qualities than others would. We may assume, as Adler has done, that the basic reason for this bias goes back to the child's initial perceptions of his own inadequacy and inferiority relative to other persons (parents, older siblings, and others). As the old joke has it his problem at this stage is not that he *feels* inferior but that he *is* inferior. We have already suggested that the child is initially not "sophisticated" enough to create his own relative standards, which means judging himself in comparison with others of his own age. He might, and he sometimes does, succeed in developing and applying such relative standards if given appropriate help, but in this respect he is very dependent upon the assistance of others.

These "others" (principally parents) may set standards that are too high for any of several reasons. They themselves may not take age into account sufficiently in appraising the performance of the child, especially after the first few years of life. They may forget or misremember how long it took them to achieve their adult degree of proficiency. They may be ignorant of or ignore maturational readiness as a factor in ability to learn. They may make inappropriate interpersonal comparisons of one child with another or of their children with themselves when young, disregarding the reality of inherent differences in general intelligence, specific aptitudes, and temperament even among persons who are closely related. Their expectations may be influenced by certain ego needs of their own: wanting their child to be "the best" in order to reflect glory upon themselves. They may imply inadequacy or inferiority by the extent to which they criticize, point out mistakes, explain how the child could do better, and so on. They may push the child so hard and so continually in the direction of achievement and perfection that the child refuses to perform out of sheer resentment. They may give him so much "help" in learning that the child begins to doubt whether he is capable of learning on his own initiative.

All such errors in parental handling or evaluation may exacerbate feelings of inadequacy and inferiority. We say "exacerbate" because the child's own tendency is to compare himself with *all* others, not just with his own age peers. The child cannot help noticing that he is smaller, weaker, more ignorant, less skilled, and more fearful than his adult associates. When the gulf seems especially wide and the child himself has no means of knowing what amount of time and effort have gone into the development of certain adult characteristics, he may decide prematurely that he will *never* be able to function as adequately as the person with whom he is comparing himself. He can bolster this conclusion with the evidence of his initial failures. Such attitudes and evaluations may then lead to avoidant behavior that precludes the possibility of successful experience.

Time indexing the self.   Hand-in-hand with this type of problem goes the matter of appropriate "time indexing" or rather the *lack* of appropriate time indexing. The child goes through an initial period of very rapid development in almost all respects between the time of his birth and his sixth birthday. Most individuals go through a somewhat similar "spurt" in the development of many characteristics in adolescence. At such times performances that would have been difficult or impossible only a few months before are accomplished at a later period with relative ease. Unless the individual is encouraged or instructed to try again later on in his development, he may accept earlier failures as evidence that he "just doesn't have it" (that is, the ability or aptitude required for successful performance). Except for the most obvious physical characteristics, the child's tendency is to equate "myself $_{today}$" with "myself $_{last\ month}$," "myself $_{last\ year}$," and so on. Some very important characteristics that we know change progressively with age, such as general intelligence, are not always noticeably different to the individual or to others from one year to the next.

Distortions of the parental image.   In addition to the real differences between the child and his adult associates, certain other "differences," more apparent than real, may be assumed. Both parent and child may contribute to this misevaluation. We must remember that the child sees himself, rather accurately, as helpless and dependent to a considerable extent. When threatened, his security is enhanced if he may rely upon the strength, wisdom, bravery, and experience of his parents. But his security is proportional to the extent to which his parents possess these desirable attributes. The more the child "sees" of these characteristics, the more secure he feels. This obviously opens the door to certain wishful or hopeful exaggerations of the parents' capacities, as manifested in the classic challenge, "My Dad can lick your Dad." In addition to such distortion serving security needs, it also serves ego or status needs, since the child through identification with the parent takes on some of the parents' positive values to bolster the value of his own ego. So the fact that "my Dad's car is better than your Dad's car" helps to make up for the fact that "your bicycle is better than my bicycle."

Parents are not always averse to such complimentary distortions. In fact, they are prone to add certain distortions of their own. Most parents are reluctant to discuss their own errors, failures, misgivings, anxieties, and so on, with their children. They may rationalize such withholding of information on the grounds that it would only disturb or upset the child. But we encounter many instances in which parents are loathe to admit that their children are superior to themselves in certain characteristics or skills. This smacks less of protecting the security of the child than it does of protecting the ego-evaluation of the parent at the child's expense. Thus, as often as not, the "real" gap between the competence of the child and of the parents is further widened by an "apparent" distance that is partially attributable to the distortions of the child and partly to those of the parents. Regardless of where the blame lies or how it is parcelled out, the result is to exaggerate the child's feeling of inadequacy over what it "needs" to be.

Absolute standards.   In discussing various reasons why the "self" is so often evaluated as inadequate or inferior, we must mention the consideration that in certain areas the child is often deliberately trained and encouraged to evaluate himself by absolute rather than by relative standards. This is especially and most significantly characteristic of what we usually refer to as "moral" training or "character formation." We can perhaps illustrate this point by reference to the controversy stimulated by the publication by Kinsey and his associates of information about sexual behavior. One conclusion which this study made immediately apparent was that what people profess to consider "proper" sexual behavior and how they actually behave sexually are by no means always the same. But the controversy we are interested in was concerned with whether or not it was desirable to continue advocating "absolute" standards of sexual morality. The "pro" argument was based on the contention that to set standards for behavior based on how people actually behaved would lead to a further "lowering" of sexual behavior. Without going into the merits of this argument, we note it as the typical rationale for setting standards that few, if any, actually live up to. However, we usually do not include this "fact" about such standards in our instructions to the young. Rather such absolute standards are generally presented with at least the implication that all "good" people always observe these standards and that only "bad" people violate them. In this way we create the very definite possibility that a person who is reasonably "good" and reasonably "adequate" may evaluate himself by standards which lead him to conclude that he is very "bad" and very "inadequate."

This bias is even built into our popular entertainment and communication media and presented in still more exaggerated form to children. In our popular myths, legends, folk tales, novels, comic strips, movies, and TV programs, the "good guys" are always "all" good. No hero ever picks his nose, belches, nurses his pennies, or leers at a woman. On the other hand, no villain ever pets dogs, remembers his mother on Mother's Day, buys Girl Scout cookies, or "respects womanhood." But principally we are concerned with the hero, who has absolutely no faults at all—or at least not any we are allowed to see. Therefore it follows, does it not, that all people with faults must be villains. Perhaps this is not what we *intend*, but does it not come out this way? And if we, as adults, "know better," does the child?

Communicative taboos.   Finally, we would refer again to the taboos on communication regarding the "self" mentioned in Chapter 6. We recognize that it is natural for the parent to be proud of his child and even to be biased in perceiving positive attributes that are perhaps imperceptible to more objective observers. It might be argued that such a positive bias should certainly tend to counteract some of the conditions we have mentioned as leading to self-depreciation. And so it might, if such appreciative evaluations were communicated *to the child*. However, we must remember that "others" whom the parent is trying to impress are rather more likely to hear such positive evaluations than the child himself. Just as the child says, "My Dad can lick your Dad," to another *child* to try to impress that child, so Dad says, "My kid can lick your kid," to another father in order to impress that father. In other words, children are bragged about by parents to other parents. When it comes to telling the *child* how good he is, parents seem to become all clutched up with anxiety about giving the child a "swelled head" or making him conceited. In any event, parents share the propensity of human beings in general to be quick to criticize and slow to praise so far as communication to the object of their appraisal is concerned. And the child is trained, in the interests of modesty, not to speak well of himself if by any chance he should happen to form a favorable opinion. A universal characteristic of the hero is his modesty, and "Aw shucks, ma'm, 'twarn't nothin'" is emblazoned on his shield.

The axiomatic nature of the self concept.   Some concatenation of the various circumstances listed above makes it highly probable that persons seen as patients will come to the psychotherapist with a distorted self-image, and usually the distortion will be an "unfavorable" direction. But, as we indicated at the beginning of this chapter, the patient does not regard his self-evaluation as an opinion or as a "map" of reality; he regards it as real, the "truth." He does not usually say: "This is my opinion—perhaps you will think differently." Rather he predicates his entire adjustment on this self-evaluation. For example, he will not attempt to do anything that he is "sure" he will be unable to do on the basis of his own evaluation. As a result, the patient is likely to be performing in life generally at a level much lower than an objective appraisal of his capacities would indicate. This has been so generally noted and commented upon by psychotherapists that "underachievement" has come to be considered almost the hallmark of persons "in need of psychotherapy."

In spite of the near universality of such depreciated self-images among patients, it would be a mistake to assume that this problem is the one usually presented to the psychotherapist by the patient. Actually, it seldom is, perhaps because his "inferiority" is so "real" to the patient that he does not consider it a matter about which anything can be done. Furthermore, we may expect the patient to carry over to his contact with the psychotherapist his habitual modes of presenting himself to others. In other words, he will make all, some, or most of the behavioral (including communicative) responses that he habitually makes in social situations. These behavioral-communicative responses rarely, if ever, permit us to see completely and from the beginning what the patient's self-evaluation is. Rather our knowledge of this self-image and self-evaluation will usually have to be built up gradually with many of the specific details depending upon inferential rather than direct evidence. Let us next consider why this is so.

"Personae": social selves.   In social and clinical psychology we speak of the "persona," the social mask, borrowing the term from the ancient Greek theater where actors actually wore masks in portraying certain characters or certain feelings. The masks of comedy and tragedy that symbolize the theater are a remnant of this classical past. In social and clinical psychology the persona refers to a person's efforts to create a particular kind of impression on others. It is the "social self" through which he interacts with others, as contrasted with the entire and "real" self as he believes or "knows" himself to be. The "self" that is presented for social inspection is determined by several considerations. For example, the nature of the relationship sought with the other person is of considerable consequence. Does the presenter of the persona seek acceptance or help, or is he trying to impress the other person? Perhaps he is trying to do all of these things, or some objective may be more important to him than others. Furthermore, in determining which attributes to "project" and which to conceal, the presenter of the persona must make certain assumptions about his "audience," specifically about the value system of that audience. We expect and find that the assumptions made are determined to a considerable extent by previous experiences with other persons which are generalized to or transferred to new social contacts. There may be varying degrees of adjustment of such expectancies based on accumulated experience with the other person in any particular relationship.

We assume that the patient is bound by habit to go through this process of selective revelation and concealment about himself, regardless of his intent to be "open" with the psychotherapist.

Problems in evaluating the self concept.   In all probability the psychotherapist will attempt to convince the patient that he will not be rejected or otherwise punished for anything he will communicate about himself. In this respect the psychotherapeutic relationship is probably unique among human relationships, at least so far as the *intent* of the psychotherapist is concerned. So we are not surprised, or should not be, if the task of "convincing" the patient is not easily achieved. Of course, to the extent that we actually *are* punitive in our response to the patient's communication, we defeat our own purpose of finding out what the patient's self concept is.

In any event we can only hope to gain at most from direct communication what the patient "knows" about himself, that is, he can only communicate about cognitive responses he is able to make as a matter of self-awareness or self-communication. When he has been severely and/or consistently punished for certain types of communication, the inhibitory habits thus created may extend to the cognitive responses most proximate to these communicative responses, so that the patient no longer "knows" these things about himself, as well as being unable to say them. The reassurance the psychotherapist is able to offer may or may not extend to the disinhibition of these cognitive responses. In other words, the patient may or may not be able to "recover repressed material." However, such repressed self-knowledge may sometimes be inferred from the patient's avoidant communicative behavior. Alternatively, we may sometimes be able to infer what has been repressed by noting what is missing in an otherwise integrated cognitive pattern, rather like being able to describe how the missing piece in a jigsaw puzzle must look from noting its sur- roundings.

Sometimes, rather than simply finding a blank, we find an incongru- ent piece in the jigsaw puzzle of the patient's self concept. Then we are led to believe that the patient has deliberately substituted a more "ac- ceptable" communicative response for the one which has been followed by punishment. Of course if this is habitually done, with an appropriate cognitive response habitually preceding the communicative response, positive reinforcement of the latter may eventually lead to retroactive reinforcement of the cognitive response so that the patient actually comes to "believe" what he is saying. At this point we may speak of compensa- tory falsification, but we must recognize that the patient no longer "knows" that he is falsifying. When such more pleasant cognitive re- sponses about the self are not only habitual but integrated into signifi- cant cognitive substructures, we may be dealing with delusions of grandeur of a greater or lesser magnitude. We call such cognitive falsifi- cation "compensatory" because the pleasantness of the delusion is as- sumed to be the result of the patient's effort to feel better about himself regarding a characteristic about which he has felt particularly disturbed.

Psychotherapeutic objectives.   What we have said regarding various aspects of the concealment of the self image should be sufficient to estab- lish the point that it is no mean achievement to determine what this image is. Yet this is only a small part of the psychotherapist's task. In this particular aspect of his work he has other significant responsibilities. The first is to form his own objective evaluation of what the patient "is." The second, and by far the more formidable, is to effect the substitution of this more objective appraisal for the patient's more biased appraisal of himself. But even this is not enough to ensure a continuing optimal ad- justment unless the therapist also persuades the patient to regard his own self-appraisal at any given time as postulational and *pro tempore*— always subject to further revision as he develops new standards and accumulates further experience of himself and others.

In case the point is not obvious there are at least three very impor- tant reasons why the psychotherapist works to correct negative biases in the patient's self-evaluation. The first is that the patient defines his goals, objectives, and aspirations with some regard to the probability of his being able to achieve them. But if he underestimates himself in significant respects, then he is inclined to settle for lesser achievements and satisfactions than he could realize. If an ultimate goal of the psychotherapist is to enhance a pleasant balance of experience, he cannot afford this kind of "loss" for his patient.

Secondly, the psychotherapist hopes to relieve his patient of the effort and strain involved in maintaining his persona or rather the various personae "needed" for various relationships. If, as is usually the case, the "real self" is acceptable to others, then the maintenance of the personae represents an unnecessary and unproductive effort. Besides, the fear of "discovery" of the supposedly unacceptable attributes of the self may contribute substantially to emotional stress within the individual. Some persons find themselves literally exhausted by social contacts because of these dual drains on their energy, and most of us pay *some* price for the maintenance of this kind of social deception. Obviously the energy thus expended might be put to more constructive use. Thirdly, the use of the personae is, in a curious way, inevitably self-defeating. What we mean is this: although the personae are created and maintained primarily either to impress others or to gain acceptance, the impression made or the acceptance gained is not for what the person feels is his "real self." How could it be, since he has not (in his opinion) presented his "real self" for evaluation? Thus we encounter the tragedy of the famous actress, more sought after and adored than any other female of her generation, who ended her own life because she felt alone and believed that no one "really" cared about her.

DISTORTIONS IN COGNITIVE RESPONSES TO OTHERS

Evaluating the personae of others.   One of the paradoxes of social and clinical psychology is that the very same patient who knows that he is presenting a carefully selected "self" to others is so universally inclined to accept others at face value, that is, to accept the personae of others as if these personae were the "real" selves. We have speculated on this point and come up with some tentative explanations of this paradox.

One of the more obvious of these explanations is that people are all so consistently defensive in social situations that sheer consistency ultimately lends conviction. If parents continually deny or ignore their own faults and shortcomings, it is difficult for the child to believe in their existence even when the evidence is reasonably clear. "After all," the child must say, "I could be wrong," as, in fact, he is about many things. Besides, as we have pointed out, the child has a vested interest in the omniscience and omnipotence of his parents, since his own security is so much dependent on their infallibility. Since the child is a less experienced (and less knowledgeable) member of his family group and the general community of "others," trust in others and distrust of self is a fairly common result of early life experiences.

Finally we come to a paradox within a paradox. If we consider most persons' self concepts as depreciated relative to objective reality but their personae as being a more favorable representation of themselves, it is conceivable that the personae might be a more accurate representation of themselves than their own self concepts. To put it more simply, Joe X tries to give the impression that he is a pretty nice guy, although secretly he believes that he is pretty much of a stinker. But by objective standards he really is a pretty nice guy, and others react to him as such. In this situation the only person seriously in error is Joe X, who probably believes that the acceptance he gets from others is due entirely to his successful deception of them.

"In-group" versus "out-group."   Regardless of the validity of these particular explanations, we consider it reasonable to assume that most patients are less negatively biased in their evaluation of others than they are in evaluating themselves. Perhaps we should qualify this assumption to limit it to what the social psychologist calls the patient's "in-group" or "in-groups," since we are well aware that members of social "out-groups" (what we might call the "other-others") may be much more *negatively* evaluated than is warranted.

Before moving on to this aspect of the evaluation of others, let us pause to note that the predominantly positive evaluation of in-group others and the acceptance of their personae at or near face value has the unfortunate effect of emphasizing the patient's feelings of inferiority. We are quite convinced that it is characteristic for the patient to compare his depreciated "secret self" with the well-groomed personae of others in his social in-group and to feel all the more inadequate as a consequence. Furthermore, the patient (person) who does this suffers a further penalty in feeling when he concludes that he must be the *only* bad apple in the in-group barrel. One of the truly moving experiences in group therapy is to watch each of the members come to realize: "But we *all* believe we are the only 'bad' one."

The problem of ambivalence.   Now how do we come by this separation of others into "good" and "bad" by groups? Again we would like to offer some speculations on this point.

We begin by noting what we have consistently observed in patients, namely, that they are extremely uncomfortable when forced to face their own emotional ambivalence toward any particular person. In evaluating others they prefer black-and-white, "go" and "no-go" types of characterization, even when such evaluations involve gross distortions or omissions of fairly obvious "facts." We can only suggest that a person's concept of another person represents some kind of integrated cognitive substructure, and it must be uncomfortable to experience the stress of pleasant and unpleasant feelings or both approach and avoidant impulses toward the person represented in this cognitive substructure. This, of course, is not much of an "explanation," but it is the best we can come up with. As indicated earlier in this chapter this "all good–all bad" division is characteristic of most hero-villain representations in popular literature and other entertainment media, so it must correspond with a deep-seated preference on the part of most people.

It becomes important to the psychotherapist because it represents a two-way bias in the patient's cognitive responses to others. Remember our ultimate concern is for the accuracy of the patient's cognitive "map" of reality, since his adjustment is based upon this map. But if the patient insists, as so often he seems to do at a more or less obvious level, upon dividing all people into "good guys" and "bad guys," we cannot be very confident that his adjustment is optimally tuned to objective reality. We suspect, of course, that in this objective reality, could we know it, we would find mostly people with some "good" and some "bad" characteristics, and rarely would we find only "good" or only "bad."

Here we have a good example of cognitive processes being controlled by emotional pressures. The patient prefers to avoid the unpleasant tension created by nearly equivalent impulses to approach and to avoid. Yet mixed feelings and hence mixed impulses of this nature would characterize (we assume) most of his relationships with others if he reacted to them as they "really are." So the patient creates his own cognitive world of black and white, omitting as many of the intermediate "grays" as possible. With his "world" thus arranged, he is able to concentrate more of his efforts on gaining acceptance by the "good guys." At the same time, he has created (in his own mind) an adequate "reason" for his hostility toward the "bad guys" and a justification for both avoidant and attacking responses. His emotional responses are thus simplified and the tension of conflicting impulses reduced. "All" he has sacrificed is a considerable degree of precision in adjustment.

Maintaining this sort of cognitive distortion is, of course, much easier when contact with the "others" being evaluated is not too intimate. Although it is possible to distort perceptual responses to conform with previous "good–bad" evaluations of other persons, there is a certain insistent reality about the sensory aspect of perceptual responses. This tends to throw the person back upon another type of cognitive response, which we usually refer to as "interpretation." Common examples of "interpretation" are: "he acts as if he likes me, but he really doesn't," or "he acts as if he doesn't like me, but he really does." Depending upon their own interpretive bias, all the children in a given family may be convinced that some other child is the "favorite."

Evaluating parents.   A really critical problem faced by each person as he grows up is that of evaluating his parents. Not only are they likely as individuals to have both good and bad traits and characteristics, but they also have mixed feelings, impulses, and responsibilities toward their children. At times they are pleased and at other times displeased by their child's behavior. Sometimes these contrary responses are even elicited by the "same" behavior. A common example would be a parent's being amused by his child's drumming on a tin pan when the parent is feeling well and screaming at the child for the same behavior when he has a headache. Another would be a parent's calling attention to a two-year-old's lisp as being cute and regarding the same lisp as a "speech problem" when the child is seven.

The parent's responsibilities to the child are also divided. To the extent that he satisfies the child's needs, he is a "good guy." But when he functions as a disciplinarian or demander of certain kinds of constructive performance from the child, he is reacted to as a frustrator, and the child's emotional response is one of hostility. But now the child faces a dilemma. If his negative feelings are followed by overt attack upon the parent, he may be punished further for such an attack. Even if he is allowed to "get away with it," the child is then in the anxiety-provoking situation of possibly destroying or at least alienating a person upon whom he depends heavily for the satisfaction of many of his own most basic needs.

Secondary distortions.   We have become convinced that quite regularly this dilemma is handled by a kind of "secondary" cognitive response which might more commonly be called interpretation, imagination, or phantasy—depending upon the degree of "distortion" involved. In conceptualizing these processes, we are assuming that cognitive responses, especially those closely associated with clear-cut sensory or verbal responses, can be united into new combinations or cognitive substructures according to the "desires" (emotional pressures) of the person involved. The problem of ambivalence toward the parents seems to be resolved by splitting the cognitive substructures representing the totality of parental characteristics into two parts for each parent. From this splitting of the cognitive substructure representing the father emerge the images of "The Good Father" and "The Bad Father"; from that representing the totality of the mother's characteristics emerge the images of "The Good Mother" and "The Bad Mother."

Dealing with dichotomized concepts.   A number of consequences seem to follow from this division of the parental images into "all good" and "all bad" aspects. For example, some children seem capable of associating both images with the real parents but alternatively rather than simultaneously. When their father pleases them and meets their needs he is "The Good Father." When he is demanding, punitive, or otherwise frustrating he is seen as "The Bad Father." Other children seem to find this kind of alternation too tension-provoking or otherwise unpleasant and will see the father only in one guise or the other, denying that the other image "fits" or is applicable. Of course such children will probably know "someone," real or imaginary, who "*is*" "The Bad Father" or "The Good Father." For reasons relating to his own security, the child's tendency is to deny that the image of "The Bad Father" ever applies to *his* father.

Sometimes we find a reversal of this situation, particularly in adolescence. As the individual becomes more sure of himself and better able to meet his own needs, he may (sometimes suddenly) reverse an earlier stand and then see one or the other or both parents as only "bad." We conclude that this has happened when we see an adolescent (as we do often enough) who seems unable or unwilling to manifest any acceptance of what the parents are or "stand for." The parents are treated as "out-groupers," "the enemy," "our opponents." Whatever they represent, this type of adolescent refuses to identify with them or with himself. It is even possible that the basic "in-group" and "out-group" distinctions that a person makes are at least partially defined by a projection of the images of "The Good Parent" and "The Bad Parent."

We have observed another significant manifestation of this dichotomized projection in childhood. This is the tendency for children to manifest quite different personalities, emotions, and behavior in different settings. Common parlance recognizes the existence of "street angels, home devils," that is, children who are models of deportment away from home and holy terrors at home. We also observe the opposite quite frequently, for example, children who are easily accepted at home but seem to go on a rampage in the school environment. Our hypothesis on this matter is that when there are appreciable differences between the demands made in one situation and another, those who are more demanding are likely to inherit the cloak of "The Bad Parents" while the less demanding come to represent "The Good Parents." If school is more demanding than home, then the people at school are "the bad guys," "the enemy," and the child's feelings, and behavior can readily be "understood" and predicted by assuming this formulation.

Culturally maintained dichotomies.   The nonmaterial aspects of culture from folklore to religion are rife with examples of the "good parent–bad parent" dichotomization. In general, there is the hero–villain distinction already referred to. Specifically, we have folkheroes representing various attributes of "The Good Father," depending upon the particular demands of the environment. Daniel Boone, Kit Carson, Jim Bowie, and others of similar ilk represent "The Good Father" on the frontier, as Paul Bunyan represents the same symbol for lumbermen and Joe Magarac for steelworkers. The Catholic religion provides a patron saint for various occupations and even for specific localities, such as cities. Santa CLAUS, in various guises, has proved a very durable "Good Father" image as the indulgent granter of wishes. On the negative, or "Bad Father," side we find an assortment of ogres, trolls, warlocks, monsters, malevolent giants, leprechauns, and werewolves. In these examples we note how often "The Bad Father" is distorted in size, being either larger or smaller than normal. We believe that most adults fail to realize how overpowering adult size and sound are to the small child. Yet we have good reason to believe, on the basis of clinical experience, that very sensitive children may be seriously intimidated by large and/or loud parents to the point of being unable to identify with them or to conceive of themselves as ever being able to be like their parents.

Of course the classical distinction between "Good Father" and "Bad Father" is found in almost all religions and reduces itself to "the forces of Good" *versus* "the forces of Evil." The protoparental qualities of the devil are indicated by the various cults of devil-worship in many lands and in various epochs. Freud has pointed out that the image of God among the Hebrew people varied at different times, and he correlates these various "faces of God" with the general prosperity and well-being of the tribes at various times. And as a final bridge between parent and religion we find various kinds of ancestor worship. It seems usually to be the case among our patients who are no longer following the Catholic religion that resentment toward the real father is rather intense and open. In a remarkably high percentage of such cases the patient has been "deserted" in childhood by the real father, either by death or divorce. The patient seems then to have retaliated by turning *his* back on "God, the Father."

The situation is, of course, analogous in folklore, mythology, and religion with respect to the mother image. In folklore the dichotomization is embodied in the images of "good fairies," "the fairy godmother," on the one side as contrasted with "the wicked stepmother and witches," on the other side. In Greek and Roman mythology a full complement of female deities accompanied their masculine counterparts. In religion the situation is not so uniform, since many major religions tend to ignore the female as a "good person." Robert Graves has suggested that masculine gods predominate in cultures where the male is dominant because of his essential role as warrior, hunter, and herdsman. According to his theory, feminine deities predominate or have high status in societies where agriculture is the most important source of food, and women are predominantly associated with agriculture either in the role of cultivators of the crops or for their magical value as symbols of fertility. He also suggests that the determination of patriarchal or matriarchal forms of family authority and government is based on similar considerations.

Personal mythology.   Returning our attention to the impact of parental "images" upon the individual in his daily and personal living, we have found it convenient to create our own kind of "mythology." Specifically, we have postulated a "quest for the Good Father" as a hypothetical dynamic that helps to bring order into otherwise miscellaneous aspects of human behavior and adjustment. We are assuming now that initially the real father (if there is one) and "The Good Father" are synonymous, that is, the real father is seen by the young child as omniscient, omnipotent, and all-giving: a combination of God and Santa Claus. However, as the father comes to function more as a disciplinarian and trainer (which he has traditionally done more for his sons than for his daughters) and as the child's experience and competence increase, the father's role as the mythical "Good Father" is increasingly jeopardized. When and if the real father is rejected as being "The Good Father" (and we believe this is more likely to happen among sons than among daughters), he may then be endowed with the mantle of "The Bad Father," and treated as an out-grouper, "the enemy." This, as we have already suggested, is most likely to happen in adolescence. Regardless of when this happens, if it happens, then many other adult authority figures (teachers, policemen, doctors) may simultaneously be cloaked with the same mantle. This we regard as characteristic of the "acting out" adolescent in general and the juvenile delinquent in particular.

This "revolution," so far as the father image is concerned, does not always or inevitably occur. However, even when there is no obvious revolution of this kind, it is quite possible for the real father to "shrink" from the dimensions required of the mythical "Good Father." Strangely enough, in either case, patients act as if they continued to "hold on" to the image of "The Good Father," and they also act as if they were looking for someone to fill the dimensions of this hypothetical role. For example, it seems as if females retain their image of "The Good Father" and typically seek to satisfy their need for such a person in the selection of a husband. They would like the husband to have all the specific attributes of "The Good Father," as each female specifically defines this image. In addition to these specific requirements the husband is also supposed generally to meet all their needs and, by so doing, "give" them happiness. The situation of the male in seeking a wife seems to be so closely analogous to this description that we shall not repeat it separately. The male does not really "want a girl just like the girl who married dear old Dad." What he would like to have is a girl with all of his mother's virtues and some additional desirable attributes to take the place of those he really did not care very much for in his mother.

Personal mythology and adjustment.   Needless to say, this quest for the perfect parent in the marriage partner represents a considerable handicap for those upon whom this expectation is projected. When this spouse fails to provide for specific needs or fails in general to make the person to whom he is married "happy," then he (or she) is in danger of also inheriting the mantle of "The Bad Father" (or "The Bad Mother"). So often marital tensions seem to be founded on this type of "failure to provide." Yet, by our formulation, much of the resentment, hostility, and downright enmity between marital partners can be attributed to a phantasy cognitive substructure—the concept or image of "The Good Parent."

We believe that this phantasy or "made-up" cognitive substructure has another type of influence on adjustment. We shall discuss it from the point of view of the male, where it is more significant, although a corre-late problem often exists to a lesser degree for the female. We are referring now to the image of "The Good Father," both as being a model for the male in his development toward adult status and as a person upon whom the male can depend for help in this development. The transition from a totally passive-dependent status in infancy to predominantly active-independent functioning in adulthood poses many challenges to and evokes many anxieties in the male. He "needs" a good model, and he "needs" various other kinds of help to make this transition. When the boy is young, the father can usually do everything the boy is learning to do and usually knows most everything his son is interested in knowing. The only real problem at this time is that the father should not appear so strong, capable, and invulnerable that the son despairs of ever being able to emulate him. However this situation may change, either because the son starts "catching up with" the father in various respects or because an antagonism toward the father develops. Again we note that even if this happens, the patient seems to "hang on" to his hypothetical image of "The Good Father," and to act as if he must really exist somewhere if only he could find him. How disturbing this illusion is to the adjust-ment of the person depends upon what proportion of his time and energy he devotes to "the quest for the Good Father" rather than to the development of and reliance upon his own capabilities.

Personal mythology and psychotherapy.   We believe that this formulation has particular significance for the psychotherapeutic relationship per se. For example, if the psychotherapist falls into the guise of "The Bad Parent," then he is forced to cope with the many negative feelings that this image evokes from the patient. Although such a projection may occur at any age, we have found it particularly likely to occur in patients between thirteen and seventeen years of age who are hostile, negative, and rejecting to various forms of adult authority. As indicated elsewhere, the psychotherapist has his work cut out for him in this type of situation. If he is to "succeed" at all in working with this kind of patient, a basic strategy must be to change his classification in the patient's eyes from the category of "Bad Parent" to "Good Parent."

But there is also a problem if the psychotherapist is classified by the patient as "The Good Parent." For one thing, the classification is not "realistic," since the psychotherapist is no more "all good" than is anyone else. Functionally, however, the significance of this mistaken identification is that it tends to perpetuate the patient's dependence upon a mythical being rather than upon himself. This problem must be very carefully understood if it is to be handled properly. For example, it is relatively useless for the psychotherapist to deny or even to attempt to disprove that he possesses all the attributes of "The Good Father." We also doubt whether it is possible to evade this attribution, regardless of the "technique" employed by the psychotherapist in relating to his patient. The patient will persist in believing in these attributes anyway, so long as he "needs" to believe in them to allay his own anxieties and feelings of inadequacy. Our usual way of handling this situation is by accepting the patient's "transference" initially and "using" it to help the patient in developing his own competence and confidence. If we are successful in this endeavor, then we find the patient more or less spontaneously relinquishing his illusions about the psychotherapist and accepting him rather comfortably as "just another human being," although often with a feeling of gratitude for valuable services performed.

OTHER ASPECTS OF COGNITIVE DISTORTION

Standards and evaluation.   There are several other aspects of cognitive structure and cognitive functioning that we believe the psychotherapist must evaluate adequately and thoroughly if he is to properly understand and help his patients. For example, we are always curious about the standards by which the patient judges both himself and others. We believe that the standards for self and for others are not necessarily the same. Some patients seem to judge others more harshly then they do themselves, in the sense that they "make allowances" or find excuses for their own "misbehavior" which they do not extend to their judgment of others. This is particularly true of what are usually called "acting out" patients, although we prefer the term "undercontrolled." However, we usually find what would generally be called the "typical neurotic" patient doing the reverse, that is, apparently judging himself by a more rigid standard than he applies to others. Moreover, we usually find that these standards are of an "absolute," rather than a "relative," nature. The standards of this type of patient are very obviously closely related to ideals and to supposedly ideal conduct for human beings with little regard for the actual achievement potential of human beings in general or of the patient in particular. Furthermore, this type of patient is unlikely to be a person who ever questions or seriously thinks about the origin of personal standards. Rather, he regards them as categorical imperatives, believed in by all "right-thinking" persons and beyond the realm of questioning or revision.

Standards and control. We can only conclude from our experience plus the relevant research in this field that the inculcating of standards is a relatively simple process which can be accomplished at quite an early age. However, we find ourselves in violent disagreement with the lay public (including our courts of law) in their apparent confidence that "knowing" right from wrong is critical in determining either the patient's behavior or his degree of "responsibility" for his own actions. In this latter respect we believe that the critical consideration is the adequacy of "control training" which, although it is obviously related to belief in certain standards of behavior, is actually quite a different matter from simply believing or "knowing" that certain acts are considered "right" or "wrong."

To put the matter simply, it serves little purpose to teach a child that "lying is wrong" if we fail to detect when he is lying and/or fail to punish him for lying. We may, if we wish (and most people apparently do), decide that at some arbitrary age the person automatically becomes "responsible" for his own behavior and should thereafter act in accordance with what he knows to be "right" regardless of the adequacy of his control training up to that point. This is a point of view that makes no sense at all to us, nor can we see how anyone conversant with even the rudiments of learning theory could possibly adhere to it.

On the other hand, we do believe in the possibility of creating adequate control habits regardless of the age of the person concerned, provided the person in charge of the "training" is allowed adequate leeway and control over the training conditions. We also believe that such training may take quite a different form with the adolescent or adult than it does with the child, but we suspect that some punitive consequence for misbehavior (perhaps self-inflicted) remains a *sine qua non* of success in these endeavors.

Standards and psychotherapy.   In any event, we regard a knowledge of the patient's standards, plus how he got them and how he regards them, as vital information for the psychotherapist. Is it necessary to add that we regard reasonable standards which the patient has some chance of "living up to" as probably better for the patient (and, in the long run, for society) than "ideal" standards which leave him feeling inadequate, hopeless, and thoroughly "bad"? In any event, if we really want to "improve" the patient's behavior, we had best expend the bulk of our time and effort on effective control training for the undercontrolled, regardless of what standards the patient ultimately "believes in." As for the "overcontrolled" patient, the same logic applies with respect to the modification of control habits, although in this situation we must consider more seriously the functional impact and significance of the standards that supposedly guide and certainly serve to rationalize his overcontrolled behavior.

Cognitive differentiation.   Another aspect of the patient's cognitive structure that the psychotherapist must evaluate in various significant substructures or cognitive "areas" is the degree of differentiation or lack thereof. Briefly, the psychotherapist should attempt to determine whether and in what way the patient is "transferring" or generalizing both cognitive and emotional responses from one relationship to another. He will, of course, concentrate his attention on relationships of major importance in meeting the needs, emotional and otherwise, of the patient. We have already devoted some time and attention to the parents and parental images as cognitive structures that are likely to remain rather fixed once they have been established, with certain new people in the patient's life then being perceived in the dimensions and characteristics of these preexisting cognitive structures. But elsewhere we have noted that lack of cognitive discrimination (or differentiation) is a much more general problem which is closely related to the development of social stereotypes and prejudices, that is, learned predispositions to feel positively or negatively about others.

Our only modifications would be to emphasize that stereotypes may be unwarrantedly favorable, as well as unfavorable, and that our concern is not only with the "prejudgment" aspect of prejudice but also (and perhaps more so) with the emotional and behavioral responses associated with the stereotype and the "prejudging." We have noted that communication and the development of cognitive structure is potentially useful in helping the person to adjust to "new" persons and situations. We have also noted, however, that when this preparation results in the person's ignoring distinctions between individuals or situations which are critical to his appropriate response to them, then the person is, to some extent, "in trouble." Therefore, in detecting such nonadjustive generalizations, the psychotherapist becomes able to perform a service for the patient in terms of being able to help him form necessary discriminations between person A and person B and between situation I and situation II.

Time indexing.   Finally, we refer again to the matter of "time indexing," also previously mentioned. We continue to be impressed (although we are no longer amazed) by the tangled "time line" of the usual patient's life. If we listen carefully, it is not difficult to detect that what happened fifteen years ago or what will happen next month often constitutes the "reality" to which the patient is responding today. Perhaps Freud was referring to somewhat the same phenomenon when he spoke of "the unconscious" as having "no time dimension." At any rate, we sometimes have the impression that certain types of patients, with their cognitive responses undifferentiated as to time referents or personal indices and with their behavior dictated by categorical imperatives, are virtually unaware of "present reality"—or at least act as if they were. For such patients we have coined a special monogram, "L.P.R.," which stands for the injunction "Live Present Reality." This would be psychotherapy enough for many patients, if they were able to follow this injunction without further assistance. Determining where such assistance is required is the essence of diagnosis, and providing the proper assistance is the essence of psychotherapy.

SUMMARY

In this chapter we discuss the types of cognitive distortion that we consider most important in determining the person's adjustment. We also indicate the *kinds* of distortion that are most often encountered in the evaluation of patients.

Foremost among such distortions are those that relate to self-knowledge and self-evaluation. These are of particular significance, since a person's objectives in adjusting are usually closely related to how competent and valuable he considers himself to be.

Quite commonly among patients we encounter self-evaluations that are quite conservative or even debased relative to the psychotherapist's evaluation of the patient. Such debasement may sometimes be covered up by compensatory assertions of worth or value.

Determining the patient's self-evaluation is usually complicated by the patient's habitual tendency to present a specific social self, or persona, in all social contacts, including his communication with the psychotherapist.

Unfavorable self-evaluation may have many sources. One such source is the setting of unrealistically high standards by the parents when the person is too young to have independent standards. The child naturally tends to compare himself with others without making allowances for age, experience, training, and so forth. The child may fail to note or to appreciate adequately the development of his own competence as he grows. He may further increase his feelings of inadequacy by unduly exaggerating the competence of others, especially of those, such as the parents, upon whom his own welfare depends.

Other invalid comparisons may be of the self with certain cultural ideals, especially as embodied in the form of "heroes." Such heroes are typically represented in a completely one-sided (that is, "good") manner.

Corrective evaluations, which might emanate from others, are often withheld as a matter of communicative taboo (see Chapter 6).

The person himself does not usually regard his self-evaluation as hypothetical or as subject to error. Rather it is treated as axiomatic in determining other adjustments. One such "adjustment" involves concealment of what is believed to be the "real self" and the substitution of more attractive social selves, personae, for purposes of social interaction.

The substitution of a more accurate conception of the self as a part of the psychotherapeutic process stands to benefit the patient in several significant ways. Primarily, he is relieved of the burden of chronic concealment of the supposed "real self" and has an opportunity to gain acceptance for the new (and improved) "real self." Also, he may be able to establish more realistic and valuable objectives for his own adjustive efforts.

People are prone to two types of distortion in their evaluation of others. "In-group" or accepted "others" tend to be seen as more valuable and fault free than they are. "Out-group" or rejected "others" are usually perceived or interpreted as being worse than they are. This division of others into distinct groups of "good" and "bad" probably stems from an attempt to avoid the unpleasant tensions associated with conflicting emotions.

This process of dichotomizing others usually has its origin in relations with parents, who "must" (for purposes of emotional security) be perceived as benevolent, omniscient, and omnipotent as long as the child is dependent upon them. From this early period of development each person retains unambivalent conceptions of "The Good Father" and "The Good Mother," as well as complementary conceptions of "The Bad Parents."

Such conceptions have become formalized in every aspect of culture from folklore to religion. Personal myths of the good and bad parents also help to explain some of the changing aspects of parent–child relationships as the child develops. We believe that such personal myths may also be highly significant in the processes of marital selection and adjustment.

Obviously the nature of the psychotherapeutic relationship will be affected by the existence of such personal myths and by how the psychotherapist is classified in terms of them.

It is always important, although sometimes difficult, to ascertain the patient's *standards* for evaluating himself and others. Patients are capable of espousing quite unreasonable standards and also of judging themselves by one set of standards and others by another. The acceptance of adequate or even idealistic standards, however, is by no means synonymous with adequate or ideal behavior. The matter of behavior is more complicated and belongs legitimately to the topic of *control training*, for which standards are a necessary but not sufficient condition.

Two topics of considerable importance are dealt with only briefly in this chapter. One is the problem of inadequate differentiation (overgeneralization) at a cognitive level relative to the specificity of adjustment required at the behavioral level of response. The other is the patient's tendency to premise today's behavior on the cognitive "reality" of yesterday or tomorrow.

SUGGESTIONS FOR FURTHER READING

Sidney Jourard (1) has devoted an interesting book to the problem of self-concealment and its implications for emotional well-being.

Most readers will find it highly instructive to compare the present chapter with Chapter 3 in Ellis (2), since these two chapters represent different ways of handling the problem of cognitive distortion. Still another way of dealing with the same general subject is presented by Wendell Johnson (3), particularly in Chapters XI and XII, but also in Chapters XIII, XIV, and XV.

Those who have not done considerable reading in personality theory should supplement their background at this point by reading Part IV of Gardner Murphy's book on personality (4). We recommend Sherif (5), Part Two, both for its presentation of "ego" theory and for its dealing with the person's reactions to "others."

REFERENCES

*1. Jourard, S. M. *The transparent self*. Princeton, N.J.: Van Nostrand, 1964.

2. Ellis, A. *Reason and emotion in psychotherapy*. New York: Lyle Stuart, 1962.

3. Johnson, W. *People in quandaries*. New York: Harper & Row, 1946.

4. Murphy, G. *Personality*. New York: Harper & Row, 1947.

5. Sherif, M. *An outline of social psychology*. New York: Harper & Row, 1948.

* Paperback edition.

Chapter 8 | Emotion: Evaluation of Problems

INTRODUCTION

Feelings and emotions.   As an introduction to the subject of evaluating emotional problems, we shall review briefly the basic definitions and assumptions about feeling and emotion that were presented in Chapter 2. As far as feelings are matters of concern to the psychotherapist, he can proceed on the basis of a simple distinction between pleasant and unpleasant feelings. Feelings are thought of here as qualitative aspects of cognitive responses in general and of perceptual responses in particular.

Psychologists generally assume that pleasant feelings are innately associated with adient behavioral impulses. Stated in somewhat different terms, perceptual responses that have a pleasant feeling quality innately evoke "approach" behavioral responses directed toward the object (person, situation) perceived. The emotion of "love" can be conceptualized as the pleasant feeling quality of a given perception *plus* the impulse to approach the object perceived.

Unpleasant feeling qualities are innately associated with abient behavioral impulses or the impulse to avoid the object perceived. "Fear" consists of an unpleasant feeling quality plus the impulse to avoid the perceived object. When the unpleasant feeling and the impulse to avoid are aspects of or are associated with nonperceptual cognitive responses (such as memories or images), the term "anxiety" is used rather than "fear." We regard fear and love as the basic emotions.

However, psychologists also note in the newborn human and in subhuman species another response that is evoked by restraint or frustration of behavior. This is the tendency to struggle vigorously. Restraint or frustration produces perceptual responses that have an unpleasant feeling quality and the "struggling" behavior is innately associated with this kind of frustration and the unpleasant feeling quality it produces. "Hostility" is defined as this feeling and this behavioral impulse.

We consider all further elaborations, refinements, and distinctions in emotional behavior to be derived from these three reference emotions as a joint function of maturation and experience (learning). We therefore limit our evaluation of emotion to these three, at least as basic points of reference.

Motivation for psychotherapy. The patient who consults the psychotherapist on his own initiative is presumably motivated by an excess of unpleasant feeling experiences and/or a deficiency of pleasant feeling experiences. However, this is *not* necessarily or, in fact, usually, the reason that he will give. Children and adolescents, on the other hand, are usually brought for failure to perform or failure to conform. It then becomes the responsibility of the psychotherapist to determine the reason for the failure.

Awareness of feeling and emotion. Up to this point our conceptualizations regarding the emotional aspects of the patient are simple. Beyond this point they become diverse, interrelated, and complex. The practical task of assessing the emotional condition of the patient is complicated by his unwillingness and (even more important) his literal inability to give a reasonably coherent and accurate account of his own emotions. This we may attribute in a large measure, we believe, to a cultural bias that strongly influences middle-class parents and teachers and, to a lesser degree, both upper and lower classes in their training of the child. This bias is that emotions are symptoms of immaturity and that lack of emotional control is detrimental to purposive effort, which is (or leads to) the ultimate value, namely, "success." In other words, emotions such as fear and hostility are considered "bad," and the child (especially male children) is discouraged from displaying or talking about such emotions. On the other hand, the manifestation of "love" in various forms is also considered unmasculine in boys and is reacted to somewhat uncomfortably when too apparent or too enthusiastic in the behavior of girls. Those who wish to speculate on the reasons for such adult attitudes and values might consider such contributing factors as the Puritan tradition, the demands of colonial and frontier societies, and the predominance of materialistic values.

Problems of communication and evaluation. At any rate, we can anticipate that most patients will be relatively inadequate and inaccurate communicators about their own feelings and emotions. We can also anticipate considerable distortion and many blank spots in their own cognitive awareness of feelings and emotion. A considerable part of the psychotherapeutic task is to infer as accurately as possible what the "real" nature of the patient's responses is, and then to communicate (often against the patient's "resistance") as much of this information back to him as he needs in order to more accurately adjust his behavior to his needs. In this instance the "resistance" referred to is the result of the training that has led to the repression or distortion of awareness of feeling in the first place.

Because of the complexity of the subject matter and the relatively "hidden" nature of the information that the psychotherapist is looking for in evaluating the emotional status of the patient, we shall attempt to be both comprehensive and specific in our consideration of this matter. This will necessarily limit the amount of time that we can devote to each topic. It may also convey an impression of certainty and dogmatism that we are a long way from feeling. Let the reader be warned on the matter of such impressions and reminded that what we shall have to say is intended primarily to encourage his own thinking along similar lines.

ANXIETY

The problem of anxiety.   For the general student of psychology there is no need here for further proof or documentation concerning the prevalence of anxiety in the patient population. Its presence has not only been noticed but even focused upon by all those who have written about psychopathology, however much they might disagree with each other as to "*the basic*" situation giving rise to anxiety. We are unable to understand this apparent need of some theorists to be able to explain all anxiety in terms of one, two, or three fundamental impulses, needs, or situations. Rather we find many reasons for anxiety and find it difficult to sort them according to their relative importance or "basic" nature.

Fear of rejection.   If, however, we were asked to choose that anxiety which seemed most universal among our patients and also most disturbing to their adjustment (in terms of their ability to achieve satisfaction of their needs), we would choose "fear of rejection" to meet these particular specifications.

As to the universality of this fear or anxiety, we might speculate that this could be attributed to the dependency of the human young upon others to meet their basic survival needs. This period of dependency extends, for all practical purposes, well into the teen years in a society with as complex a material and nonmaterial culture as our own. During this long period of necessary or seminecessary dependency, the presence of others is consistently associated with the gratification of all the more basic biological needs and with the pleasant feelings that accompany such gratification. This association creates a positive "value" for being with others, so that the presence of others becomes desirable, comfortable, reassuring or rewarding in its own right regardless of whether or not more basic (biological) needs are being satisfied. In this way, acceptance by others "stands for" (or represents symbolically) potential gratification of all survival needs. Or in a situation such as our own at present, when relatively few are seriously in want of the basic means of survival, the "need" for others may assume an importance from which it would be displaced were survival needs more difficult to satisfy. At least so we would speculate.

We see the negative side of the need for others—the fear of rejection—as disturbing to the patient's adjustment in various ways. For example, it adds immeasurably to the emotional consequences of self-evaluations of inadequacy or inferiority, since such self-evaluations are seen as incongruent with acceptance by others. The fear of rejection provides a strong motivation toward conformity and acceptance of the standards of others regardless of their reasonableness or logicality, especially when the person is young and lacks independent standards for evaluation. At the very same time the fear of rejection is divisive in human relationships. Often patients will isolate themselves from others or avoid attempts to initiate relationships because they regard such passive isolation as preferable to (less anxiety-provoking than) the explicit and unequivocal rejection they are afraid they will receive if they are more active in approaching others. Thus we encounter the tragedy of a society of lonely people, each able to see the others to whom he would *like* to relate but isolated by the glass shell of his own fears of rejection, and pathetically waiting for the others to make the first move through their common barriers.

Fear of failure.   We can even relate two other forms of anxiety that we also encounter very frequently to this fear of rejection. The fear of failure is disturbing enough in its own right, even when the evaluation of others is not involved. We suspect, however, that fear of failure arises initially through fear of being rejected because one has failed to meet the expectations or satisfy the demands of others. We note that fear of failure is similar to fear of rejection in that it also is enhanced in intensity by self-evaluations of inferiority and inadequacy. Finally, we note another similarity in that fear of failure is inhibitive, that is, it tends to stop the person from doing things he might be able to do and would gain satisfaction from doing.

Anxiety about hostile impulses.   A very common anxiety, yet one which often must be probed for, is the patient's fear of his own hostile emotions. We know, on the one hand, that much of the social training of the child is frustrating in either forbidding him to do what he wants to do or requiring him to do something for which he lacks intrinsic motivation. We expect such frustration to give rise to hostile feelings and impulses and note the frequency of overt displays of such impulses in the infant and young child. But we also observe such behavior leading to reprimand and other forms of "punishment" (including rejection) as the child grows older. Such negative reinforcement for hostile behavior creates an emotion of anxiety that tends to follow closely upon cognitive responses closely associated with hostile impulses. The anxiety serves to inhibit the hostile response and quite frequently the cognitive response preceding it as well. In the latter instance, the person is left with a cognitive awareness of anxiety but does not "know" what has provoked it.

"Free-floating" anxiety.   This leads us naturally to the topic of "free-floating anxiety," which is so often referred to in the literature on psychotherapy. We assume that anxiety, like the punishment from which it is ultimately derived, is primarily inhibitive in its effect upon responses of all kinds. Either through deliberate intent or through simple inadvertence, the creation of anxiety through negative reinforcement often inhibits the cognitive responses preceding behavioral responses as well as inhibiting the behavioral responses themselves. Quite frequently those who train others *want* to eliminate the cognitive as well as the behavioral response. This orientation is based on the assumption that if the person being trained does not even "know" what he wants to do, this provides an additional safeguard against his doing it. From the point of view of the psychotherapist, however, the end result is a blank space in the trainee's "cognitive map." Not only is the psychotherapist opposed to such blind spots in the person's cognitive map on the general principle that ignorance seldom leads to a better adjustment than knowledge; he is also more aware than the "trainer" that the impulse which is denied expression through a "deliberately selected" behavioral response may nevertheless be "acted out" through behavior that is habitually associated directly with perceptual responses without any intermediate cognitive links. In other words, the person may "unconsciously" do what he wanted to do anyway, even though punishment and/or anxiety has caused him to "repress" awareness of the impulse. Or to put the matter still more simply, the subject of punitive training may lose his capacity to control behavior that otherwise he might have been able to direct.

We suspect that sometimes the "free-floating anxiety" may be related to a threat so cosmic yet so fundamental that the patient is unable to formulate a "reason" for his anxiety. We would regard a persistent predominance of unpleasant over pleasant feeling as such a basic kind of threat, in fact *the* basic threat to the survival of the individual as a "normally" functioning "system."

A note of caution.   We would like to add a note of caution to the novice evaluator before concluding our emendations to the theory of anxiety as related to psychopathology. This is an area of evaluation (or "diagnosis") where "things are seldom what they seem." We have just given a theoretical explanation of how the "reason" for an anxiety might become "repressed." However, anxiety which is completely "unattached" from any reason the patient can give for it is not all that commonly encountered. Usually the patient has "a reason" for feeling anxious; the crucial question is whether it is "the right reason." Hypochondriasis is an excellent example to illustrate our meaning. All too often the hypochondriac is treated unsympathetically by physicians, because the physician "knows" that the patient's anxieties about his health are unfounded. What should be given equal consideration by both the physician and the psychotherapist is that the *anxiety* is "real." Only the "cause" has been changed to protect the patient from still further anxiety.

HOSTILITY

The problem of hostility.   The general student of psychology who goes on to specialize in the evaluation and treatment of emotional problems should be prepared for frequent encounters with the problem of hostility. If he is not already familiar with these books, a perusal of *Frustration and Aggression* (1) and *The Neurotic Personality of Our Time* (2) should be instructive. As we have already suggested, the process of socialization provides recurrent and frequent provocations to hostility. Yet the most characteristic response of parents to the aggressive behavior of their children is to be punitive, thus further complicating the problem of hostile emotions by discouraging any overt response. Also, as we have indicated in Chapter 7, the person who feels hostile toward another person whom he also likes, has his own problems in deciding what to do with or about his hostile impulses. As a child, adolescent, or even adult he may be reluctant to attack and thus either "destroy" or alienate a person upon whom he may want to depend at another time. Yet the "task" of perpetual suppression of hostile behavior can apparently also become prodigious; at least we have seen patients whose chronic "fatigue" would seem traceable to such a situation.

It is true that most societies make some provision for the expression of hostility. The "in-group, out-group" distinctions mentioned in Chapter 7 serve the purpose (among others) of defining those (the "out-group") toward whom the expression of hostility is more acceptable or more likely to be accepted. However, with the growing recognition that many hostile phenomena, from neighborhood discrimination and riots to world wars, are traceable to such direction of hostility "outward," even aggression against an "out-group" is becoming increasingly less "fashionable." In a revision of the maxim that marriage is recommended because it combines a maximum of temptation with a maximum of opportunity, we must face the dilemma of social living, which offers a maximum of provocation with a minimum of opportunity—for the expression of aggression.

Diversions of hostility.   In *Frustration and Aggression* Dollard and his co-authors point out that aggression may be overt or covert, immediate or delayed, and directed against the frustrating agent, an "innocent bystander," or the self. Obviously these devious and manifold manifestations are motivated by the need to avoid punishment for direct, overt, and immediate expression. Obviously, also, they suggest the tangled trail the psychotherapist must pursue in running down his patient's major hostilities.

A common and deceptive problem arises when the patient, for lack of a "safer" object, turns his hostile impulses inward upon himself. The resulting self-criticism, excessive feelings of self-blame or guilt, and/or depression are difficult to trace to their source in hostility towards others. These reactions are also difficult to separate from other similar reactions that may have quite a different sort of origin. For example, this type of self-criticism is often not clearly distinguishable from self-evaluations of inadequacy or inferiority. Excessive self-blame or guilt may be traceable to excessively high standards of behavior as well as to inwardly directed hostility. Depression likewise may have other sources than hostility toward the self. The beginning of wisdom, when responses of any of these three kinds are encountered, is to consider the possibility that redirected hostility is involved. Differentiation may depend upon certain observations or inferences. For example, the less obviously hostile the patient is in his reaction to others, the greater the probability that hostile reactions are being diverted toward the self. The person who is already socially isolated but wants to be accepted is usually strongly motivated to suppress all outward manifestations of hostility. We suspect a hostile motivation for such self-destructive tendencies when we note that there may be a "secondary gain" of punishing others via one's disabilities. We consider the possibility of hostile motivation when the patient tends to change from one to another of these patterns of reaction at various times or under different circumstances.

The evaluation of hostility.   Often the matter of "where the hostility went" cannot be settled by any of these evaluative means. It is then that we are forced to rely upon the broadest possible evaluation of the patient, including not only the total configuration of his communicative behavior and the cognitive structure which we can infer from this, but also the major aspects of his developmental history. To illustrate what we mean here, we would consider any of the following kinds of communicative behavior as indicating a possibility that hostile impulses are being inhibited or redirected. (a) We note in our relationship with the patient that he avoids expressing irritation or disagreement with us under any circumstance. (b) The patient denies feelings of frustration or hostility in situations in which his own desires have obviously been thwarted. (c) The patient expresses concern or guilt over his own hostile behavior that seems out of proportion to the "offense." (d) The patient manifests "disguised" forms of hostility in ways he does not define as being hostile. In the patient's relationship with the therapist this can take the form of canceling appointments, being late for appointments, and not paying his fees. In communicating, the patient can manifest hostility in the form of humor, satire, irony, and so on. The patient may indicate hostile impulses in dream content or in accidental happenings where he does not consider himself "responsible."

There are, of course, still other kinds of clues to the distortion of hostile impulses in the patient's behavior. These are simply some of the more common and obvious things to look for. We hope it is apparent that in making many of these evaluations, the psychotherapist is using his own reactions as a standard in evaluating distortion in the behavior or communications of the patient. We shall take this opportunity to emphasize once more how crucial is the objectivity and freedom from bias of the psychotherapist if he is to make such evaluations with reasonable accuracy.

CONTROL

"Over-control" and "under-control."   We would like to introduce the subject of evaluating emotional control at this point. Traditionally, the psychotherapist has dealt so predominantly with "overcontrolled" individuals as patients that "psychotherapy" is regarded by some as practically synonymous with "disinhibition." However, the psychotherapist who works with children and adolescents soon becomes aware that the "problems" of many of his younger patients are essentially problems of "undercontrol," so far as emotion and behavior are concerned. This impression is confirmed by experience with that group of adult patients whose "problems" are those of repeated violations of legal, moral, or social regulation. Granted that we do not see so many of this latter group because they are not always "disturbed" by their own lack of conformity, we still consider it a serious distortion of the psychotherapist's role to see him as only concerned with and potentially helpful to the "overcontrolled" person.

Let us stop for a moment to attempt some definition of terminology. When we speak of the "overcontrolled" patient, we do not intend to imply that any degree of self-control over emotional behavior is undesirable or harmful. Obviously other human beings would not tolerate for long any person who consistently "acted out" all his impulses, emotional or otherwise. Freud also suggested in *Civilization and Its Discontents* and elsewhere that if man were free to act out all his impulses, he would be unlikely to indulge in any behavior having social value. When we speak of "overcontrol," then, we are referring to a situation in which the inhibitory training of the individual along with the standards and values with which he is indoctrinated so restrict his behavior that it is very difficult or impossible for him to obtain sufficient satisfactions from his behavior to counterbalance negative or unpleasant feelings. We note by way of amendment that it is quite possible for a person to derive satisfaction from activities which are socially valued, so that "pleasant" and "impulse oriented" are not necessarily one and the same thing. At the other extreme we would define as "undercontrolled" the person whose impulse-oriented behavior evokes punitive responses from others to an extent that offsets the pleasure gained from impulse gratification. These are not rigorous definitions and the logically minded will be able to detect some rather obvious flaws, but they will serve well enough to convey our meaning.

Definition of control.   Let us also specify what we mean by emotional or behavioral "control." We consider a behavioral response "controlled" when a behavioral response that has previously followed upon a perceptual response and/or cognitive response is inhibited. We speak of "voluntary control" when cognitive responses precede the inhibition of the behavioral response. We speak of "involuntary control" when the inhibition of further (cognitive) responses, as well as inhibition of the behavioral response itself, follows immediately upon a given perceptual response.

Control: persons or behavior?   Although it is convenient for certain purposes to differentiate between undercontrolled and overcontrolled patients, the distinction begins to break down in practice. What we note instead is undercontrolled and overcontrolled *behavior* in any given person. To illustrate, our first example would be the adolescent who is under heavy and persistent pressure to conform and to achieve according to very high standards that his parents have established for him. The adolescent actually conforms and achieves in many areas and in a way that implies very good self-discipline at most times and in most respects. However, he is given to outbursts of temper that get him into fights at school. He also impulsively destroys some of his own possessions. Finally, he cannot deal with his feelings in a way which enables him to achieve the grades in school which his aptitudes would indicate he might be able to earn. Our evaluation might be that here we have a problem centering around overcontrol and conclude that if we could mitigate the frustrations imposed by excessive demands and restrictions, our patient might then be better able to control the hostility attendant upon a lesser degree of frustration. What efforts, if any, might be made toward increasing "control" in the three areas where hostility is now "acted out" or at least adversely influences behavior? Can the psychotherapist himself do anything to aid in increasing "controls" in these areas? Would this be advisable if there were no mitigation of other sources of frustration?

Our second example also involves an adolescent, this time a girl. She comes from a home in which the mother adhered to a very rigid moral code. As a child this girl attempted to gain acceptance at home by being very "good." However, she never felt accepted at home and began dating boys at a very early age. This led to conflicts with the mother that resulted in her running away from home. She was taken to court and placed, through the court, in a foster home. Here again she tried to be "perfect" in her behavior. However, the foster mother considered it her "duty" to note lapses and discuss them with the girl. The girl felt that she was losing the "love" of the foster-mother and left this home also.

By legal standards this girl would be considered a "juvenile delinquent" because of her running away from adult supervision, violation of probation, failure to observe curfew laws, and other legal violations. She says she is unable to control certain aspects of her own behavior and asks us to help her in this respect. Is this, then, a case of "undercontrol"? Obviously there is some connection between her premature relationships with boys and her need for acceptance, affection, and love. To meet her own request literally would presumably involve us in criticizing or otherwise responding negatively to her "bad" behavior. Yet we know that when the foster-mother essayed this role, the girl interpreted her behavior as if it were a withdrawal of acceptance and left the situation. Also we note that the girl responds in a strongly self-punitive way to her own "acting out" of emotions and emotional needs. What are the basic differences between the girl, who "has been in a lot of trouble" and the boy, who "has never been in any 'real' trouble"?

Voluntary versus involuntary control.   Obviously, if we cling to the dichotomy of "overcontrolled" and "undercontrolled" patients it is easy to become confused. Furthermore, our attention may be diverted by criteria, such as whether the person has been arrested by the police, that may have only a certain probability relationship to the actual behavior involved. What seems to us much more critical to the psychotherapeutic process is to evaluate those situations in which "control" of responses is automatic (habitual) and involuntary. When we find such involuntary inhibition "blocking off" too much of the behavior of the individual which would otherwise produce personal gratification, we may want to make such inhibition a cognitive "matter" by communicating with the patient about the inhibition and discussing with him the *pro's* and *con's* of the "reasons" for that particular inhibition.

When *lack* of control or inhibition is the problem and the resultant behavior is disturbing to the patient and/or others, the situation of the psychotherapist is considerably more complicated. We shall try to deal more comprehensively with this problem in our discussion of treatment. Our purpose here is to indicate two things. First, lack of control is a problem that may be found in *any* patient, whether such persons are generally regarded as "undercontrolled" or "overcontrolled." Second, lack of effective control over behavior is a legitimate and necessary concern of the psychotherapist. Therefore he should be alert to such lacks in the behavior of *any* patient and should consider the evaluation of specific kinds of "undercontrol" as a vital part of his evaluation of the patient.

LOVE

Definitions.   Now it is time to consider the positive aspect of the emotional picture. Our definitions here are very simple and general. At a perceptual and cognitive level we assign the symbol of "positive" to a perceptual quality that we call "pleasant" or "pleasure" without further attempt at definition. We assume that what is innately perceived as "pleasant" is determined more or less accurately by the biological survival needs of the individual. In other words, we assume that by approaching, touching, eating, and so forth those "things" responded to perceptually as pleasant, the individual's chances of survival are enhanced (as a matter of probability). In addition to meeting individual survival needs, some pleasant perceptual experiences are associated with behavior that leads to mating and reproduction.

The need for others.   Just as we have defined "fear" and "hate" in terms of feelings (unpleasant) plus behavioral impulses (avoidant and struggling, respectively), we also define love in terms of a feeling or feeling quality (pleasant) plus a behavioral impulse (approach). We attribute the rapid association of this emotion with specific persons among the human young to their helplessness and dependency in meeting their basic survival needs. Most pleasant experiences of the infant are associated with the presence of other persons and specifically with the thermal, tactile, olfactory, gustatory, visual, and kinesthetic stimuli they provide. In this way the child usually comes to "love" those who care for him. However, we also note that under similar conditions the child also comes to "love" the teddy bear he holds as he rests and falls asleep, and a dog comes to "love" the master who feeds him. We believe that the "special love" and need the child usually seems to develop for the parents or others who care for him can be explained simply in terms of the repeated association of the person or persons involved with the pleasure accompanying the gratification of many kinds of needs.

We might put it crudely that the presence and attention of those closely and continuously associated with many kinds of need reduction is like "money in the bank." Either attention (acceptance, contact) from others or money can "stand for" or represent the potential satisfaction of many needs. By the same token, loss of attention, contact, or acceptance from others can be threatening to the dependent individual because such a loss may indicate that the means he has habitually relied on for the satisfaction of needs or the enhancement of pleasures will no longer be available. He then faces the prospect of deprivation and "unpleasant" feeling states unless or until he has available other means to the same (pleasant) end result.

Attention, acceptance, approval.   The attention, acceptance, and approval of others thus becomes "coin" of considerable motivating significance. What we mean is that the individual will modify his behavior in response not only to the positive "reinforcing" effect of sensory pleasure but also in response to the reinforcement provided by the attention, acceptance, and approval of others. Similarly, he will also modify his behavior in response to the "negative" reinforcement or unpleasant feelings associated with rejection, disapproval, and criticism. In the technical jargon of the learning theorists, such acts would be considered "secondary reinforcements," which means that their capacity to influence behavior depends upon some consistent prior association between these acts and pleasant or unpleasant experiences for the child. We must remember, however, that the negative reinforcement value of disapproval or rejection depends ultimately upon the association of such behavior from others with the enhancement of unpleasant feelings. To leave a child alone when he does not "need" the adult or to criticize the child but continue to give him whatever he wants would mean that such responses would have no significant deterrent "effect" upon behavior.

These associations (of pleasure with acceptance, approval, and attention, and of unpleasantness with rejections, criticism, and disapproval) are obvious in the early behavior of the infant. However, as his experiences multiply and become more varied, it is no longer necessary for approval to be immediately associated with some sensory pleasure or for disapproval to be immediately associated with some sensory unpleasantness. We might say then, in a figurative way, that the on-going bonds of habit or learning supply a certain degree of autonomy to the pleasant quality of attention, acceptance, and approval from others and to the unpleasant quality of rejection, criticism, and disapproval (3). The individual then acts as if he needs or wants approval and as if he wished to avoid disapproval without any apparent regard for immediate pleasant or unpleasant perceptual experiences.

The need to love.   Now if we are willing to assume (and in popular parlance we apparently *do* assume) that attention, acceptance, and approval are the result of "others'" love for the individual, we have accounted for each person's "need for love." Actually here we mean his "need to be loved," if we assume that "being loved" is the equivalent of being approved of, accepted, attended to, and so on. When we talk about the need "to love" someone else or to "have someone to love," we are talking about something different. Remember, we have assumed that love for someone else originates in childhood with the other person's providing "primary" (perceptual) pleasure. Once this association has been established, however, it may (as is true of any other learned association) be transferred or generalized to others, depending upon their similarity to the original "love object." In other words, we "fall in love" with another person because of that person's similarity to some one who has already been "loved." We enjoy the experience of "falling in love" because (whether we "know" it or not) we expect to experience the "same" (similar) pleasures with the "new love" as we have already enjoyed with the old.

When this "transfer" of feeling occurs quickly and on the basis of superficial but readily apparent characteristics (such as appearance) we commonly refer to the attachment as "infatuation." When the "love" is based upon a more reliable evaluation of the other person's ability to provide gratification and pleasure, we are inclined in common parlance to regard this as "true love." Being utterly pragmatic about the matter, the difference would seem to rest largely on the accuracy of our original (and perhaps noncognitive) anticipation of the gratification to be realized by further association with the person "loved." Until this issue is settled, however, it "feels good" to be in love because of the pleasures we anticipate (whether rightly or wrongly), and it "feels good" to be loved for essentially the same reason. As we have said, love, like money, is symbolic of ("stands for") many potential forms of gratification. Those who have it feel "rich"; those who lack it feel "poor." And, of course, everyone would like to be rich.

The avoidance of love.   But would they? Doesn't all this depend upon what a person's actual experience with others has been? Suppose we have found others critical, demanding, or in other ways punitive or unpleasant in terms of their effect upon us. Might we then "decide" neither to love nor expect to "be loved"? Actually no cognitive decision would be required. Innately we tend to avoid situations in which we have experienced predominantly unpleasant feelings.

Evaluating "love" experiences.   In evaluating the "love-seeking" or "love-avoiding" behavior of his patient, the psychotherapist can never afford to be misled by certain conventional beliefs about love. For example, he cannot afford to assume that all parents love their children any more than he can afford to assume that all children love their parents. Also, the psychotherapist may be grossly misled in his task of evaluation if he is satisfied with a verbal profession by his patient that he loved, or was loved by, another. There are strong social taboos against expressing lack of love or feelings of hostility or fear in many relationships, such as parent-child, child-parent, and marital relationships. Whenever we are aware of such taboos we are also aware of the possibility of the inhibition and/or distortion of cognitive and communicative responses. In fact, we cannot always be sure of the accuracy of information to the effect that the patient was *not* loved. Such a statement represents a judgment by the patient, and judgments (as we have noted earlier) are especially subject to distortion according to the feelings actually associated with the situation being judged. We might, however, be willing to accept the patient's statement as to whether or not he thought he was loved or "felt" loved, with due regard for the possibility of distortion in accordance with social pressures regarding such communication.

Regardless of our evaluation of the accuracy of the patient's statements about being or not being loved or about loving or not loving, it is always necessary to examine in some detail the nature of the interaction between the persons involved in the relationship. For example, we are very accustomed to having parents tell us how much they "love" their children. Yet a parent who tells us this may also supply information indicating that he spends very little time with his children, that he pays little attention to them when he is with them, and that when he does pay attention it is usually to reprimand, criticize, or punish. If this is true, then what does it mean when he says he "loves" his children? And is the child supposed to feel "loved" when this is the nature of the actual interaction between the parent and himself? Is the child supposed to "love" this parent enough to modify his behavior in the interests of further "strengthening" this type of relationship? To go to the opposite extreme, how are we to evaluate the "love" of a parent who manifests his affection for his child by letting the child do whatever he wants when the child is young and later is angry and disturbed because the child continues to act in the same way?

Love and marriage.   Let us shift our attention to the question of love in marriage. Presumably the person who "marries for love" does so on the basis of an assumption that the person loved will "make him happy." If, however, we analyze this assumption it may boil down to the expectation (not always represented by cognitive responses of sufficient habit strength to "register" in awareness) that the person loved will provide certain types of gratification, especially those to which the "lover" has become accustomed in prior relationships with others. But this expectation may be based on inadequate, incompetent, or irrelevant experience with the other person. Sweetheart may resemble mother in physical appearance but she may cook and keep house more like baby sister. She may have the "same" face as the current "love goddess" on the drive-in movie screen, but she may react to sex in the manner one might expect of Ma Kettle. She may know as much about English literature as one's favorite professor and still be unable to balance a checkbook.

Marital expectations.   The plain and discouraging fact of the matter about marital expectations is that these are usually based on an acquaintance with the other person which occurs under conditions only remotely resembling those of marriage. Feelings may be strongly aroused by characteristics that have much less significance or will actually change in marriage as compared with courtship. Finally, for our brief survey, the person whose anticipations, whether accurate or not, are predominantly pleasant, tends to reduce the uncomfortable conflict of ambivalence by minimizing the evidence suggestive of unpleasant consequences in marriage. No wonder love is called "blind"!

Of course these expectations become the criterion by which the person also judges how "good" the marriage is once he is in it. Therefore we can expect to find considerable bias in the patient's evaluation of how "good" his marriage is. We once performed the trick of describing to two very unhappy wives the characteristics of the other's husband. Having met both men, we considered them very similar. We also had reason to believe that they functioned very similarly as husbands. Both women responded to my "objective" descriptions plus a few "detail" differences in specifications by assuring me that she could be "perfectly happy" with the other woman's husband. Perhaps these biases "before and after" also help to account for the fact that close friends can often notice only what appear to be insignificant differences between a man's first wife and his second, although he assures them (before the marriage, at least) that there is all the difference in the world between them.

The significance of love. To summarize our comments on love relative to the evaluation of the individual, one of the basic things we need to know about the patient is whether and to what extent unpleasant feelings outweigh pleasant ones both in his present experience and in his anticipations of the future. In this evaluation, what we can discover about the patient's experiences of loving and being loved (or the opposites) are particularly crucial because what we might call "personal love" represents the potential fulfillment of many significant specific needs. We look for primary or direct evidence on this point because social taboos and social requirements tend to create both cognitive and communicative distortions. We should be prepared to find that our patient's dissatisfaction with certain relationships is based less on what they fail to provide in the way of need satisfaction than it is upon whether the needs met are up to the expectations of the patient. There are many reasons why these expectations may be unrealistically high.

DEFENSIVENESS

"Openness" to love. Besides evaluating the lack of love and pleasure in a patient's life, we also need to investigate his "openness" to love relationships and pleasurable experiences in general. Furthermore, if we find (as we usually do) some degree of constriction in the person's openness to love and other pleasant experiences, we want to know why it came to exist, why it is maintained, and how it is maintained. All these evaluations are made with a view to determining how we can "reopen" the patient emotionally.

At one point we were not sure that this "reopening" process was always desirable or necessary. Our position then was that it was the psychotherapist's responsibility only to make the patient aware of his emotional defensiveness and to point to some of the consequences, specifically the symptoms of the patient that were most obviously related to this defensiveness. The patient was then free to decide whether he wished to make small emotional investments in life and in others and thus keep his potential losses to a minimum or to "go for broke" on the possibility of winning the emotional jackpot.

A psychotherapeutic position.   Further experience and thinking have converted us to the position of usually (if not always) working for more emotional receptiveness in the patient.   A defensive or conservative approach to life is oriented toward reducing "losses," that is, minimizing negative or unpleasant feelings. However, the most the patient can do in this respect is to minimize his emotional involvement with other things and persons. If he succeeds in isolating himself completely, so that what happens to "others" does not affect him in any way, it is obviously impossible to derive pleasure from relationships with others. But one can still be "cut down" by purely personal misfortunes, such as accidents, illness, and aging. Thus it looks as if the defensive, emotionally uninvolved person must always "lose" in the game of life. He can be hurt, but he cannot be helped.

We recognize, of course, that the isolated person is capable of providing pleasant experiences for himself. But this requires an effort on the person's part. We question whether there is usually or consistently any net gain when the pleasure enjoyed is measured against the (unpleasant) effort required to gain it. If a person "loves" (enjoys) his work and is able to enjoy also what he can buy with the money he earns, he would perhaps have no "need" for others. We believe the answer to this argument is that few of us can afford to buy all the things and services we need or from which we might derive pleasure. On the other hand, we have a fighting chance to come out ahead in "love" relationships. On the one hand we can enjoy doing things for those we love, perhaps, basically, because this enhances our feeling of security about the continuance of the relationship. Then, also, we can enjoy what is "done" for us by the other person. Besides actual services performed, this usually includes many intangible sources of pleasure, such as assurance that our needs will be taken care of in the future and the enjoyment of the presence of the other person because of his association with pleasures enjoyed in the past.

Actually we do not believe we can make a perfectly logic-tight case for emotional involvement with others as against emotional defensiveness. There are, however, other points to be made on the "pro" involvement side of this argument, such as the possibility that mankind is so constituted genetically that the presence of people we like is pleasant and their absence is unpleasant. (Relatively few mammals live completely solitary lives, and we know of no primates that do.) Perhaps a significant consideration is that society "approves" of "belonging" and "disapproves" of those who lead a solitary existence. Undoubtedly the degree of dependent orientation in a person's life adjustment *versus* the ability to function independently is of some consequence in determining the value of "love" relationships. But fundamentally our position rests on a very simple basis: by and large people seem to be happier and better satisfied when involved in relationships and emotional interchange with others than when alone.

In fact, this observation is so general that it is usually safe to assume that any patient who comes into psychotherapy does so at least partly because he feels the need for more satisfying relationships, whether he says this explicitly or not.

Defenses against involvement.   The only obvious and complete means of defense against emotional involvement is emotional withdrawal, that is, neither subjectively wanting nor objectively seeking relationships with others. However, only when we see that the patient's experience in relating to others has been so consistently and predominantly unpleasant as to "convince" him that no future relationships could be rewarding can we begin to believe in the "genuineness" of his desire to remain solitary. Otherwise we shall suspect that his apparent rejection of the need for others is based more directly and functionally upon his fear of being rejected by them. And why does he fear rejection? Very often we find feelings of inadequacy and inferiority involved in the basis for this fear. Such feelings plus actual experience with rejection (real or imagined) from others will almost always account for the anxiety that motivates defensiveness.

We must mention two major forms of what we call "partial defensiveness." The partially defensive person seeks acceptance, approval, and love but does so in a way that provides a degree of protection against the fear of rejection. One defensive maneuver is to create a false image of the self, designed to meet the tastes, needs, and so on, of the other person whose acceptance is being sought. There are three major "penalties" that this device entails. The first is the effort required to maintain the disguise. The second is the anxiety that is generated by fear of being "found out." The third is that even when the disguise "works" in securing acceptance and is successfully maintained, it is, after all, the disguise (persona) which is apparently loved and not the "self."

A second major defensive maneuver in love-seeking is to substitute services for "self." (We sometimes wonder whether this is not the characteristic defense of the service-oriented occupations, including psychotherapy.) In this "ploy" of "lifemanship" the tactic is to distract attention from the supposedly undesirable nature of the self by setting up a screen of valuable services rendered. Again, we find three potential hazards to this mode of adjustment. First is the effort involved, which may outweigh the benefits received. Second is the possibility that the services will be accepted or even taken for granted without any assurance regarding acceptance of the "self" which provides the service. Third is the danger that when the "other's" need for the service ceases, so will his acceptance or apparent acceptance of the "server."

A scale of defensiveness.   We are reluctant to leave this brief discussion of "defensiveness" without offering a simple but useful scale for evaluating degree of defensiveness in attempting to relate to others. We note that only the extremely disturbed individual makes no effort to relate to anything outside himself. One step less defensive is relating emotionally to objects. One more step less defensive is relating emotionally to animals. Next in order is relating to other humans, with relating confined to the very young being more defensive than relating to age peers. Finally, among age peers, the more defensive person tends to seek acceptance primarily from persons whose status he sees as inferior to his own, while the less defensive person seeks acceptance without this degree of concern for status. If we direct our attention to the relative amounts of time and effort our patient devotes to seeking acceptance in these various categories, we may have not only a useful indication of his emotional defensiveness but also an indirect index of his anxiety about attempting to relate.

DEPRESSION

"Disguised" depression.   At first blush it might appear that little need be said concerning the evaluation of depression in persons who present themselves for psychotherapy. It is obvious that the patient must be unhappy; otherwise, why would he be a patient? Like most apparently "simple" matters in psychotherapy, however, the problem is rather more complex than this.

First of all, *how* depressed the person is can be of considerable importance. This is by no means always obvious at first view. Many patients are reluctant to be completely open about the intensity of their depression. They may wish not to face the matter themselves. They may want (strange as it seems) to make a "good" impression on the therapist. They may feel embarrassed because they cannot see how their "real" life circumstances justify the intensity of depression they feel, or at least they do not expect others to accept the validity of their reasons. For these or other reasons the patient may give a superficial impression of lesser disturbance than actually exists.

On the other hand, we have also seen the reverse situation: the patient who talks as if he were more depressed than we would assume on the basis of other evidence. In some instances, this is simply a bid for the psychotherapist's attention and concern. Of course, the need for attention and concern may present a legitimate problem in itself, but it is important to know *which* problem is of paramount importance. At other times communicating about feelings of depression is the patient's way of getting into the therapeutic relationship before bringing up his "real" reason, which he may disclose later. In our experience patients who tend to "cover up" depression have outnumbered those who exaggerate it by a considerable margin. What we have been particularly impressed with, however, is how frequently some "disguise" along these lines is attempted.

Depression and hostility.   Aside from the matter of more or less deliberate deception, another question is how much depression is "really" depression. This question arises because of the possibility of a kind of "disguise" which the patient may not be aware of himself. The literature on psychotherapy includes a number of references to a form of depression that is primarily a matter of hostility turned inward upon the self. We see this "adjustment" in an early form when we note the child blaming himself for the parents' failure to accept him. In childhood and adolescence it may be fairly obvious that "depression" begins with an episode in which the individual is thwarted but under circumstances where an overt expression of hostility could bring down reprisals. In such situations the child or adolescent may wind up just being "very unhappy."

What has led us to accept the hypothesis that depression can be a "converted" form of anger is experience similar to the following. We note in the patient's accounts of his life various frustrating circumstances and/or persons, but when we question him about his feelings toward the situation or person, he denies having felt or now feeling any anger. We may also note the same with respect to contemporary experience and perhaps be able to observe that increases in depression follow frustrating episodes. If, in conjunction with these two observations, we also see that encouraging the patient to be more expressive of hostility tends to reduce the frequency or severity of his depressions, then we may feel reasonably sure that a part (at least) of this depression has been due to "hostility turned inward."

The significance of depression.   If we keep this exception and these "disguises" in mind, then we may regard depression as the most fundamental and basic symptom of all. What it should indicate to the psychotherapist is that his patient has lived and is now living his life in such a way that unpleasant feelings consistently predominate over pleasant feelings. The patient's consulting the psychotherapist indicates that he believes that he will be unable to redress this balance without assistance. A fundamental task and responsibility of the psychotherapist is to provide this assistance.

SUMMARY

The ultimate reason for seeking psychotherapeutic assistance is an unfavorable balance between unpleasant and pleasant feelings. This situation is often not readily detectable from the patient's verbalizations, however, because of training that has encouraged him to "play down" emotional experiences and expressions of feeling. It becomes the responsibility of the psychotherapist to recognize, interpret, and attempt to change the nature of emotional experience.

All psychotherapists recognize the significance of anxiety in determining the unsatisfactory nature of their patient's affective life, although therapists are inclined to disagree about the most important sources of anxiety. The most obvious conclusion is that patients are anxious about different things and for different reasons. We tend to stress the following sources of anxiety: fear of rejection, fear of failure, and anxiety about hostile impulses.

When the patient has inhibited the cognitive responses that would represent the intermediate links in the arousal of anxiety, the psychotherapist must deal with the problem of anxiety without an apparent specific cause: so-called "free-floating" anxiety. Sometimes the patient attributes his anxiety to a source that is not the real source. Before the psychotherapist can help to allay anxiety, he must determine its real origin.

Hostility is also often difficult to track down to its original sources. Society is responsible for many frustrations, yet it offers only a limited number of "approved" outlets for the aggressive impulses that are created by frustration. The expression of hostility may be delayed, disguised in form of expression, or directed against objectives other than the original source of frustration.

So far as the control of emotional behavior is concerned, the psychotherapist must be alert both to problems of undercontrol and to problems of overcontrol. He will do a better job of evaluating emotional problems if he is concerned with under- and overcontrolled *behavior* rather than with under- and overcontrolled *persons*, since persons are not consistent in this respect. The psychotherapist attempts to develop a situation of voluntary control over emotions as the "safest" situation for the patient.

The development of love for others is dependent upon pleasant experiences with others. If others are helpful in meeting a person's needs, then the attention, acceptance, and approval of others becomes "valuable" to the person. "Loving" another person correlates closely with expectancy of pleasant experiences with them. Sometimes these expectancies are highly unrealistic and would be recognized as such if they were "spelled out" cognitively. Since they seldom are, it is possible to "fall in love" and "fall out of love" without being aware of the real reason for either experience.

The person who has been disappointed with the outcome of his relationships with others is motivated to avoid relationships. The psychotherapist should usually try to overcome this "defensiveness," because negative feelings are unavoidable, and interpersonal relationships are potentially the most significant source of pleasant feeling experiences with which to counterbalance unpleasant experiences.

Depression is a pervasive "symptom" of patients, which patients themselves may either conceal or exaggerate. In many instances depression turns out to be a form of hostility directed toward the self. Most basically, however, depression indicates that unpleasant experiences predominate over pleasant ones and that the patient sees no way to redress this unfavorable balance.

SUGGESTIONS FOR FURTHER READING

The problem of suggested readings for this chapter is one of having too many resources to choose from. However, we suggest reading Freud (4) on the problem of anxiety, Horney (2) on the problem of hostility, and Reik (5), Part 1, on the problem of love.

Dollard and Miller (6) discuss the development of the need for others in Chapter V. Those who have more time to devote to the subject, however, may profitably read all of Part II in Murphy (3).

REFERENCES

1. Dollard, J., Doob, L. W., Miller, N. E., and Sears, R. R. *Frustration and aggression.* New Haven, Conn.: Yale University Press, 1939.
2. Horney, K. *The neurotic personality of our time.* New York: Norton, 1937.
3. Murphy, G. *Personality.* New York: Harper & Row, 1947.
4. Freud, S. *The problem of anxiety.* New York: Norton, 1936.
*5. Reik, T. *Of love and lust.* New York: Noonday, 1963. (Farrar, Strauss, 1949.)
6. Dollard, J., and Miller, N. E. *Personality and psychotherapy.* New York: McGraw-Hill, 1950.

* Paperback edition.

Part Three | PSYCHOTHERAPY

Chapter 9 | *Psychotherapy: Objectives*

INTRODUCTION

The scope of modern psychotherapy.   Our objective in this extended essay on psychotherapy is to provide a theoretical framework for understanding the individual that will both provide a guide to evaluation and also indicate what the psychotherapist should do about conditions that he considers detrimental to the welfare of his patient.

We come now to the most challenging aspect of this effort, namely, to extend theory and methods of evaluation in such a way that they indicate logically what the psychotherapist is supposed to do about the conditions evaluated. There are two problems associated with this task that make it especially difficult. The first is to select a level of discourse that is sufficiently general to cover a wide variety of problems in a wide variety of patients and yet specific enough to be of concrete value to the person who will himself be confronted with the specific problems of specific patients.

This problem would be much simpler (although by no means simple) if one were to confine his scope to a more homogeneous set of problems or a more homogeneous set of patients. Yet it is quite apparent that the practice of psychotherapy is already past its fledgling years. With these years has gone the prerogative that the psychotherapist once enjoyed of accepting only those patients who happen to respond well to a specified "technique." Some psychotherapists somewhere at this hour are engaged with patients and problems that were perhaps only dimly envisaged as objects of psychotherapeutic concern at the turn of the century. These include patients both older and younger, more and less "disturbed," more (perhaps) and less intelligent, more and less well educated, and from a greater variety of cultural and socio-economic backgrounds than the "classical" patient.

A greater variety of approaches to "treatment" has also been proposed, utilized, and evaluated (not always rigorously). Many of these have survived at least casual evaluation to qualify for the attention of those psychotherapists who are more concerned with improving their effectiveness than with maintaining their "orthodoxy" in the exclusive use of a specific technique. It is no longer easy to be *comprehensive* when discussing psychotherapy, and (if we are to judge by the available literature) it has never been obviously easy to be *specific* without resorting to the hyperspecificity of a particular case. This *apologia* we extend not only on our behalf but also on the behalf of all those who attempt the broader rather than the narrower view.

The problem of sequential exposition.   The second problem is that any verbal exposition must be serial or sequential: we must talk about some "things" before we can talk about other "things," although in fact the "things" or "events" referred to may occur simultaneously. This can be illustrated from our own material.

It has certainly occurred to many readers that although the concepts used in the preceding section on "evaluation" were perhaps a little strange, what we have "really" been discussing in the last four chapters has been "diagnosis." So why not call it "diagnosis" rather than "evaluation"? To dispose of the reasons less relevant to the present purpose first, the first two reasons for the use of this terminology were: (1) to minimize analogous thinking that relates psychotherapy to the treatment of physical disorders (we would have eliminated the terms "patient," "psychopathology," and "psychotherapy" for the same reason if we could have thought of convenient substitutes); and (2) to break away as far as possible from what we consider the sterile, static, and misleading *classification* of patients that seems to be the prime purpose of classical diagnosis.

Our third purpose is illustrative of the problem of serial communication that we mentioned above. It is and has been customary for "diagnosis" to precede "treatment" in psychotherapy, perhaps because this is the customary procedure for the treatment of physical disorders. But any experienced psychotherapist either is or should be aware of how inappropriate such a model is for procedure in psychotherapy. The psychotherapist is not (or should not be) interested in what the patient "has"; he is (or should be) concerned with what the patient "is" and "does."

We do not have, and perhaps we shall never have in psychotherapy, specific remedies to "cure" a particular condition. Rather we have people who function more or less adequately as total organisms. We must communicate with these people. We must establish relationships with them. Why? Because (as we shall see) these two processes, relating and communicating or, more accurately, relating through communication, are our only means of access to the patient and his problems. Therefore establishing a communicative relationship must be our first concern and our first endeavor. All else, evaluation and psychotherapy, depends upon the success of this initial effort. Evaluation can wait on this, and, in a certain sense, it must. Even effective testing can only be accomplished when there exists a certain "rapport" with the subject. But what do we mean by "rapport" except a relationship in which the subject accepts the examiner and the evaluating situation?

It is important for the psychotherapist to keep in mind that psychological testing was first devised for evaluating large numbers of subjects in a minimum of time by persons with minimal psychological training. None of these considerations is relevant to the psychotherapeutic situation except, perhaps, in the screening of patients in institutional situations. The reasons for the routine use of psychological tests or even the formalized and detailed case history as a prelude to psychotherapy escape us, unless we assume that (1) this helps fit psychotherapy to the irrelevant model of medical procedure in cases of physical disorder, and/or (2) it helps reassure the psychotherapist who is doubtful of his ability to evaluate the patient properly without such "tools."

"Diagnosis" and "treatment."   To return to our subject, one of the reasons we have used the term "evaluation" rather than "diagnosis" is to escape as far as possible from the pattern of thinking that one first "diagnoses" and then "treats." What actually comes first is that the psychotherapist is face to face with another person with whom he establishes a relationship by the process of communication. From the moment of this face-to-face meeting (or even prior to it in the case of telephone contacts), the psychotherapist is simultaneously evaluating and affecting the patient. From that moment forward, the processes of evaluation and psychotherapy are simultaneous and coterminous. Yet the serial nature of communication makes it necessary for us to discuss one or the other of these processes first, and so we have done.

In the same way and for the same reason we shall be forced to discuss certain aspects of psychotherapy before we discuss others. This is awkward, inconvenient, and irritating. Both the order and the interval between certain aspects of psychotherapy can be completely critical to the success of a particular venture. We do not see how these aspects of psychotherapy can be stereotyped and prescribed at present, if only for the reason that we must start at different levels and perhaps end at different levels of adjustment with different patients. Further, we cannot deal with all patients as if any aspect of their cognitive structure, emotions, and behavior were equally "accessible" and it were only up to us to decide where to begin. Rather the patient provides us a point of access through his initial communicating and relating to us. We must proceed from this point because there is no other point from which to proceed. We can now turn to a consideration of psychotherapeutic objectives and the means by which they may be accomplished.

COMMUNICATION: GOALS

Communication and adjustment.   There are several objectives or goals that we have in mind so far as the communicative behavior of the patient is concerned. Basically it is important that the patient be or become an effective communicator, both as a "sender" and as a "receiver." We sometimes talk glibly about a person's "adjustment" in such a way as to minimize the fact that "adjustment" always means "adjusting to" some particular situation. If other persons are involved, so that we talk about "social adjustment," then we are concerned with the patient's ability to modify his behavior in such a way as to maximize need satisfaction and/or to minimize frustration and anxiety, in interpersonal contacts. "School adjustment" implies a concern with the ability to derive rewards and satisfactions from the patient's presence in and behavior in a school situation.

In other words, when we speak of "adjustment," we should keep in mind both specific requirements that certain situations impose upon the person and certain needs that the person may be able to satisfy in the situation. Knowing what the requirements are involves the patient's functioning as a communicative "receiver." Indicating his needs and desires, as well as meeting the requirements, usually involves the patient as a communicative "sender." Obviously his ability "to adjust" can be significantly affected by his effectiveness in either communicative role.

Competence in communication.   Most basic to "effectiveness" is the simple matter of competence. Can the person adequately "understand" all communications to him? Can he adequately express whatever he is required to express or must express in order to represent himself adequately? This basic competence may be lacking in the young, the undereducated, the mentally retarded, those with a bilingual or foreign language background, and others. The negative emotions, fear and hostility, may block effective communication. The stutterer may often be considered an example of such emotional blocking. Also, the patient has often been trained to avoid certain types of communication, so that he is either unable or unwilling to communicate freely. Our objective here is to enable the person to say what he wants or needs to say and to understand what he needs to understand.

"Openness" in communicating.   In most cases a particular need will be to increase openness in communication, that is, to encourage the person to be more expressive and more receptive in communicative behavior. Here we have in mind two different types of restriction. One is that the person is afraid to say what he thinks, feels, wants, needs, or intends because of an excessive fear as to what effect such communication will have on others. Most people as children have heard too frequent admonitions to the effect that: "You shouldn't *say* that. It is naughty (impolite, disrespectful, rude)." All too often such warnings are generalized into a habit of keeping quiet unless a particular kind of communication is requested. One direct advantage of the psychotherapeutic situation is that this tendency to minimize communication is offset by the request or even the requirement to communicate plus "approval" for increasing communication and "disapproval" for withholding communication.

In addition, the psychotherapist can facilitate communication in various more specific ways. He can accept free-associations, dreams, jokes, drawings, and various kinds of nonverbal behavior in lieu of more direct and purposive communications. He can take the initiative in verbalizing certain thoughts for the patient. He can put certain concepts into concrete terms for the patient via "interpretation." He may, under certain circumstances, use facilitative means such as drugs and hypnosis. This is getting a little ahead of our story, but we cite these various "techniques" here to illustrate the function and value of the psychotherapist as a facilitator and encourager of communicative "openness." Of course, and most significantly, he usually refrains from "punishing" the patient for being open and communicative.

Accuracy in communicating.   In addition to being concerned with increasing the patient's communicative tools and his willingness to use them, the psychotherapist is also concerned with *accuracy* in communication. The communicative "sender" selects from a certain structure of cognitive responses, certain symbolic responses to represent the significant dimensions and characteristics of the entire structure. This book is such a selection of symbolic responses arranged in a particular sequence with the objective of communicating at least the major dimensions and significant characteristics of our experience with the process of psychotherapy. It is obviously impractical to attempt a complete reconstruction of that experience. But if the attempt to communicate is reasonably successful, then at least the reader's conceptual framework should coincide with ours, and appropriate details from his own life experiences will be appended at appropriate places to help fill in the outline. We will thus have achieved a certain communality of cognitive responses regarding the subject of psychotherapy.

This same type of communality is one of the objectives of communication in psychotherapy—that is, to have the communication "land" in a context of cognitive responses in the "receiver" similar to that from which they were selected in the "sender." Where this is not true at the outset, then it becomes a significant objective in psychotherapy. Of course the value of this effort to the patient in his extra- and post-therapeutic communicating depends very largely on how representative the communicative behavior of the psychotherapist is of the communicative behavior of people in general. It should be noted here that the psychotherapeutic relationship affords the psychotherapist the opportunity (and the requirements of his work impose the obligation) for him both to check and to increase his own communicative accuracy.

Accuracy of affective communication.   We should not forget that the concept of communicative accuracy can be applied to the affective connotation of words as well as to their informative connotation. Here the situation in psychotherapy is somewhat delicate in those instances where the affective or feeling impact of the patient's communication is greater than he expects it to be. If the psychotherapist responds with the "appropriate" (most common) feeling reaction, he runs the risk of inhibiting communication from the patient. On the other hand, if the psychotherapist's response is atypical in terms of "feedback" to the patient, then he allows the patient to run the risk of being "misunderstood" in extra-therapeutic situations. Quite often this dilemma can be resolved by the psychotherapist's indicating his own personal acceptance of the communicative effort of the patient while also informing him of what he believes the reaction of others would be to the same communication.

Usually, however, the psychotherapist deals with those who are overanxious concerning others' emotional reactions to their communicative efforts. For example, the patient says: "I can't tell you about that (certain details of sexual behavior) because I don't know the right words." Here the patient is saying, in effect, "If I told you about what I have done in the only words I know to describe it, I am afraid you would be shocked and would have a bad opinion of me." Such attitudes in the patient are encountered especially often when or while the patient is relating to the psychotherapist as an "out-grouper" or one of the "others." From this point of view, the patient's attitude toward communicating with the psychotherapist is indicative of inadequate rapport. One approach to the problem, then, would lie in the general direction of improving the relationship, or, to use other terms, "working through the negative transference." However, the psychotherapist may also approach this attitude instructively, pointing out that words themselves are neither "good" nor "bad" and that the value of accuracy and adequacy in communication often warrants some risk regarding what emotional impact a particular form of communication may have on others.

COGNITIVE STRUCTURE: GOALS

Emendations to the map concept.   We have previously discussed some problems in cognitive structure in terms of certain aspects of cognitive structure constituting the patient's "map" of reality. We have pointed out that the map may be blank or inadequately detailed where more information is needed for optimal adjustment. The map may also indicate details that have no counterpart in reality. Thirdly, there may be distortion so that portions of the map do not correspond accurately with analogous aspects of reality. We shall repeat that an important objective of psychotherapy is to help to correct the patient's conception of reality.

It is not enough, however, to be concerned with whether the patient's conception of reality is corrected up to the contemporary moment. On the one hand, we must make the patient aware of the dangers of using old, out-dated orientations, so that he will continue to devote time and effort to revising his conception of reality after he leaves therapy. On the other hand, he needs to be aware of what errors he has made in the past if he is to have an appropriate perspective on his present adjustment and problems. Explaining to the patient where and how he has previously erred in perceiving reality can be both instructive and reassuring to him.

However, it is important to avoid the error of concentrating so exclusively on the past that the patient, like the "phillylulu bird," flies backwards, more interested in where he has been than in where he is going. As was indicated in Chapter 1, the amount of time that Freud devoted in psychoanalysis to past events could be justified in terms of his need to learn about certain aspects of childhood and development which, until Freud's advent, had been ignored by psychologists. The emphasis in contemporary psychological theory on "being" and "becoming" (1, 2, 3) suggests that psychotherapy should be much more present and future oriented than has been typical of psychoanalytic psychotherapy.

We should say, then, that what the patient needs is, in effect, a stack of maps extending from the past through the present into the future. These should be properly time indexed. The errors in old adjustments should be clearly indicated. The tentative nature of anticipations of future events should also be clearly indicated. Furthermore, the map representing the contemporary situation should be clearly labeled: "*Use me most.*"

Both the patient and the psychotherapist, however, are concerned with more than what was true, what is true, and what will be true. The patient is also (and even more) concerned with "what to do," "can I do it," "may I do it," and "must I do it." In considering questions such as "may I do it" and "must I do it," the most important aspect of reality to consider is the probable behavior of others. But it is impossible to make such an evaluation definitive, because we cannot assume homogeneity among all the "others" involved, nor is it even safe to depend upon complete consistency from a given person at various points in time and in various circumstances. In other words, conclusions about "may do" and "must do" can only be reached in terms of probability and contingency. Absolute certainty on such matters cannot be guaranteed by the psychotherapist and should not be expected by the patient.

The significance of the self concept.   Of the two remaining questions, "what to do" and "can I do it," the answer to the latter sets the outer limits for answers to the former. This is because the patient is hardly likely to consider responses to situations that he believes are beyond his capacity. In fact the patient's evaluation of his own incompetence or inadequacy needs to be carefully considered as a possible basis for his cognitive and behavioral rigidity. If the patient is concerned to conceal such negative self-evaluations from others, the reasons for what is sometimes called "persistent nonadaptive behavior" may not be immediately apparent to the psychotherapist. Such negative self-evaluations may also help to account for the patient's rejection of direct suggestions from the psychotherapist or others as to how he might proceed in a given situation. When this type of problem arises, it is important to determine what the *patient* considers possible.

The most common error here is for the psychotherapist to base his approach to a given situation the patient faces on his *own* evaluation of the patient's ability rather than upon the patient's evaluation of himself. In the most typical case, the psychotherapist's evaluation of the patient will be more optimistic or favorable than the patient's evaluation of himself. In such cases, the alternative ways of dealing with a situation, which the therapist "sees," are not functionally perceptible to the patient until he accepts the psychotherapist's evaluation of himself.

For this reason a considerable amount of "education," "information giving," "direct suggestion," and similar psychotherapeutic efforts may be wasted. Such efforts to inform and direct the patient are often ridiculed or ignored by certain theoretical approaches to psychotherapy, either on the grounds that "they don't work" or on the premise that such direct intervention "violates the integrity of the patient." Where the former reason is given, we consider it important to analyze the reason for the ineffectiveness of an informative approach. If the reason is lack of self-confidence on the patient's part, then of course this condition must be remedied *before* the psychotherapist suggests alternative modes of response; otherwise his suggestions will have no value for the patient. The other objection concerning "violation of the patient's integrity" makes no sense to us. It seems obvious that when the patient approaches the psychotherapist for help, he has invited the therapist to become involved and to participate in his decision making. One might almost go so far as to say he expects it.

Evaluation.   Although the point should be more than obvious by now, we shall state once more that a major objective of the psychotherapy must be to give the patient a realistic evaluation of himself. Scarcely less important is the necessity for the patient to have a realistic evaluation of others, although the importance of such evaluations of others varies according to their degree of involvement with need-gratification in the patient's behavior. The term "evaluation" that we have used here implies two different aspects to this portion of the psychotherapeutic task. On the one hand, we deal with the matter of what *are* the characteristics, abilities, and attributes of the patient. On the other hand, we deal with their value. The task of evaluation involves a review (and usually some revision) of the standards by which the patient judges himself and others. Such standards may be absolute or relative. They cover the entire range of social coercion from current fads and fashions, through manners and morals, to legal and religious codes for conduct. They are, in fact, synonymous with the "may I's" and the "must I's" just referred to, except that they include static or structural characteristics (such as appearance) as well as standards for behavior.

While psychotherapists may differ widely in their opinions as to which standards (if any) are the legitimate concern of the psychotherapist, certain generalizations along these lines can be made. For example, in order for the patient to evaluate both himself and others more accurately he should have access to information concerning what others *do* as well as what they profess to do or to believe in. In other words, it is patently "not fair" for the patient to have to compare himself in terms of his own intimate knowledge of desire, impulse, and private behavior with the public masks or personae of others. This matter can be considered independently of whether absolute or relative standards are involved in the goals and objectives the patient chooses for his own future strivings.

It is also in order for the psychotherapist to indicate standards that have become outmoded. For example, many of the standards that are still used in evaluating masculinity or masculine adequacy belong to an era that is now past in our society. Physical strength and physical skills that had pragmatic or "survival" value in a frontier society may be at best

useless and at worst detrimental to adjustment in an increasingly urban-
ized and mechanized culture. Being "the fastest gun in the West" butters
no parsnips in Denver, Cheyenne, or Calgary these days, and the man
who is overly quick to "defend his honor" may find that he has just lost
the prime account for his advertising agency and, with it, his job.

Furthermore, it seems always appropriate to bring to the patient's
attention the fact that the categorical imperatives of his own particular
upbringing are not so regarded by all people everywhere. The "must be
done's" and "thou shall not do's" vary not only as a function of time but
also as a function of culture patterns in different societies, geographical
location within a particular society, and with caste, class, religious, sex
and age characteristics. Psychotherapists in certain areas, such as Los
Angeles, may find that the majority of the patients with whom they deal
are "displaced" from the culture area and social class in which they were
raised. In these circumstances, the psychotherapist would find it difficult
to avoid devoting attention to standards and their relation to particular
social milieus.

Controls.   Finally, we come to the matter of "controls." With respect
to this aspect of cognitive structure, the psychotherapist's attention is
directed toward increasing the degree to which control is exerted as a
matter of deliberate choice rather than as a matter of habitual conformity. There are several reasons for this orientation. Most generally, certain
controls that may have been imposed at an habitual level before the
patient was capable of "thinking things through" for himself may involve
matters about which he is now capable of making his own decisions.
Some such automatic controls may have been imposed to meet the
wishes, needs, or standards of persons who are no longer of primary
importance in the patient's life. When such controls are no longer appropriate to the environment in which the patient functions, they represent an unwarranted and nonadjustive restriction upon his behavior.

In addition to these considerations, the patient may have, through
contact with others besides those responsible for his primary control
training, learned to accept standards and values different from theirs. He
may have developed different ideas about "good–bad," "right–wrong,"
and so on, than those with which he grew up. Yet often such individuals
come to us with the complaint that although they now "think" differently,
they are unable to function in accordance with these newer convictions.
It then becomes the psychotherapist's responsibility to help the patient
act the way he wants to.

This definition of goals so far as control is concerned will, incidentally, apply as well to the under-controlled patient. Except for children, institutionalized persons, and other semivoluntary patients (such as

husbands and fathers), we can assume that all other patients who consult us because of the inadequacy of their control over behavior do so because some new integration of cognitive responses has convinced them of the nonadjustive value of their present behavior. The psychotherapist's function is then to work toward the development of adequate controls. However, he should also consider it his responsibility to evaluate the patient's desires in this respect with respect to their long-run consequences for the patient. We have, on occasion, considered it necessary to discuss with a patient the matter of whether his new ambitions about "being good" were not rather extreme and perhaps impractical in view of our own evaluation of human potential in this respect.

In the case of the semivoluntary patient who is deficient in control, a more difficult assignment for the psychotherapist is presented, in that he must then attempt to achieve that integration of reason and attitude which will give the patient a motive for desiring more adequate controls. Only then can he proceed with the remainder of the task with some assurance of success.

"Reasonable" behavior.   Those who have read this section carefully and have considered the implications of the various objectives defined may have certain questions at this point as to whether our emphasis is not really more "rational" than we have maintained elsewhere. It would seem (and this may become more obvious in the remaining chapters) that a considerable part of therapy may be devoted to creating an "awareness" of matters about which the patient has not been aware. Further, it would appear that the psychotherapist wants the patient to relinquish certain automatic, habitual ways of responding to situations in favor of conscious, deliberate, and (if you will) rational choices. Such conclusions, if arrived at, are correct as applied to the position that we take and advocate.

Because this is true, we wish to emphasize again that there is considerably more to the psychotherapeutic process than "reasoning with" the patient or than getting the patient "to listen to reason." While it is accurate to say that we want the patient "to be reasonable" or "to act in a reasonable way," the definition of rationality in psychotherapy has to do primarily with the appropriateness of the patient's behavior to the satisfaction of his needs or to the avoidance of unnecessary frustration. We are concerned at the outset with why the patient does not behave in a reasonable way, and our evaluation of these reasons is synonymous with diagnosis. Treatment, however, involves much more than telling the patient what to do. After deciding which changes in response (cognitive, physiological, or behavioral) will most benefit the patient, the real challenge of psychotherapy is to create adequate motivation, provide appropriate "cues," elicit satisfactory responses from the patient, and provide sufficient reinforcement to ensure the continuity of the patient's new manner of dealing with the world in which he lives.

EMOTION: GOALS

The effects of negative emotions.   Before discussing specific emotional goals in psychotherapy, let us consider certain basic assumptions with respect to the negative emotions, namely fear and hate. If we consider the physiological responses related to unpleasant feelings (including all the organic effects of activation of the sympathetic branch of the autonomic nervous system) it would appear that these physiological changes do indeed prepare the individual "for fight or flight." It is also apparent that sympathetic stimulation gives rise to conditions within organs and cells which are antithetical to optimal anabolic activity and which, in fact, create both chemical and mechanical "tensions"—if that term may be applied to conditions of chemical balance. The situation is similar to the use of JATO (Jet Assisted Take-Off), in that the entire structure is subjected to a temporary overstress (relative to normal operating conditions) in order to minimize the dangers of power failure during the critical moments of getting the airplane into the air.

In subhuman survival problems the functional analogy holds up well enough. Normal metabolic activities are disrupted in an "emergency situation," and cellular and organic structures are subjected to greater than normal "stress." Such stress states are seldom maintained for more than minutes, however. In the human young we note the same pattern: ready arousal to a tension state, intense muscular activity, and return to quiescence—the whole sequence taking perhaps not more than fifteen minutes. It seems to be generally agreed that the muscular activity is a necessary condition (or, at least, is conducive) to the subsequent "quieting."

But many of the "thou shalt nots" of society are directed against such energetic discharges of tension. Furthermore, the intellectual capacities of the more mature human enable him to respond to purely symbolic threats, frustrations, and so on. In this way he can "borrow trouble," which may or may not actually confront him at some future date. Also, via complex cognitive processes the human being can be restimulated to emotional response by events that are past in time. Finally, the human can be stimulated to intense feelings by purely cognitive responses, such as self-evaluation according to standards the person accepts as applicable.

All of these conditions give rise to situations where feelings are evoked but where there is no obvious need or even opportunity for vigorous muscular response. Under these conditions we expect (and often find) that the duration of emotional upset is much more prolonged in the older human than it appears to be in younger humans and among sub-human species.

The possible consequences of this situation are many. One such consequence is structural deterioration in cells and organs subjected to repeated and prolonged stress. The resulting deterioration in functional efficiency can produce any of a variety of psychosomatic symptoms. Another consequence may be awareness of uncomfortable tensions within the body that can serve as a basis for hypochondriasis or other manifestations of anxiety. Such tensions can lead to habitual use of chemicals that tend to counteract them, thus paving the way for addiction or "compulsive" problems such as overeating. Regardless of the particular symptom produced, it seems obvious that we cannot usually expect a socially valuable or personally valuable outcome of such tension states, although such outcomes must always be considered possible.

Emotional objectives.   The general alternatives open to the psychotherapist in dealing with the undesirable effects of prolonged tension states are rather simple and obvious. When the provoking situation is an on-going aspect of the patient's real environment, we can (1) change the environment, (2) remove the patient from that environment, or (3) change the cognitive and/or behavioral response of the patient to the environment. When the principal stimulus to feeling consists predominantly of cognitive responses, then either these must be altered or the way in which the patient responds to the resulting tensions must be altered.

As simple and as obvious as these conclusions may be, we feel that they are too often ignored or considered too casually as the starting point in developing a psychotherapeutic strategy. We would point out that the novice psychotherapist has a strong inclination to be somewhat "technique happy." He is most anxious to learn and master the "how to" aspects of psychotherapy. But "how to" should always depend upon, and therefore follow upon, certain decisions concerning "what to." Further, there is usually truth and merit in the general and the obvious that needs to be realized before proceeding to the specific and the esoteric. To repeat, there are only a limited number of general alternatives open to the psychotherapist and at least tentative decisions relating to these alternatives logically should precede decisions relating to the technical aspects of procedure.

We can now give another illustration of the limitations of sequential exposition. Emotional goals in psychotherapy are being dealt with last because they represent our ultimate concern, the *raison d'être* for the other goals that we have already discussed. We have pointed to cognitive and/or behavioral changes as the only literally psychotherapeutic mode of dealing with those situations in which unpleasant feelings are adversely affecting the patient. Yet an awareness of emotional objectives is necessary in order to determine a plan of procedure, including a specification of communicative and cognitive objectives. What the psychotherapist must do, in other words, is to define his emotional objectives first, then develop that level of communication which gives him effective access to cognitive structure, then use communication to produce certain preconceived changes in cognitive structure and behavior in order to reduce the tensions associated with unpleasant feelings and to increase the incidence of pleasant feelings.

Yet while this is the sequence with respect to any specific objective, at any actual point in time during therapy the psychotherapist may be involved with quite different stages of this sequence with respect to different objectives. He cannot hope to know at the outset of therapy all of the feeling problems of the patient, if only because the patient himself is not fully aware of them and could not communicate about them even if he would. Rather the therapist will find some problems obvious. These he can "go to work" on immediately and even achieve considerable progress while still in the process of establishing adequate awareness of and communication about others.

Emotional experience in psychotherapy.   It must also be understood that while emotional *objectives* may be the last to be realized, the psychotherapeutic process is, in itself, basically dependent upon emotional experiences, and these are continually involved in the psychotherapeutic interaction. Specifically, it is impossible to change either communicative interaction or cognitive structure without changing existing habits in the patient or creating new ones. The psychotherapist cannot either create or change habits without evoking feelings that motivate and feelings that reinforce. Furthermore, in the process of creating change he must deal continually with what is commonly called the "resistance" of the patient. But this resistance can always be analyzed into and defined in terms of feelings that serve as either motive or reinforcement to sustain the existing habit structure. "Dealing with resistance" can likewise be defined as the task of bringing in stronger feelings to motivate and reinforce change to offset those feelings that support the *status quo* of the patient's prepsychotherapeutic adjustment.

Objectives: anxiety.   Returning to the matter of emotional goals, we should like to be a little more specific with respect to these so far as the two unpleasant feeling states are concerned. It would not be accurate to leave the impression that the psychotherapist is only concerned with the reduction of anxiety without further qualifying this conclusion. Actually he is concerned only with the reduction of excessive anxiety, that is, anxieties which are disproportionate to "real" dangers or calculable threats. The person in danger *should* be afraid: otherwise there would be nothing to motivate him to adjust appropriately to the danger. It is true that the sudden onset of significant threat may produce enough feeling to "paralyze" the thinking or even the moving capacities of any human being. This, however, is not the psychotherapist's problem. Rather he must consider it a design defect in the "system" with which he is dealing. However, the psychotherapist should take into consideration the amount of anxiety that a given patient can tolerate and still function adaptively, because he can help the patient in this respect through influencing the type of environment in which the patient must function or chooses to function.

Objectives: hostility.   As far as hostility is concerned, the psychotherapist's responsibility is to help the patient in minimizing the amount of frustration he must endure. Again, however, the ultimate objective cannot be realistically defined as a state of zero frustration. Basically, the process of maintaining life is one of attending to certain compulsory needs of the body. Beyond this, the hazards of injury and disease prevent life from running smoothly, and there is always the inevitable frustration of death. The satisfaction of any need or the achievement of any goal involves a necessary effort that the person might not otherwise choose to make. Also, some goals are incompatible with others in such a way that the satisfaction of one need involves the frustration of others.

The patient may also need to be trained in the proper use of his own hostility. What we mean, specifically, is this. A common, perhaps universal, characteristic of patients is that they do not know how to be hostile. At one extreme is the undercontrolled patient whose "acting out" of his hostile impulses places him in continual danger of retaliatory measures from others, including especially rejection and social isolation. At the other extreme is the person who wants acceptance from others so much that he attempts to inhibit any obvious outward manifestation of hostility. But in order to do this he must "put up with" additional frustrations that others will impose when they evaluate him as nonaggressive and therefore a "safe" object for exploitation. Furthermore, as a non-aggressive person he loses status, which is, in itself, a deterrent to acceptance. Finally, if any aggression "leaks out," it is quite likely to do so under circumstances that make the patient's response inappropriate, thereby creating feelings of guilt and further fear of hostile impulses.

In Chapter 2 and in Chapter 8 we have discussed the various means by which the patient attempts to control or redirect his hostilities. It is sometimes possible for the psychotherapist to help the person with whom he is working to find more adequate or less destructive ways of expressing hostility than those he has already developed. However, our own position is to consider hostility as having a potential adaptive value in much the same way that fear or anxiety has.

To illustrate the potential adaptive value of hostility, let us consider one of the basic problems of relationships. The continuation of a relationship on the basis of mutual satisfaction depends upon some kind of communication being established about how each feels about what he is getting or giving. Otherwise the relationship lasts only until one person or the other finds it intolerable and discontinues the relationship. If inhibitions about expressing hostility prevent either person from communicating adequately about the frustrations he experiences in the relationship, then the probability that the relationship will not continue is increased (4).

More generally, we believe it is realistic to consider the hostility-motivated threat as a significant means of influencing the behavior of others. The word "threat" itself has unpleasant emotional connotations that cause both patients and psychotherapists to avoid it. In essence, however, a threat is only a particular kind of promise. Each is a statement about future action, usually based on a qualifying premise: "If *you* do this, then *I* shall do that." As such, it is a legitimate and potentially useful form of communication. Relatively few authorities on matters of psychotherapy seem to have taken a clear stand on this issue. We, however, feel that aggressive behavior is a fundamental requirement for normal adjustment. Our goal in this respect is an appropriate degree and appropriate modes for the expression of hostility through aggressive behavior.

Objectives: pleasure and love.   Our final objectives with respect to emotion have to do with the need for experiences having pleasant feeling qualities, generally stated as the "need for love." We are indebted to George Bach for some of his formulations in this area (and also on the constructive uses of aggression). There is a strong tendency, as we have noted previously, for rest, recreation, and other forms of pleasure-seeking to be regarded as, at best, permissible and, at worst, sinful in large segments of the population of the United States. Put another way, having fun is nothing to be proud of. Yet considering the inevitable tolls of anxiety and hostility, the "pursuit of happiness" would seem to be a necessary endeavor if we are to strike some kind of favorable balance in our emotional bookkeeping.

It is not enough to assume that the pursuit of socially-approved goals will automatically provide pleasure, at least of sufficient magnitude to compensate for the effort involved. If examined thoughtfully, many such socially-approved goals have to do more with the allaying of anxiety than with any actual increment of pleasant experience, so that their realization is not accompanied by intense feelings of happiness so much as it is followed simply by a sense of relief. An example would be the feelings accompanying graduation from college. Although this is supposed to be a glorious occasion, the culmination of many years of striving and therefore the cause for intensive celebration, the most universal reaction among the participants seems to be "Well, we made it." The "others" involved—parents, relatives, and friends—may feel like celebrating. The graduate is more inclined to be too exhausted to feel any great sense of exhilaration, and he is probably already concerned with the next social requirement, finding gainful employment.

Still other social requirements make no great pretense of being anything except "other-oriented." Requirements for politeness, decency, responsibility, and other social virtues may be rationalized in terms of ultimate benefit for the person who must meet these requirements. This "ultimate benefit", however, is usually only that the person who meets these requirements avoids social censure or punishment.

The simple fact of the matter seems to be that while others may pay a great deal of lip service to their concern for the "happiness" of a person, the bulk of their efforts are devoted to insuring that the person will do what he is "supposed" to do. Perhaps this is as it should and must be, especially in the years before maturity. But in these same years, the controlling "others" are also the source of considerable and direct need gratification, which is quite incidental to their function as social conditioners. When the person is "on his own," he may find himself restricted, on the one hand, by the effects of his social training, yet have no one who is responsible for supplying his needs except himself. If he then assumes that personal gratification will automatically follow upon diligent performance, he may well find himself "overworked and underpaid" (5).

A more reasonable position would be that as soon as the person begins to function independently, he also becomes responsible for planning for his own happiness. He has no right to expect someone else to provide for this happiness nor to "make him happy." The more practical aspect of the matter is that he will, in all probability, be hard put to find anyone who is particularly concerned with his personal gratifications, except on a more or less obvious *quid pro quo* basis. Defects in the person's training for adult life show up in his reasons for resistance to facing the problem forthrightly. He protests that an orientation of self-interest is "selfish," "egocentric," "asocial," and so on, all of which add up to "bad." If, however, we ask him who he expects to "look out" for him and to assure his personal gratification, he is usually unable to come up with a satisfactory answer.

If we can convert the patient to the point of view of being actively responsible for his own pleasure (or if he already has this attitude), the problem of pleasant experience is not necessarily solved. For example, the person may have been so trained that the value of money is greater than the value of things or services for which the money may be exchanged. Problems of this nature, although significant in some cases, are generally less important than problems that relate to deriving satisfaction through relating with others.

Problems of love.   In the psychotherapeutic literature the problem of loving is usually counterpoised with the problem of hate. We would like to suggest, however, that the more basic problem is "love versus anxiety," or rather, the need for love versus the avoidant tendencies which are associated with anxiety. In Lewinian terms, this would be designated as an "approach–avoidance" conflict.

Let us use a specific case to illustrate the various emotional dynamics involved. An attractive young female patient comes into the office and begins her hour by stating: "I'm so damn mad. That fool who works for my boss wants me to go out with him Saturday night." We are somewhat surprised by this outburst, since the patient had never spoken of this man except in either neutral or approving terms. So we ask: "Why are you so angry?" The answer is: "Because I don't have anything to wear, and I don't know what to say to him, and I can't dance, and I'll make a fool of myself."

In this situation, although the anger is manifested first, the emotion that is more basic is the patient's fear of inadequacy and rejection. These anxieties prevent her from making active attempts to relate to others except in situations (such as work) where her adequacy has been established. In other words, the response that is associated with anxiety is avoidance. It is only when someone else breaches this "defense" by making overtures for a relationship which she must respond to in some way that she feels frustrated enough to become angry.

We do, of course, see persons who have given up all hope of acceptance and who will not, therefore, make any effort to relate. Some of these will use others only as objects for their hostility. But these are the "hopeless" ones, the ones who feel they have nothing to lose by expressing their hostility, since it is inconceivable to them that they would be accepted by others regardless of how they acted. Even in these cases, it is the supposed "refusal" of others to grant acceptance that accounts for much of the hostility they express toward these others.

For many reasons we must regard the need for acceptance by others as basic and fundamental to human existence and postulate that hostility is a secondary manifestation arising from the frustration of this need. We see hostility, not so much as a deterrent to relating, but rather as a complication in relating. The arousal and existence of hostility is only possible when a relation exists, or at least is contemplated or desired. We conclude, therefore, that the primary "antagonist" of love is not hate, but fear.

For this reason we shall define our emotional objectives (so far as love is concerned) in terms of reducing the anxieties of the patient to the point where he will pursue activities that will yield pleasure, including especially those activities that involve relating to others. With respect to hostility, we work toward the objective of avoiding those frustrations that generate hostility. Since, however, it is inconceivable that all frustrations can be avoided, we suggest that the residual hostilities can be put to constructive use in influencing the behavior of others so that relationships have a better chance to continue.

SUMMARY

There are two problems to be coped with in discussing psychotherapeutic techniques and objectives. The first is to be general enough to cover all psychotherapeutic problems while being specific enough to be useful. The second involves the difficulty of presenting simultaneous events in terms of sequential exposition. For example, evaluation and treatment are continual and parallel processes in psychotherapy, although the classical procedure involves diagnosis first and then treatment. This medical model is inappropriate for psychotherapy.

Our basic objective with respect to communication is to help the patient become a more effective "sender" and "receiver." This may involve the development of communicative skills. We can also talk about "accuracy" in communicating, defining this in terms of whether the sender is able to evoke the cognitive and/or behavioral responses that he intended to evoke. The psychotherapeutic situation provides an opportunity to deal directly with these aspects of communicative behavior.

Our objective with respect to cognitive structure is to see that the patient has a cognitive map which is sufficiently detailed and accurate enough to meet his adjustive needs. The map concept of cognitive structure must be amended when it comes to discussing psychotherapeutic technique. First of all, we must "time index" our maps in order to differentiate clearly "present" from "past" and "future." We must further find means for indicating the "permeability of boundaries," indicating what is possible, easy, difficult, or impossible. This requires us also to employ a probability index, especially with reference to future events.

Evaluations of the self and of others are prime determinants of what the patient believes is "possible." Direct suggestions from the psychotherapist are useful to the patient only when he regards them as "possible" in terms of his own evaluation of himself, others, and situations. The nature of the patient's evaluations depends, of course, upon the standards he uses to evaluate. We believe it is important that the patient have normative standards in addition to whatever other kinds of standards may be considered relevant.

Our objective in the area of "controls" is to enhance the degree to which behavior is a function of conscious decision and effective behavioral execution of cognitive "plans."

Human beings do not function well when physiological stress is intense and prolonged, yet human characteristics make such stress possible. Our basic emotional objective is quite simple: to reduce such emotional stress by whatever means are available and appropriate to the psychotherapeutic relationship. Often this involves the use of or the arousal of countervalent feelings to offset the emotional "resistance" of the patient to situational, behavioral, or cognitive changes.

We are not concerned with the elimination of all anxiety, but only with the removal of anxieties that are disproportionate to the danger the patient faces. We cannot hope to eliminate all frustrations, but we can hope to avoid unnecessary frustrations. Furthermore, we can direct the patient in constructive uses of hostility, especially for his own protection in relating to others.

Finally, we can attempt to help the patient by augmenting his opportunities for pleasurable experience. We must make him aware that his happiness is his own responsibility and that the "pursuit of happiness" may require deliberate planning and diligent effort on his part. The greatest potential for pleasant experience probably lies in interpersonal relating. Most patients must be helped with their anxieties about being rejected before they are ready to realize maximum benefits from attempts to relate.

SUGGESTIONS FOR FURTHER READING

We feel that the reader should sample other ideas about the objectives of psychotherapy at this point. We shall refer him to a number of different sources, most of which are relatively brief.

We recommend, as a starting point, Freud's thoughtful essay, "Analysis Terminable and Interminable" (6). Others representing the psychoanalytic point of view are Menninger (7), Chapter VII, and Fromm-Reichmann (8), Chapter X.

Wolberg devotes six pages (Chapter 46) to the goals of treatment (9). Carl Rogers handles the topic more generally and freely in Chapter 9: "A Therapist's View of the Good Life: The Fully Functioning Person" (10).

Julian Rotter provides a treatment that is different from any of these in Chapter IX of his book (11), wherein he discusses various conceptions of the psychotherapeutic task.

REFERENCES

*1. May, R. (Ed.) *Existential psychology.* New York: Random House, 1961.

*2. Maslow, A. H. *Toward a psychology of being.* Princeton, N.J.: Van Nostrand, 1962.

*3. Allport, G. W. *Becoming.* New Haven, Conn.: Yale University Press, 1955.

4. Bach, G. A theory of intimate aggression. *Psychol. Reports,* 1963, XII, 449–450.

5. Becker, E. *The revolution in psychiatry.* New York: Free Press, 1964.

6. Freud, S. *Collected papers,* 5. New York: Basic Books, 1959.

*7. Menninger, K. *Theory of psychoanalytic technique.* New York: Science Editions, 1961.

*8. Fromm-Reichmann, F. *Principles of intensive psychotherapy.* Chicago: Phoenix, 1960.

9. Wolberg, L. R. *The technique of psychotherapy.* New York: Grune & Stratton, 1954.

10. Rogers, C. R. *On becoming a person.* Boston: Houghton Mifflin, 1961.

11. Rotter, J. B. *Social learning and clinical psychology.* Englewood Cliffs, N.J.: Prentice-Hall, 1954.

* Paperback edition.

Chapter 10 | *Communication:*
Techniques

INTRODUCTION

Communicating and relating.   To introduce this chapter, we shall
repeat a statement made in the preceding chapter. What the psychotherapist must do is to define emotional objectives first, then develop that level
of communication which gives him effective access to the cognitive structure of the patient. He then uses communication to produce certain pre-
determined changes in the patient's cognitive structure and behavior in
order to improve the balance between his pleasant and unpleasant feelings. This statement will serve well enough to indicate in brief and in
general the role of communication in the psychotherapeutic process.

However, in order to convey at all accurately the critical role of
communication in psychotherapy, we must point to quite a different conception of the function of communication that is equally valid. This conception centers around the statement that psychotherapy is a communicative relationship, with the emphasis placed on "relationship."
When we place the emphasis on "relationship," we do so in order to emphasize once again that the psychotherapist must create new feelings in
the patient in order to motivate and to reinforce the cognitive, behavioral,
and physiological changes he hopes to achieve with and for the patient.
If the *relationship* is conceived of as the principal source of such new
feelings, then we may emphasize "relationship" and subordinate "communicative," although the relationship would not exist without communication and is therefore completely dependent upon it.

The psychotherapist has room for choice between these two positions, depending either upon the preference of the psychotherapist or
upon the different needs of different patients. To illustrate the latter
point, patients may be more or less emotionally involved in their relationship with the psychotherapist. Those who are less involved may not be so
much influenced or so readily influenced by his comunications to them.

Such a situation would indicate that the nature of the communication itself would be of relatively more importance than in other cases where the patient responds with strong feeling to any indication of the psychotherapist's own beliefs or attitudes.

As to the preference of the psychotherapist, it seems quite reasonable to assume that different persons occupied in this activity may feel varying degrees of comfort or discomfort in dealing with the feelings of their patients about them. Some may choose for this or other reasons to minimize feelings in the relationship, while others may deliberately seek to strengthen such feelings for psychotherapeutic purposes and because they prefer working in an atmosphere of emotional involvement. We believe that a basic orientation toward the process of psychotherapy should be able to encompass a variety of positions on the involvement–non-involvement continuum.

In this chapter we shall be primarily concerned with the communicative process per se. However, we shall note again that no communication can take place without creating a relationship, and no relationship can exist without communication.

Verbal and nonverbal communication.   In order to make this statement meaningful and valid, we shall point out once more that the concept of "communication" includes nonverbal, as well as verbal, behavior. If there is any question on this point, a review of Chapter 4 would be in order.

We suggest a possible correlation between the position of emphasis on the communication-relationship dimension and the use of verbal *versus* nonverbal means of communication. We believe that psychotherapists who emphasize "communication" rather than "relationship" are inclined also to be more verbally than nonverbally oriented in their interaction with the patient. We would expect them to be more aware of "content" than of "expression," both in communicating to and receiving communications from the patient. Finally, we would expect them to be more aware of informative than of affective connotations in their verbal communication with the patient.

We wish to make our own position on these matters clear. *If* such correlations as we suggest above *do* exist, the effectiveness of the psychotherapist who follows this more "intellectualized" orientation toward psychotherapy may be seriously affected and curtailed.

To see why this may be so, or when it will be so, let us once again consider the basic conception of motivation, cues, response, and motivation as the conditions necessary for habit formation or reformation. The strictly "informative" aspect of communication has relevance to only one of the four required conditions, namely, "cues." To put the matter somewhat differently, psychotherapy that is primarily "content" oriented, so far as communication is concerned, is also primarily concerned with the structural aspect of cognitive responses. It is true that we rely on changes in cognitive response and cognitive structure to produce changes in behavioral and physiological response. But such changes will not occur unless the patient is appropriately motivated and reinforced. Motivation and reinforcement, we repeat once more, are matters of *feeling*.

If or when either the patient or the psychotherapist elects to concentrate on the communicative rather than the "relationship" aspects of their interaction, the attention devoted to the nonverbal, "expression" and affective aspects of the communicative process should increase, rather than decrease. It is only by being a good "receiver" with respect to these aspects of communication that the psychotherapist can become aware of the patient's feelings when the patient cannot or will not talk about them as a part of the "content" of his communication to the psychotherapist.

The importance of emotional interaction.   It is only by creating an affective impact (or, to put it another way, by evoking cognitive responses with appropriate feeling qualities) that the psychotherapist himself is able to participate directly in the process of readjustment so far as motivation and reinforcement are concerned. But "affective impact" depends more upon the affective connotation than upon the informative connotation of communications. Nonverbal means of communication (such as slapping the patient or kissing the patient, to cite two extremes) may have considerably more "affective impact" than verbal communication. Along the "expression–content" dimension of communicative activities, it is predominantly "expression" that is affect-determined, affect-loaded, and has "affective impact" on the receiver.

What we are saying here tends, of course, to break down any distinction between "communication" and "relationship." What we are saying implies that however much the psychotherapist or the patient may prefer to "talk to" each other rather than "relate at an emotional level," the psychotherapeutic objective cannot be achieved unless the patient's feelings are affected by his contact with the psychotherapist. We consider it the psychotherapist's responsibility to be fully aware of this requirement and to be at least as concerned with the affective impact as he is with the informative content of his communication with the patient.

To put the matter still another way, we are now on the verge of considering technique in psychotherapy. Choices of technique, we believe, should be determined predominantly by the characteristics and needs of the patient as we evaluate them. These needs, in turn, define certain therapeutic objectives that we hope to achieve through an appropriate selection of techniques for interaction with the patient. However, even when our attention is centered on techniques that have to do with communication, we should evaluate these with respect to their affective import as well as with respect to their informative effectiveness.

ELICITING COMMUNICATION

Patients' communicative limitations.   One of the basic maxims we adhere to is that the psychotherapist must start with the patient where the patient is, so far as his development is concerned. Many potential patients are poor communicators in a verbal sense. In many instances this deficiency may be considered "normal," in the sense that the deficiency can be readily understood in terms of obvious characteristics of the patient, such as age, intelligence, or education. In other instances where none of these "obvious" criteria apply, we may reasonably assume that reticence in verbal communication is a part of the patient's "problem." Under these circumstances, it is scarcely reasonable to require verbal fluency as a necessary precondition for successful psychotherapy. To do so would be tantamount to saying that only effective people can become effective patients. Although such a dictum is conceivable and perhaps defensible, we consider it much too restrictive in terms of techniques now available.

Note that in the preceding paragraph we have clearly limited our remarks to *verbal* communication. It is quite inconceivable that we could spend any reasonable length of time with a patient, even when he does not speak, without learning something about him and communicating something to him. Often with children between two and five years old, the child may not say a word until quite a bit of "communicating" has gone on, and until he has enough "information" from and about the therapist to decide whether he wants to relate to the therapist. Perhaps we can use this age group to illustrate various techniques of communication.

An illustration of communicative technique.   Usually when we enter the waiting room the child simply looks at us. We say "hello" to the parent (whom we have talked with previously) and then immediately turn our attention to the child while asking the parent, "Is this John?"— or whatever the child's name is. We seldom shift our attention from the child for the next few minutes, even though the parent may attempt to engage us in conversation and talk "around" the child, as it were. The reason for this is very simple. If we engage in conversation with the parent, even though it is about the child, we are "relating" to the parent and not to the child. At this point we are interested in establishing a relationship with the child, which we indicate by making him the focus of our attention. So our next remark is directed to the child also and consists of saying "hello" and introducing ourselves and offering to shake hands with the child.

By the time this simple routine is finished we have had fairly clear indications from the child concerning his readiness to accept us. For example, if the child rises or approaches us, returns our greeting without prompting and offers his hand, we ask him if he will come into the office with us, which he will usually do. Even if he asks a question at this point, such as "What are we going to do?", we usually consider that he has actually accepted the relationship. We therefore answer the question briefly and generally. We then tell the parent at what time we shall be finished and go into the office with the child. The child may hesitate at the moment of separation from the parent, at which point we might say, "We won't need them for awhile. You and I are going to do some things together, and when we are through your mother (or father) will be waiting for you."

What has been accomplished.   In addition to what has been said, several other things have been communicated to the child. First, and most important to establishing rapport, is our indication that we are interested in him rather than in the parent. We have focused our attention on him, learned his identity, volunteered our own, and offered to be friends by extending our hand. If he accepts our offer, we indicate that we would prefer to be alone with him, but we also let him know that this will be for a limited period, and we have aranged for his reunion with his parent at the end of that period. If he is still "with us" at this point, we indicate our knowledge of his acceptance by not going into any great detail to answer a more or less "conversational" question (provided this is how we actually evaluate it). We further this orientation by using terms such as "we will (or won't)—," "you and I are going to—," and so on. Given this kind of response from the child, the procedure as described will usually serve to establish the initial phase of a relationship with any person up to adult age.

Dealing with reluctance.   Suppose the child is more reluctant to respond to our initial approach. Careful observation of the child's behavior should indicate to us whether he is simply waiting for more information before committing himself, whether he is anxious about the situation, or whether his response is directed toward evoking further response from the parent. These differences we note for the purpose of determining further interaction once we are alone.

Regardless of this evaluation, our next move is to make a statement designed to allow the child time for further consideration while still focusing his attention upon ourselves. Usually this involves asking if he would like to see some of the things we will be using. Provision for this is made by storing play and art materials in the reception room. We then devote ourselves to showing these materials to the child, explaining the uses of each. This removes pressure from the child for making an immediate decision about us, and gives him a chance to relate to "things," which are less anxiety-provoking. Yet these things belong to us, and his degree of interest in and contact with them is a fairly good indication of how his feelings are progressing. He may clearly indicate an interest in something we have shown him. If so, it is usually safe to use the material as a "bridge" to relating to us, by telling him that he may use it, but it would be better for "us" to use it in the office rather than in the reception room. When no clear choice has been made, we may ask the child what his preference is and follow up his choice as if his expression had been spontaneous.

Avoiding "forcing the issue."   With these more cautious children, we do not force the issue of establishing a relationship by making obvious attempts to win their friendship. This would be a dangerous tactic, since if we push the child for a decision, it may very well be "no." Instead we try to indicate our awareness of his indecision by giving him additional opportunities to observe us in the process of showing him the material. Since it is our material, it also gives the child another basis on which to evaluate us and the potentialities of the relationship in terms of *his* interests and *his* needs. The fact that he has some choice in (and therefore some control over) the situation is brought out. He may also learn something about the psychotherapist and the "rules" of the situation by the way in which we handle the matter of where the materials are to be used.

With the most anxious children, we allow the parent to come into the office with us but maintain primary contact with the child ourself. We join with him in preparing or setting up the material we have brought with us and become engaged in activity with the child. When the child has begun cooperating with us in this way, especially after we begin talking about what we are doing, we choose an opportune moment to tell the parent that he may go to the reception room. If necessary, we promise the child that he may have access to the parent there.

The use of observation.   In discussing the evaluation of the child we usually use the term "observe the child" to refer to the basis for our evaluation. We use this term in a rather literal sense. Children generally are not adept at relating to adults by means of conversation, and even when they are *able* to relate in this way, it is usually not their preferred mode of interaction. For this reason we frequently permit them to relate in the psychotherapeutic situation by allowing them to use art, crafts, or toy materials and by participating with them in their chosen activities. Consequently much of our communication *from* the child may be of a nonverbal nature. Since we are also doing things with the child, much of our communication *to* him is also of a nonverbal nature. For example, we can set limits, show acceptance, praise, disapprove, and in other ways influence cognitive processes and behavior without extensive verbalization. For those who are not sure how this can be done, we suggest raising a child from birth or, as an alternative, raising a puppy and volunteering for baby-sitting assignments, especially with children under two years of age. This will circumvent the need for extensive reading, as well as being considerably more informative than a purely verbal learning experience.

Communicating with adolescents and adults.   Incidentally, any of these techniques for relating to children may legitimately be considered as means for communicating with older patients who are limited in their ability or desire to relate primarily through verbal means. For example, we have been able to establish an effective therapeutic relationship with a seventeen-year-old girl who was reluctant to talk with us by getting her cookbooks (after we learned that she wanted to know how to cook) and teaching her how to read and use recipes. We sometimes allow or encourage adult patients to use art materials as a means of expression. Most readers will be aware of psychodrama as a medium for nonverbal as well as verbal communication. Some adult patients are allowed to communicate at times via written notes or letters. Some patients will communicate more readily if allowed the freedom and permissiveness of a "free-association" type of verbal communication while others are made very anxious by such lack of limits and lack of communicative structure. The latter type of patient may become virtually mute if required to communicate in a manner that is unfamiliar and, to him, frightening.

Dreams as a form of communication.   At this point we should like to insert a note on the relating of dreams as a form of communication. Our theory is that as the psychotherapist is learning to "interpret" the symbols of the patient's dream material (assuming the patient provides such material, since not all do), the patient is learning the psychotherapist's way of interpreting dreams. The patient uses this knowledge in two different ways. First, he "learns" to interpret his own dreams. Second, once the patient knows the psychotherapist's "system," we believe he uses the relating of dreams as a method of communicating about matters that he is still too anxious to discuss as a matter of direct communication. In this way the patient can pre-test the psychotherapist's response to certain kinds of communication. The "safety-factor" from the patient's point of view in this approach is that he can disclaim any "reality-value" for the communication should he be made anxious by the psychotherapist's response to it.

Extreme measures: hypnosis.   Perhaps the most extreme measure within the realm of psychological techniques to which the psychotherapist may resort in eliciting verbal communication is to place the patient under hypnotic influence for this purpose. We consider this technique "extreme" in the sense that under these conditions the psychotherapeutic relationship is one in which the therapist acts out a dominant, active, and controlling role while the patient accepts a subordinate, passive, and submissive role. If we assume that the ideal relationship is equalitarian and that the general progress of psychotherapeutic relationships should be toward this ideal, the use of hypnotic procedures would place us rather far in the opposite direction.

Our own recommendation would be that hypnotic influence be used only when other psychotherapeutic techniques are obviously inadequate to elicit comparable and essential information, although we know that there are those who would disagree strongly with this opinion. Rather than going into all the issues and viewpoints involved, we shall confine ourselves to commenting that we are not impressed by arguments which assert that "material can be got at more quickly" in this way. If we consider the psychotherapeutic task as involving an appreciable amount of habit formation and reformation, we are not apt to handle any deep-seated problems very quickly in any event. We would consider that any patient who can only be communicated with on significant subjects via hypnosis has some very deep-seated problems.

Extreme measures: drugs.   We would adopt much the same reasoning with respect to the use of chemical agents as disinhibitors so far as verbal communication is concerned. We can hardly regard scopolamine, LSD, Rityline, and similar psychopharmacological agents in any other light. We regard these as measures of desperation from a *psychotherapeutic* point of view, and consider it highly appropriate that their use should be confined to medically trained psychotherapists who are also experts in the field of psychopharmacology or to teams having a combination of such skills among them. Such forms of practice are beyond the scope of this essay. However, we cannot resist tossing in the observation that if chemical means of disinhibition are being conscientiously sought and considered, we should not overlook the rhymed advice that "candy is dandy, but liquor is quicker."

Controlling communication.   Going from one extreme to the other, we must also mention the problem of the overly free, glib, or compulsive talker. Some authorities have left us with the impression that they consider any form of interference with the spontaneous verbalizations of the patient one of the cardinal sins of psychotherapy. After some years of experience we have been forced to conclude that they must have been either very lucky or very perceptive in their choice of patients. We, on the other hand, have encountered situations with patients where we were convinced that the patient was talking in such a way as to avoid certain subjects about which they were very anxious. In some cases we felt they were also "using" their verbalization to avoid the problem of relating with the psychotherapist. Under these circumstances a policy of non-interference with the communications of the patient could represent a neglect of psychotherapeutic responsibility.

Principles of the communicative relationship.   Having mentioned several means of eliciting communication from the patient and several forms which such communication may take, let us now see whether we can make any generalizations. First, our primary objective is to establish a communicative relationship with the patient. Second, patients vary in their ability to participate in communicative relationships. We are now faced with the question of whether the psychotherapist should have a set pattern for such relationships and accept only such patients as are able to fulfill their designated role in his pattern.

What we have been suggesting as an alternative is that the psychotherapist should evaluate the patient's capacity for communicative relationships and establish his initial relationship with the patient on the basis of this capacity. Depending upon the needs or limitations of the patient, the communication may be more or less nonverbal. Depending upon the needs or limitations of the patient, we may indicate much freer limits for verbal communication than prevail in normal social talk, as we do when we express an especial interest in the patient's accidents, humor, dreams, or free associations. On the other hand, to insist upon such communications can be disturbing to some patients, whose limitations at the outset we can respect by accepting a much more conventional type of conversational interaction.

Objectives of the communicative relationship.   If we consider a communicative relationship as basic to all further psychotherapeutic endeavor, then we can afford to be, in fact we must be, flexible in our means of establishing this relationship. Does this mean that we are completely permissive or *laissez-faire* with respect to the patient's communication in psychotherapy? Not at all! In the first place, we attempt to establish the communicative relationship at the highest level of directness and openness of communication about self of which we consider the patient capable. Secondly, regardless of where or how we establish the relationship, we continually encourage, direct, and reinforce progress toward *more openness of* communication about self and others. We consider that what is crucial about the patient's communicative behavior is not where or how we begin our communicative relationship with him, but how this communication develops, in what direction it progresses, and where we are at the end of the psychotherapeutic relationship.

Naturally we shall achieve our objectives more quickly if we attempt to elicit the most honest, open, and direct communication of which the patient is capable at any and every stage of the relationship. However, it is important to remember that we are limited in our progress not only by what the patient will say, but also by what he *can* say. In this sense we are always dependent in the process of psychotherapy upon nonverbal or indirect verbal communication. By the latter, we mean verbalizations from which we can infer (interpret) conclusions about the patient beyond the limits of those conclusions he has drawn about himself. The literary judgment, "Style is the man himself," is our most general guide to efforts in this direction. It directs our attention to the nonverbal aspects of the patient's behavior because it suggests that in this mode of functioning we shall discover much of the true individuality of our patient unhampered by traditional taboos on verbal communication. It suggests that the wider the limits we allow our patient or encourage him to utilize in verbal communication, the more leeway there is for "the man himself" to be manifested beyond the restraints of conventional communication.

What needs to be rigorously defined is not method but objective. The question that the novice should be asking himself is not: "What am I going to do?", but: "What am I trying to accomplish?" With this question clearly in mind, the psychotherapist can then consider the experience of his predecessors and colleagues as suggestive rather than coercive. If he has no ideas of his own, he may be well advised to follow the counsel of others. If his judgment is defective, he may find it necessary to follow a fairly set routine, although this may involve a considerable sacrifice in versatility. If, on the other hand, with his objectives clearly defined and the ethical standards of his profession carefully memorized, he decides to attempt new variations on the theme of establishing communicative relationships, only timidity can stop him.

COMMUNICATIONS TO THE PATIENT

Voluntary and involuntary communication.   In considering the psychotherapist's communications to the patient, we must make one further distinction beyond that between verbal and nonverbal communication. From the therapist's point of view we are concerned with the distinction between voluntary and involuntary nonverbal communication.

Let us see why this distinction is important. We began the preceding section of this chapter with an example of initial interactions with a child patient. It may be instructive to reread this material and see how much of the "communicating" that we do (or believe that we are doing) is nonverbal. However, all of this is intentional and voluntary; we "know what we are doing" and why. What we do *not* know is what else we are communicating about ourselves by nonverbal means. This, of course, is the involuntary or "giving ourselves away" aspect of nonverbal communication.

Involuntary communication.   It is this involuntary aspect of (usually) nonverbal communication that imposes upon the psychotherapist the requirement of being both open and honest with himself about his own feelings with respect to various kinds of people. It is what he cannot help "giving away" about himself to all those who are sufficiently perceptive to be aware of what he is doing. It is what gives his professors (and sometimes his colleagues) the right to judge his suitability for the very delicate and personal interactions of psychotherapy. Just as we suppose that we can find out more about the patient than he knows about himself by careful observation and accurate inference, we must also allow that the patient may find out more about ourselves than we necessarily "want" him to know. We consider it naive to ignore this point.

The only safeguards against such involuntary disclosure of a nature detrimental to the psychotherapeutic relationship are two. First, the psychotherapist must determine whether his own personal attitudes, values, and standards are consistent with those required for therapeutic relationships. When and where they are not, and cannot be changed with reasonable effort, then the second safeguard must be invoked, namely to avoid those relationships and/or those types of interaction in relationships for which he is not personally suited.

It is seldom safe to leave so significant an appraisal solely to the skill and presumably biased judgment of the potential psychotherapist himself. Appraisal by others, especially by those with considerable experience with the psychotherapeutic task and its requirements, would seem to be a minimum precaution. Psychotherapy for the psychotherapist serves the dual purpose of a prolonged opportunity for appraisal plus the possibility of changing characteristics that may become serious obstacles to psychotherapeutic effectiveness. In addition (although aside from our present concern), such an experience can also serve useful didactic or instructional purposes.

We suggest that this preliminary appraisal be supplemented by periodic reviews of one's work, once the psychotherapist is actively engaged in practice. (We assume, of course, that his work in training will be adequately supervised.) This may be done alone, but it will probably be more adequately done in collaboration with a trusted colleague. Similar consultation regarding persistent or recurring difficulties in the handling of cases is also advisable. Such consultation may indicate the need for further psychotherapy for the therapist.

Voluntary nonverbal communication.   It is interesting to note the predilection for verbal communication in the psychotherapeutic literature, especially that dealing with adult patients. Books dealing with psychotherapy with children have never been so biased in this respect, for the reason (we suspect) that children do not usually respond well to purely or predominantly verbal means of relating. As we have indicated earlier, the child first learns the "meaning" of nonverbal aspects of communication, since these are considerably more consistent and probably easier to discriminate than the verbal or "word" aspect. We believe this to be a reason for the child's orientation toward "expression" on the "expression–content" continuum in communication.

Another reason could be that "expression" is probably more directly and consistently associated with the emotions of the communicator and so yields the more useful clues regarding his further behavior than does "content." Those who work closely with children quickly become aware that the child himself is a great pantomimist and tends to use words only when necessary, especially in the first two or three years of life.

Working with children.   Working with young children provides good training in the nonverbal aspects of communicating with the patient. The child patient tends to watch the psychotherapist closely in order to receive clues for his own behavior. Facial expression, gesture, movement, and posture are all sources of significant information to the child. He is also extremely sensitive to voice quality—pitch, timbre, loudness, and pace. Candor about one's feelings is especially significant in relating to the child, because he is virtually certain to "read" the psychotherapist's feelings correctly and often even before the therapist himself is aware of them. Consequently it is our policy never to deny a child's allegations about our feelings without pausing for a certain amount of introspection, and to do so then only if we are quite sure of what those feelings are. The policy of never lying, even inadvertently, to the patient is quite crucial in maintaining relationships with children, since they tend to be both critical and unforgiving about this aspect of adult behavior. On the other hand, the child's realization that you will try always to be truthful with him is a quick way of "gaining points" in your relationship with him—which probably does not say much for his experience with adults in general.

Working with adults.   In contrast with children, who are rather uniformly sensitive at a given age to the nonverbal aspects of communication, adult patients may show an extreme variation in this respect. Although not strictly germane to the subject of communication, the following story will help to illustrate the point of patient obliviousness.

At one time we had quite a large collage, possibly three by five feet in dimensions, framed in dark brown but with some bright colors and reflective materials in the picture itself. It was hung on the wall that patients first saw as they entered the office. We finally decided that this picture was rather overpowering and replaced it with a picture about half as large with subdued colors in a vertical composition (rather than horizontal) and framed in white. After several months a patient who had been seeing us regularly asked, "When did you change the picture on that wall? I didn't notice until today."

At another extreme among adults are the patients who seem to even outdo the child in their sensitivity to variations in the psychotherapist's moods and feelings. It was such patients as these who may have caused Freud to justify the use of the couch for patients and staying out of their field of vision by saying that it was intolerable to be stared at for eight hours a day. We, at least, have deliberately used this arrangement for patients who were hyperattentive and hypersensitive to our moods and feelings. In all honesty we must admit that this strategem only partially solves the problem, since some patients are quite capable of picking up all the cues they need from their initial contact with the therapist plus subsequent impressions from voice alone.

An interactive episode.   However, rather than regarding such nonverbal communication to the patient only as a problem to be guarded against or resolved (which might be appropriate for certain involuntary communications), we should also consider their potential value as a means of communicating with the patient. This is true even of some involuntary responses. For example, recently we were helping an eight-year-old boy assemble a model kit. The model was too difficult for the child to assemble successfully himself (which was our mistake), and we were momentarily preoccupied with the model rather than with the child (a very major error). While we were so occupied, the boy picked up an awl from the tool kit and gave us several "playful" but rather sharp jabs in the buttocks with the awl. A moment later he was saying (with complete justification), "You're mad at me!" Our response was, "You are *right*, and anyone else will be angry if you do the same thing to him." Having become involved in an involuntary response that the patient correctly interpreted, we took advantage of the situation to verify his interpretation and generalize upon it. (Incidentally, we also apologized to the child, not for becoming angry or for what we had said, but for neglecting him in the therapeutic situation. In this way we acknowledged our awareness of his reason for being angry and the validity of his feelings under the circumstances.)

The importance of nonverbal communication. We are particularly concerned with nonverbal means of communicating to the patient because of our impression that such means may be especially potent as motivators and reinforcers. In the example just given it seems obvious that our anger was a much more impressive form of "communication" than a restrained verbal comment would have been. Generally speaking, however, we are more concerned with voluntary rather than involuntary responses on the therapist's part. We recall a clever bit of research which indicated that the experimenter could influence the frequency of a certain type of response in his subjects by nodding his head at appropriate points in the subject's communication (1). We believe that considerably more research along such lines is needed to clarify and to emphasize the potency of such nonverbal behavior on the therapist's part in influencing the subsequent behavior of the patient.

In lieu of such research the psychotherapist should consider carefully the potential value of facial expression, bodily movement, and posture as means of affecting the patient even when the therapist is not speaking. When he *is* speaking, then the voice qualities of pitch, timbre, loudness, and pace are means by which he can emphasize and increase the impact (especially the affective significance) of the words he is also using as a means of communicating with the patient.

VERBAL COMMUNICATION

The subject of verbal communication to the patient is embarrassingly complex to go into in any limited scope. We shall attempt to serve the purpose of this essay by indicating some of the more common kinds of communication to the patient along with some indication of the circumstances in which each might be appropriate or helpful.

Instructions to the patient regarding the therapeutic situation.   This is a type of communication that is sometimes overlooked or inadequately performed. It is especially important with the young, the less intelligent, and the more naive or uneducated patient. Every patient has a right to know what the "rules of the game" are, and no psychotherapist has the right to assume that he knows. This applies especially to "ground rules" that may be relatively peculiar to a particular therapist or to a particular approach to psychotherapy. "Rules of the game" include such mundane details as length of the psychotherapeutic appointment, the fee for each appointment, expected methods of payment, policy with respect to broken appointments, how vacation periods (both the patient's and the psychotherapist's) will be handled, and so on. Going beyond this, patients usually need some orientation as to what they are supposed to do during their appointment and what the psychotherapist will be doing. We may even, in certain cases, explain some of the reasons for the psychotherapist's activities and inactivities. The patient also needs some indication of limits for both his own and the psychotherapist's behavior in relating to each other, both during the appointment and at other times. Finally, the patient should know where his responsibility to the psychotherapist begins and ends and where the psychotherapist's responsibility to him begins and ends. Needless to say, all of these instructions should not be lumped at any single point in the relationship although there are good reasons for some of them to be given somewhere near the beginning.

Reflection, restatement, summarizing.   In "reflection," the psychotherapist repeats back to the patient some part of what he has said in the same words the patient has used. In this way the psychotherapist can indicate what he considers most significant in the patient's preceding communication and/or the subject about which he would like the patient to continue talking. "Restatement" involves the psychotherapist's repeating what he has understood the patient to say but reformulated in different words. This technique is useful for checking accuracy of communication between patient and therapist. It can also be used to emphasize a somewhat different facet of the subject under discussion than the patient has emphasized. The meaning of "summarizing" is obvious. It can be used to serve the same purposes as reflection and restatement. In addition, it can be helpful to the patient whose thinking and/or language tends to become confused, by clarifying "where he has been" in the communicative process.

These techniques may be used at any time with any kind of patient for the purposes indicated. How much of the psychotherapist's communication to the patient is of this nature may vary considerably with different types of patients. It may be used predominantly or almost exclusively with intelligent and verbal young adults whose problems are peripheral to basic character structure, as in counseling college students on matters of academic or vocational choice. Younger, less intelligent, less sophisticated, and more disturbed patients tend to be upset by the psychotherapist's apparent lack of participation or contribution if this approach is used without adequate explanation. We find ourselves usually using these techniques relatively less at the outset of most patient contacts and relatively more as he progresses in the development and use of verbal communicative skills.

Evaluation.   Evaluation involves the making and communicating of value judgments, including approval and disapproval. Many psychotherapists are radically opposed to the use of this technique, at least in theory. However, it seems rather unlikely that these same psychotherapists have no values of their own and do not evaluate the patient and his environment, whether or not they voluntarily communicate such judgments. We believe that most psychotherapists do, in fact, communicate their evaluations and may even do so verbally and voluntarily when the judgment involves *approval* of the patient. We are inclined to the use of evaluations because of our concern about motivation and reinforcement as necessary conditions for habit formation or reformation. However, we are aware that evaluations have little or no value in affecting the behavior of the patient until a considerable degree of rapport has been established. The need for a considerable acceptance of the psychotherapist by the patient is especially acute when negative evaluations are involved; otherwise, of course, we run the risk of alienating the patient from the relationship.

Since evaluation always is relative to some specific standard or criterion, the patient should (we believe) usually be told what standard is involved. Examples: "I (the psychotherapist) think that was a hostile thing to do"; "They (the others involved) probably thought you were being hostile"; "Would you consider your behavior in that situation hostile?" "Perhaps most people would think you were being hostile if you behaved in that way."

Interpretation.   As the examples that we have just used will indicate, it is sometimes difficult to draw a hard and fast distinction between evaluation and interpretation. Generally speaking, when we interpret we are making an inference, drawing a conclusion, or creating an abstraction about the patient's communication that the patient himself has not made (or at least has not communicated.) Sometimes interpretation involves interpolation or extrapolation from information the patient *has* given us to indicate other things, which might be or probably are true. Since interpretations are always in fact hypothetical, we consider it important that their tentative nature be indicated to the patient in most instances. The psychotherapist can use such phrases as "it is possible," "we might conclude," "this would seem to indicate," and so on. However, we allow some variation in practice when such qualifications might be interpreted by the patient as indicating that the psychotherapist is basically uncertain about his own conclusions. Actually, we usually avoid making interpretations to the patient until we have enough evidence to be reasonably sure of our conclusions.

An equally critical consideration is the matter of when the patient is ready for an interpretation. The clearest guide we can give to this matter of timing interpretation is to point out that the patient usually has at his disposal the same (or an even more adequate) basis for interpretation, in terms of knowledge about his feelings, past experiences, dreams, and so forth. Assuming a reasonable degree of intelligence on the patient's part, why does he not do his own interpreting? The client-centered therapists assume that he will, in fact, do this. In some cases, however, the patient may lack the necessary intelligence, suitable frames of reference, or other attributes necessary for the formulation of interpretations. In such cases (with children, for example) a certain amount of informing or educating the patient may be a necessary prelude to interpretation. In still other instances, what seems obvious to the psychotherapist and by any reasonable criterion should also be obvious to the patient, is categorically rejected by the patient. Such instances illustrate the psychoanalytic concept of "resistance," or more specifically emotional resistance. When the psychotherapist encounters this type of reaction to interpretation, he should recognize that some change in feelings or attitude will necessarily have to precede any change in the patient's cognitive structure based on his "acceptance" of the interpretation.

Sharing experience.   The possibility of the psychotherapist's sharing some of his experiences with the patient by communicating about himself to the patient was suggested to us by our experience in group therapy. We believe that in group therapy the sharing of experiences among patients and between therapist and patient has value, especially in helping each person to distinguish between the social mask (persona) and the "inner self" of the various individuals involved. We have found it a rather tricky technique that can backfire to the detriment of the psycho-therapeutic relationship, especially early in that relationship, when only a single patient and the therapist are involved. There can be little question but that some patients initially "prefer" to maintain their own opinions and evaluation of the psychotherapist and are resentful of any communication which would tend to change the image they apparently "need" at that point. It has been interesting to observe this attitude change very considerably as a function of (what we have evaluated as) progress toward self-sufficiency.

We have also used this technique in working with those adolescents and other patients who seem to take forever in deciding whether they will accept the psychotherapeutic relationship in any truly functional sense. Such patients often seem to want as much information as possible about the psychotherapist before committing themselves, even to the extent of their communicating adequately. We are less certain of the justification of using the "sharing" technique for this purpose except that it seems "to work" in quite a few cases, especially among adolescents. Perhaps this is because the adolescent who reacts to adults primarily as "hostile others" must be given some specific bases for positive identification with the psychotherapist before he will include the therapist in his own personal "in-group."

Information giving.   Giving the patient information that he does not (apparently) have but that is relevant to a situation with which he is involved can be either very helpful or a waste of time. It may be a waste of time, for instance, if the patient already has the information but has not communicated it, although there may be some value in the psycho-therapist's knowing that he has had the information. Information giving may be largely a waste of time if the patient is not properly or sufficiently motivated to use it or fails to see the relevance of the information to his situation. We have found, however, that the value of information given cannot always be judged by the patient's immediate or short-run response. In many instances we believe that information which the patient has appeared to ignore has actually been retained and may be used by him weeks, months or even years after the original communication.

When, to whom, and how to give information to patients is a topic of considerable complexity, which would merit an extensive treatise in its own right. We happen to believe that it is a legitimate psychothera-peutic technique which can have significant value for most patients if properly used, although it tends to be overlooked and underused by most psychotherapists (if we judge only by what they say and write). We tend to use this technique more often with younger, less intelligent, and less educated patients, although we probably use it with most patients to some extent. We may also rely rather heavily on information giving when we have reason to believe that our contact with the patient will be brief.

Suggestion.   We include under the heading of "suggestion" all communications of the psychotherapist that tell the patient, either directly or indirectly, to do some particular thing. As a means of helping the patient, suggestion does not seem to be highly regarded by most professional psychotherapists, although it is probably the technique most frequently used by laymen in attempting to help others. Perhaps the fact that most of us have been given "good advice" we ignored has tended to bias most psychotherapists against its use. We might also consider the possibility that the person who uses suggestion definitely "goes out on a limb," in the sense that if the suggestion is followed but the results are not those predicted, the person who makes the suggestion will usually be held responsible.

We, however, consider it irresponsible to ignore the fact that suggestion, when properly used, may provide the most direct means of influencing the patient's behavior. It can function as motivation, cue, and reinforcement (provided by the suggestor's tacit approval), leaving only the matter of response to the initiative of the patient. Obviously this makes it a very "powerful" means of controlling the patient's behavior under optimal conditions. Naturally, a commensurate degree of responsibility must go along with the use of this "control" over the patient. We may allow that some psychotherapists would prefer not to assume this degree of responsibility. However, we would consider it only ethical for those who prefer to avoid such responsibility also to avoid handling cases where the use of suggestion could produce results superior to those obtainable by other techniques.

We cannot be sure that we have been exhaustive in considering the various ways in which the psychotherapist can communicate to the patient verbally, but we have tried to suggest some of the more commonly used techniques and a few we believe might profitably be used more frequently than they are.

SUMMARY

In order to appreciate the significance of communication in psychotherapy, we must realize that "relating" and "communicating" are virtually synonymous. We can stress either the relating or the communicating aspect of psychotherapy within certain limits, depending on the predilections or limitations of either therapist or patient. What we cannot afford to ignore is the emotional interaction that is both an inevitable and a necessary part of the psychotherapeutic process.

If we conceptualize the scope of psychotherapy in terms of those who might be benefitted, rather than in terms of those who are easiest to work with, we begin to encounter the problem of eliciting communication from the patient. Many potential patients (in the first sense) have limited skills in verbal communication and/or lack appropriate motivation. However, the psychotherapist *always* has one source of information about the patient: the patient's nonverbal behavior. To illustrate this point, we have included a description of an initial contact with a child to indicate the psychotherapist's observation of, interpretation of, and response to the child's nonverbal behavior.

Many years of experimentation and research have yielded a variety of methods for eliciting information from the patient. Working on projects, artistic productions, psychodrama, and written communications are illustrative of some of these means. Free association helps some patients to communicate but seriously hinders others. The relating of dreams can be conceptualized as a means by which the patient can communicate information about himself to the therapist when he has questions about whether the therapist will accept the information without rejecting him. The use of hypnosis or of drugs to facilitate communication is regarded as an extreme measure because of the gross distortion of the psychotherapeutic relationship that occurs under these conditions.

With some patients the psychotherapist's problem may be one of controlling or limiting verbalization rather than the problem of eliciting adequate communication.

The attitude we recommend is one of flexibility in attempting to adapt communicative techniques to the limitations of the patient. The psychotherapist who is unable to do this may find his usefulness as a therapist unduly limited. Our general objective, however, is constant: more complete, open, and effective communication from the patient.

In considering the psychotherapist's communications *to* the patient, we must be aware of both voluntary and involuntary communication. The latter (involuntary communication) means that we must insist upon certain precautions in the selection and training of psychotherapists if the welfare of patients is to be safeguarded.

The deliberate use of nonverbal communication by the psychotherapist is a subject that has been largely neglected. Those who work with children find themselves relying on nonverbal communication as a matter of necessity, because of the child's limited tolerance for verbal communication. Adult patients, on the other hand, vary greatly in their sensitivity to the psychotherapist's nonverbal behavior. We stress the importance of nonverbal communication because we believe it can be a useful therapeutic tool and also because it may have more affective impact under certain conditions than verbal communication.

In the last section of the chapter we take up techniques of verbal communication. We have not tried to be especially comprehensive, since the references given in the suggestions for further reading will supply detailed discussions of technique. Rather, we have taken up some techniques that are often used (such as summarizing, reflecting, restating, and interpreting), some that are seldom used (such as sharing), and some (such as suggestion and information-giving) that may have fallen into undeserved disrepute or neglect. All of these should be given further critical clinical and experimental consideration in view of the diverse needs of today's more heterogeneous patient population.

SUGGESTIONS FOR FURTHER READING

For the reader's information regarding the psychoanalytic means of dealing with communication, he may consult Freud's *Collected Papers*, Volume 2 (2), especially Chapters XXXI and XXXII. Menninger (3) discusses interpretation and other communications to the patient in Chapter IV. Fromm-Reichmann (4) devotes all of Part II to the psychotherapeutic process, with Chapters VIII and IX being particularly relevant to communication.

Much information about "interview" therapy with children will be found in Rogers (5), Chapters X and XI. Axline (6) offers a good description of play therapy in Part III of her book.

Those who want an economical survey of communicative techniques should consult Brammer and Shostrom (7), Chapters 7, 9 and 10. Bach (8) provides an excellent discussion of communication in group therapy in Chapters 6 through 10. Rosen (9) discusses "radical" means of communicating with very disturbed patients in Papers 1 and 7. Frank's entire book (10) in concerned with suggestion (our term) or persuasion (his term) and its role in psychotherapy.

Dollard and Miller (11) offer a brief chapter (Chapter XXV) on "Techniques of Therapeutic Intervention." Ruesch (12) presents a very sophisticated and detailed analysis of the same subject. If the reader must be selective, we recommend Chapters 4, 8, 10, and 11.

For those who have ample time we strongly suggest the reading of Sullivan's *The Psychiatric Interview* (13).

REFERENCES

1. Greenspoon, J. The effect of two nonverbal stimuli on the frequency of two verbal response classes. *Amer. Psychol.*, 1954, *9*, 384.

*2. Freud, S. *Collected papers*, vol. 2. New York: Basic Books, 1959.

*3. Menninger, K. *Theory of psychoanalytic technique*. New York: Science Editions, 1961. (Basic Books, 1958.)

*4. Fromm-Reichmann F. *Principles of intensive psychotherapy*. Chicago: Phoenix, 1960. (University of Chicago Press, 1950.)

5. Rogers, C. R. *The clinical treatment of the problem child*. Boston: Houghton Mifflin, 1939.

6. Axline, V. M. *Play therapy*. Boston: Houghton Mifflin, 1947.

7. Brammer, L. M., and Shostrom, E. L. *Therapeutic psychology*. Englewood Cliffs, N.J.: Prentice-Hall, 1960.

8. Bach, G. *Intensive group psychotherapy*. New York: Ronald, 1954.

9. Rosen, J. N. *Direct analysis*. New York: Grune & Stratton, 1953.

*10. Frank, J. D. *Persuasion and healing*. New York: Schocken Books, 1963. (Johns Hopkins Press, 1961.)

11. Dollard, J., and Miller, N. E. *Personality and psychotherapy*. New York: McGraw-Hill, 1950.

12. Ruesch, J. *Therapeutic communication*. New York: Norton, 1961.

13. Sullivan, H. S. *The psychiatric interview*. New York: Norton, 1954.

* Paperback edition.

Chapter 11 | *Changing Cognitive Structure*

USING COMMUNICATION TO CHANGE COGNITIVE STRUCTURE

Receptive versus passive attitudes toward the patient.   A brief review of the ways in which the psychotherapist may respond to the patient will indicate that the psychotherapeutic relationship begins with the therapist in a predominantly receptive role. This role is obvious when we speak of reflection, evaluation, and interpretation because such responses require that the psychotherapist first be communicated *to*. However, a moment's thought will suggest that even those responses that involve more initiative on the part of the psychotherapist (such as sharing, giving information, and suggestion) require a considerable knowledge of the patient if they are to be used most constructively and effectively. We would go so far as to suggest that the tendency to avoid the use of such techniques may be based upon their being easy to misuse.

Such misuse is, in turn, quite likely to be associated with the possibility of using such techniques before knowing the patient well enough. For example, the psychotherapist may try to impress the patient or to satisfy a patient's desire for quick results by making suggestions about what the patient should do early in the relationship. However, until the therapist knows the patient thoroughly, the chances are that his premature suggestions will be little, if any, more useful to the patient than the "advice" he has already received from others or considered on his own initiative. Such a response on the therapist's part might, in such circumstances, cause the patient to lose confidence in him or to become prematurely discouraged with the potentialities of the psychotherapeutic approach to his problems.

To say that the psychotherapist is initially predominantly *receptive* is not at all the same thing as saying that he is predominantly *passive*. In fact, it is quite detrimental to the psychotherapeutic task for the therapist to have anything like a passive attitude at this stage or to create such an impression upon the patient. The psychotherapist should be aware of the importance of establishing a relationship with the patient as quickly as possible. He must react to the patient in order to do this, and yet he needs information from the patient before determining his own reaction. To illustrate this point, it may be instructive to reread the material in the preceding chapter about our handling of an initial contact with a child. Our responses are determined by the child's response to the situation. If we are not actively and intensely receptive in these initial moments, the child may be alienated beyond any hope of establishing effective rapport.

When we have observed students under our supervision making errors in initial contacts, it has usually been evident that the student was concerned with *his* responses to the situation in a manner and to an extent which precluded his being sufficiently receptive to the patient's responses.

"Reactive" versus "active."   Various "schools" of psychotherapy have taken different positions as to how "active" the psychotherapist should be in the therapeutic relationship. We believe that this issue and others could be resolved or simplified if we defined the psychotherapist's role as predominantly *reactive*. We find it impossible to designate any specific sequence of maneuvers in the psychotherapeutic relationship, because we find ourselves reacting differently to each person according to his own behavior and the particular needs he manifests. If he needs help in communicating, we help him to communicate, but only after we become aware that he needs help. We may even help him to communicate by taking the initiative in communicating. However, taking the initiative is then a reaction, and only one of several possible reactions, to his difficulty.

Our respect for the integrity of the patient as an individual is manifested, then, in treating him as an individual with his own particular attributes and needs. We do not treat him as a classified object in terms of what is considered beneficial for persons classified in a particular way. Nor do we have certain "rules and regulations" for psychotherapeutic interaction that the patient must learn and agree to (and be able to) follow if we are to help him. Rather we believe that with the variety of interactions which are possible between two persons within the limits of the psychotherapeutic relationship and with well-defined general objectives, the psychotherapist should be able to use the former to achieve the latter without following a rigidly prescribed formula.

An individualized orientation.   But how does one explain an infinitely variable process? Obviously we must resort to generalizations. However, it is important for the reader to note that the generalizations we employ are always limited or conditional. Whether *all* patients have a poor sexual adjustment or problems in expressing hostility or feelings of inadequacy are not matters of primary concern to us. What we are concerned with is whether this particular patient has any or all of these problems and (if he does) the extent to which each is responsible for his unfavorable emotional balance.

The task we set for the psychotherapist is, of course, made more difficult by this individualized orientation. We insist that the psychotherapist learn enough from his patient about the nature of the patient's communication, cognitive structure, and feelings so that he can make certain crucial decisions regarding the therapist's function in the psychotherapeutic process. He must decide which problems in communication and which distortions in cognitive structure are most consequential so far as the patient's feeling balance is concerned. He must decide upon a certain sequence or order of priority in which these problems can most readily be corrected. Finally, he must decide for each patient the maximally effective means of communicating (and relating) in order to produce the required changes.

The use of verbal techniques.   In this chapter we shall illustrate the use of the communicative techniques described in Chapter 10 in dealing with some of the more common distortions in cognitive structure (including omissions and additions) that have been discussed previously. We shall be primarily concerned with verbal communication because it is easier to talk about. Our concentration of attention upon verbal communication, however, does not imply any contradiction of earlier statements regarding the significance of nonverbal communication. So far as eliciting communication from the patient is concerned, the psychotherapist's expression of interest, attention, acceptance, and approval are at least as important as any verbal communication that he can make to the patient, although all of these attitudes may be conveyed more or less adequately without the use of words.

Such nonverbal reactions are especially important at the outset when the psychotherapist's function may be primarily receptive so far as verbal communication is concerned. The patient will usually not proceed very far in discussing himself without looking for indications of reaction from the psychotherapist. How he proceeds (and, sometimes, whether he proceeds) will certainly be affected by the kind of "feedback" he gets from the psychotherapist, yet this may involve very little verbal communication.

Similarly, in dealing with cognitive structure, the reactions of the psychotherapist (especially expressions of attitude) are of considerable significance in motivating and reinforcing changes and even in indicating what changes might be made. Smiles, frowns, approving nods, laughter, silence, and so on are means of expression, but they are also means of communication that the psychotherapist can use to the advantage of the therapeutic process. It would be naive to assume either that such expressions do not occur or that they have no significant impact on the further responses of the patient.

Viewed the other way around, if the psychotherapist has his procedures and objectives clearly in mind (based, of course, on his knowledge of the individual patient), then even his involuntary reactions may serve the purposes of therapy. This assertion is based upon the assumption that if the therapist's thinking has a certain directional emphasis so far as the patient's development is concerned, his involuntary reactions will tend to reinforce positively the patient's "movement" in that direction and to reinforce negatively regressive or irrelevant movement.

The self concept.   Aside from limiting our consideration in this chapter primarily to verbal means of communication, we shall be concerned predominantly with the self concept. The importance of the self concept in determining the patient's mode of functioning, goals, and feelings, we have tried to indicate in preceding chapters. There we have also suggested that most often we expect to encounter in the patient a self-evaluation which represents a distortion of the true characteristics, value, "goodness," and so forth, of the self. The task of changing the self concept is therefore usually of considerable significance in the psychotherapeutic process. By concentrating on the self concept, rather than the totality of cognitive structure, we can attempt to be both specific and concrete about procedures in psychotherapy without coming down to the hyperspecificity of the individual case.

Caveat.   Our expository concentration upon changing the self concept is not to be interpreted as indicating an exclusive interest in this problem nor necessarily a predominant interest in this problem in all cases. It is a common problem in psychotherapy, and usually an important one, but the process of psychotherapy also involves a number of other challenging aspects. We shall discuss the more important of these in our final chapter.

THE INITIAL INTERVIEW

Expressing interest.   In our first contact with the patient we try to indicate by both verbal and nonverbal means that we are interested in whatever he has to say. This may be considered our first active psychotherapeutic effort on behalf of the patient. It is not unusual for patients to apologize for coming in with their problem. This takes the form of their saying that they are aware that others have much more serious problems and theirs are really not so important, but . . . We may consider that such statements really constitute an inquiry to the psychotherapist as to whether *he* feels that they are justified in taking up his time. We assure the patient that we are interested in hearing more about what he has to say. In this way we tell the patient that we consider him worth at least an hour of our time, without being forced to make a premature evaluation as to how significant the problem really is.

Actually we know that in most cases his problems must be of considerable importance to the patient, otherwise he would not have taken the trouble to secure a referral, phone for an appointment, and keep it at some inconvenience and expense to himself. However, immediate assurance on this point may be misunderstood or mistrusted by the patient, who will ask himself how the therapist can *really* consider himself or his problem important until he knows more about them.

Such apologies, when they are made, are usually a reliable indication of negative self-evaluations on the patient's part and serve as an early clue to the importance of this factor in the patient's total problem situation. Other early indications of such self-depreciation, at least relative to the status of the psychotherapist in the patient's eyes, are an excessive formality or restraint in behavior, formality in speech (attempting to talk the therapist's "language"), frequent use of the therapist's title, use of the term "sir" in addressing the therapist, and so on. Such responses from the patient also may indicate rather clearly that he is reacting to the psychotherapist as an "authority" or "quasi-parental" figure and is using modes of communication and behavior he is accustomed to using in relating to such persons. The degree of distortion involved in such a transfer depends upon the "real" differences between therapist and patient in age, education, socio-economic status, or whatever dimensions of comparison the patient may be using in making his evaluation. In such a situation verbal assurances and nonverbal expressions of interest on the part of the psychotherapist make some contribution to the patient's feeling of being of some significance or importance.

Receptive attitude.   The psychotherapist's playing a predominantly receptive role in this initial contact may be considered another means by which he enhances the patient's feeling of value or importance. The patient may indicate that he does not know what to say. By telling him that whatever he wants to say will probably be of value, we indicate confidence in his intelligence and judgment.

Actually we have rather effective means of controlling the content of the patient's communication without obviously correcting or redirecting him in a manner that may tend to make him feel inadequate or "in the wrong." The communicative techniques of reflection, restatement, and summarizing are very useful at this stage for this purpose. By these means we can indicate what we are more interested in by including such material in our reflection, restatement, or summary and not including in such responses that information which we consider less relevant.

More directly, but in a positively reinforcing way, we can use evaluation, for example: "What you were just saying about your relationship with your boss is very interesting. I would like to hear more about that." In this manner we can elicit particular information that we may want for our preliminary evaluation while still complimenting the patient on his discernment in bringing the topic into his conversation.

Generally we avoid more active intrusions into the communication during the middle part of the initial appointments. We have found that inclinations to evaluate (prematurely), interpret, share, give information or make suggestions at this time are likely to be due to feeling somewhat threatened in our own ego-evaluation as compared with our evaluation of the patient. We interpret our own impulse to intervene in these ways as indicating that we are anxious to do something to assert or establish our own value. Such competitive impulses are injurious to the self-esteem of the patient if successfully acted out and injurious to the relationship (status of the psychotherapist in the patient's eyes) in any event.

Ending the first interview.   Different considerations, however, govern our communication at the end of the initial interview. One of the most significant of these concerns the patient's need or desire for "closure." This has several aspects. First, the patient has risked his ego in initiating the contact and seeking a relationship with the psychotherapist. If he is still interested in pursuing that relationship at the end of the initial appointment, he wants to know as soon as possible whether he has been "accepted" by the psychotherapist. Second, he wants to know whether he has done the right thing in seeking psychotherapeutic assistance with his problem. Third, he wants to know whether the psychotherapist thinks his problems can be successfully handled. He may also intrude other questions about the total amount of time and money involved, although most of our adult patients are aware that such questions cannot reasonably be answered except, perhaps, in terms of minima.

Our usual procedure is to deal first of all with the significance of the problem and the suitability of a psychotherapeutic approach to it. If our evaluation is at least tentatively positive in both respects, we inform the patient of this evaluation. We next evaluate for the patient the assets and liabilities that he may have relative to the goals he has indicated. Here, if we have considerable confidence in the outcome of psychotherapy, we may so indicate and stress primarily the patient's assets as a further measure to improve the patient's self concept. Finally, we deal with the matter of our own suitability for working with the patient and by this means indicate our acceptance (or rejection) of the patient. In the case of acceptance, this may be done very simply by saying that we believe we should be able to help the patient and would be interested in working with him. Our final step is to relieve the patient of any feeling of inadequacy about how to proceed by taking the initiative in arranging for the next appointment and giving basic information about payment of fees and similar procedural matters.

Obviously we are pursuing several objectives in these procedures and communications. So far as the patient's self concept is concerned we attempt to communicate the following:

(a) We are glad that he has contacted us.
(b) We are interested in what he has to say and want to know more about him.
(c) We consider him competent to communicate adequately about himself and his situation.
(d) We have received adequate information to make certain basic evaluations.
(e) He has acted correctly in seeking psychotherapeutic assistance.
(f) He is probably capable of benefiting from psychotherapy.
(g) We would like to continue the relationship with him.
(h) It is our responsibility, rather than his, to make appropriate arrangements for the continuance of the relationship.

EARLY PHASE: FIRST ASPECT

Establishing a communicative relationship.   Once a mutual agreement to attempt to establish a psychotherapeutic relationship has been arrived at, the initial phase of psychotherapy begins. In general, we characterize this early phase as that in which a relationship is established and adequate communication starts to develop. We must discuss the nature of this relationship briefly in order to explain why certain communicative techniques tend to predominate in this phase of psychotherapy.

Actually we are concerned with two different relationships, one ostensible and one hidden. The ostensible relationship is one of equality between patient and therapist. The inadequate self concept of the patient is "defended" at this point by both the patient and the psychotherapist. The patient cannot tolerate any further depreciation of the self concept and defends this self concept by insisting (in various ways, both verbal and nonverbal) that he is relating to the therapist as an "equal" and does not "need" an emotional relationship with him. The therapist respects the patient's need for this defense by not discussing the "other" aspect of the relationship at this point.

This "other" aspect of the relationship is that the patient *must* feel inadequate or he would not have sought the psychotherapist's assistance in the first place. Furthermore, he must also *want* something from the psychotherapist, so he will like the therapist and be pleased with him if his needs are met, and he will be frustrated and angry with the therapist if his needs are not met. There must, then, be an emotional relationship involved. It may be only potential at the outset, but these basic emotional reactions *must* be involved before the psychotherapeutic relationship comes to an end. So the "hidden" relationship *is*, in fact, an emotional relationship between patient and therapist.

More specifically, however, the patient comes to the psychotherapist to have something done for him that he cannot do for himself. Therefore the patient's position in the relationship is a *dependent* one, in the sense that the patient needs and expects certain kinds of assistance from the therapist which the therapist does not need or expect from the patient. (The psychotherapist is ultimately dependent upon his patients for his livelihood, but he is not dependent, even in this respect, upon any specific patient.) In this sense the psychotherapeutic relationship involves the therapist in a quasi-parental role with the patient.

Communicative problems. The communicative problem of the early phase of psychotherapy is largely related to the discrepancy between the ostensible and the hidden aspects of the therapeutic relationship. Briefly, this problem is that if the psychotherapist dominates this phase, the patient will retreat from or escape from such an obvious indication of his own inadequacy. If, on the other hand, the psychotherapist is passive, the patient will feel that he is not getting the help he needs and wants and may terminate the relationship for this reason. Therefore the psychotherapist must communicate with the patient in such a way as to avoid creating either the impression of domination or the impression of passivity.

We handle this problem by encouraging or allowing the patient to continue telling us about himself, much as he has done in the initial interviews. This places him in temporary "control" of the relationship and helps to allay any initial anxieties about being dominated and dictated to. If the patient is very explicit about his dependency, to the extent of indicating that he needs help in order to communicate at all, we give the minimal assistance required and encourage the patient to do as well as he can on his own. During these initial interviews of the early phase, we rely heavily on reflection, restatement, and summarizing as forms of communication to the patient. These techniques represent the least obvious kinds of intervention on the therapist's part, while still providing him with means of directing the patient's communication to some extent. Furthermore, they serve the valuable function of enabling the psychotherapist to check the accuracy of his understanding of the patient's communication. Restatement is particularly valuable for this purpose. Reflection and summarizing are useful techniques for clarifying the basic "structure" of the patient's communication, that is, for distinguishing more significant from less significant aspects of the patient's communication and for clarifying relationships between different parts of his communication.

Giving help.   During these initial interviews we respond to the "hidden" aspects of the relationship (the patient's need for help) by remaining alert, interested, and attentive and by using the techniques mentioned above as our "active" contribution to the process of communicating. As each interview comes to a close, however, the patient seems to become rather acutely aware that another appointment has passed and that a certain amount of time must intervene before he has another opportunity to receive help from the therapist. In other words, having defended his autonomy and his adequacy by communicating actively during most of the hour (with the therapist's cooperation), the hidden aspect of the relationship now comes to the fore, and he wants the therapist to do something for him.

Almost any kind of communicative response from the psychotherapist may be appropriate at this point, so long as it represents an adequate recognition of and response to the patient's desire to receive something useful from the therapist. However at this stage in therapy, we prefer some form of ego-enhancing evaluation. To illustrate, suppose we say: "You brought out some very important points this time. What you were saying about your relationship with your older brother seems to be especially significant." What might be accomplished by such a statement? We indicate to the patient the following: (a) some progress has been made today (important to his need for help); (b) he (the patient) has been largely responsible for the progress (therefore we regard him as functioning adequately). On the other hand, (c) we have been actively involved ourselves (since we can make this evaluation). And, (d) we have some concrete plan for procedure (indicated by our saying what we consider most significant). In addition, we may have helped to direct further communication into an area where we need more information.

Ending the defensive phase. Sooner or later this "defensive" aspect of the early phase comes to an end. Occasionally such termination occurs on the initiative of the psychotherapist. This must be done when the patient seems inclined to prolong this phase indefinitely as a means of avoiding his anxiety about facing or acknowledging the "hidden" relationship. The psychotherapist should be able to recognize the essentially defensive nature of the patient's behavior when he notes that a considerable amount of time has gone by without any significant addition to his knowledge of the patient or his environment. (Of course the psychotherapist must be reasonably sure that he has done everything possible to facilitate such advancement.)

More generally the "defensive" aspect of the early phase of therapy comes to an end when the initiative of the patient in communicating with minimal active help from the psychotherapist has been exhausted. The psychotherapist's objective, however, is to extend the patient's progress in communicating as far as possible before assuming active control. There are two reasons for this. If the patient is sufficiently competent and/or his difficulties are not too complicated, he may be able to resolve them with minimal assistance from the psychotherapist. When this is possible, the patient's self-esteem is enhanced rather than undergoing some further temporary depreciation as will otherwise occur. The second reason breaks down into two parts. First, we want the patient to see how much he can do before involuntarily relinquishing control to the psychotherapist. Second, it is quite important to the subsequent relationship between patient and therapist that the patient realize that the therapist assumes control *when* the patient cannot go further and *because* he cannot go further without more active assistance. In other words, the psychotherapist tries to make it as obvious as possible that his more active intervention is in response to the patient's need rather than being a manifestation of his own need to dominate and to control.

So far as the self concept is concerned, the defensive aspect of the early phase ends when the patient has communicated all he "knows" (or is willing to tell) about himself. During this defensive phase the patient may follow one or more of three patterns. One pattern is to avoid discussion of the self as much as possible while directing the therapist's attention toward external agencies as the "cause" of his problems. Another pattern is to deny weakness, inadequacy, or inferiority. The third pattern is to expose his own conception and evaluation of himself—in other words, to stress and emphasize what is wrong with him to the exclusion of any positive evaluation. In practice, only rarely do patients communicate about themselves exclusively in any one of these three modes. Various mixtures may occur, depending upon a number of variables. For example, the same patient who has made very negative statements about himself on his own initiative may deny the same statements when the therapist later communicates them back to him.

EARLY PHASE: SECOND ASPECT

Transition to the second aspect.   In any event, the patient cannot account for his own behavior in terms of what he "knows" about himself. Still less can he point to the logic of his behavior in terms of what he communicates to the therapist during the defensive aspect of the early phase. When the psychotherapist points to illogicalities or discrepancies, the patient does not account for them adequately or says that he "doesn't know." As indicated before, the psychotherapist may use reflection, restatement, or summarizing as "gentle" means of exposing the inadequacies or illogicalities in the patient's communication about himself. If such relatively "passive" probing still leaves the patient confronting the unresolved enigma of his own behavior, then the psychotherapist must assume a more active role if further progress is to be made. Just as obviously, the patient must be able to accept the "hidden" relationship, which can no longer remain hidden.

To help the patient in accepting this new definition of the relationship (which may be painful for him since it is a "real" indication of his inadequacy), the transition should be made gradually. The reasons are: first, the patient is less likely to be so threatened as to leave the therapeutic situation prematurely; second, psychotherapy is like surgery in that the therapist attempts to accomplish his purpose with the least radical procedure which will be effective. Unless he is extremely skilled, the safest procedure is from less to more extreme measures until "something gives."

Communicative techniques.   The communicative techniques which best suit this "transitional" situation (in addition to reflection, restatement, and summarizing) are probably sharing, giving information, and interpretation—in that order. *Sharing* involves equalitarian roles in the communicative process, but it does require the patient to accept the psychotherapist as a real person, in contrast with the patient's own projections about the therapist, which he can (and does) arrange in accordance with his own needs. *Giving information* changes the communicative relationship from an equalitarian to an authoritative one, with the psychotherapist obviously functioning as the "authority." Although this is a direct and obvious reflection of the "hidden" relationship, giving information does not involve coercion of the patient in any way, except perhaps by implication. The psychotherapist is serving as the "authority" in the sense of "expert." The patient is not required to *do* anything as a result of this kind of communication.

Interpretation takes us one step further in this direction. Actually it is a form of information giving. One distinction, however, is that the "information" is hypothetical rather than "factual." It represents the psychotherapist's own reaction to the "facts" presented to him by the patient. The other distinction is that there *is* an element of coercion implied in interpretation, since the interpretation (if used correctly) is something which the patient must accept as a part of his own cognitive structure if further advances are to be made. (Any other use of interpretation would cause us to reclassify it either as information giving or as suggestion.) Of course interpretations which are so clearly and obviously related to the "facts" or are so nonthreatening that they are easily accepted by the patient involve this "coercive" element less than interpretations the patient has difficulty in accepting.

This leaves "evaluation" and "suggestion" as the most "controlling" communicative techniques. The reason for including "evaluation" so near the top of the "controlling" continuum is perhaps obvious. The psychotherapist cannot evaluate, by definition, without creating emotional reactions, which is the same thing as saying that he cannot evaluate without setting up motivational valences. Although the specific action or direction of movement may not be *explicitly* defined by evaluation, it is strongly and clearly defined nevertheless. For example, to say to the patient, "You do not allow yourself enough time for recreation," clearly indicates that you want him to allow himself *more* time for recreation.

In order to cross the border over into suggestion, where the desired response is explicitly stated, we need only say, "You must allow yourself more time for recreation." Here the psychotherapist is obviously telling the patient what to do, which is about as far as we can go in controlling the subject in terms of the informative connotation of verbal communication. (We might, however, conceivably affect his behavior more by means of the affective connotations of verbal communication or by means of nonverbal communication—such as expressions indicating extreme repugnance or disgust.)

Objectives in the second phase. What specific objectives are we pursuing by means of these techniques? So far as the self concept is concerned we enter into a fascinating task in the latter aspect of the early phase of psychotherapy. Usually we find evidence in the initial phase that we are dealing with three different self concepts rather than one. We pick up bits and pieces (occasionally a fairly whole and clear picture) of a conception of the self as inadequate, inferior, "bad," and so on. This conception is most obviously related to the patient's evaluation of himself and other's evaluations of him as he has been, especially in infancy and childhood. Clearly related to this depreciated self concept we find a second conception of the self, representing compensatory phantasies that involve positive feelings about the self to "neutralize" or compensate for the negative feelings created by the depreciated self concept. There is still a third conception of the self in terms of the person's contemporary or still pertinent attributes that constitute a more or less valid or realistic image and an evaluation of valid characteristics by "reasonable" standards.

We may conceptualize the second aspect of the early phase as involving the clear and complete delineation of these three aspects of the self. In other words, we want to bring out, in as great detail as possible, all the attributes of these three selves. We want to determine the patient's evaluation of each self. We want to create, through the communicative relationship, an "awareness" of these three "selves" and appropriate verbal responses to enable the patient to communicate about them to himself or with others. Finally, we want similarly to explicate the relationship of these "selves" to the patient's feelings and behavior, including his emotional "problems" and his frustrated aspirations for his own behavior.

Resistance.   The second aspect of the early phase is a time of strong feeling and therefore of active resistance on the part of the patient. His negative feelings about the depreciated self create strong impulses to avoid awareness of and communication about the characteristics of *this* self. He is also reluctant to accept the evaluation of the compensatory self as fictional, since the compensatory self is the "equalizer" that the patient needs to balance off the negative feelings aroused by the characteristics of the depreciated self image. In the typical patient the concept of the real self is not strong enough or clear enough at this point to afford the patient any great amount of assurance or security. Besides, in order to fit the definition of "real," this concept of the self must include "real" inferiorities, inadequacies, and so on. The patient is ultimately limited not only because he "feels" inferior but because he "*is*" inferior, in certain respects.

What the patient needs.   During this stage of therapy the patient has several kinds of very strong "needs" for the psychotherapist. First of all, he "needs" the psychotherapist to see those negative aspects of the depreciated and real self that his feelings strongly motivate and direct the patient to avoid thinking about. Secondly, the patient "needs" the psychotherapist as a communicator and as a teacher of communication to help him develop appropriate verbal labels both for characteristics of the various selves and for the feelings associated with these characteristics. He also "needs" the help of the psychotherapist in determining the relationship between these various selves and his emotional and behavioral responses (or his inhibition of response). Finally, the patient "needs" the approval, acceptance, and emotional support of the psychotherapist to motivate his investigation of all those negative aspects of his depreciated and real self images that he would prefer to avoid. There are, in fact, still other purposes for which the patient needs the psychotherapist, but these are the principal and most readily described ones.

The psychotherapist's controlling role.   Toward the end of this early phase of psychotherapy, the psychotherapist may need to exert strong controls and to exert considerable coercion in order to get the patient to face and communicate about the "worst" aspects of the depreciated self concept. He may also have to deal rather "forcibly" with the patient's reluctance to admit the fictional nature of those phantasied attributes of the self that are most necessary or effective for neutralizing the anxieties associated with the patient's depreciated self. For example, the woman who sees herself as a drab housewife, but who tells herself that she could have been a glamorous opera star if she had not married, is extremely reluctant to face the fact that she had neither the talent nor the motivation required for such a career.

It is helpful to the therapeutic process that this period, when the psychotherapist may have to control the communicative relationship, coincides with the patient's strongest need for the therapist's acceptance, support, and help. Otherwise, patients with strong negative feelings about accepting control by others would leave the relationship prematurely, and, of course, if this aspect of the relationship is not handled adroitly, some do leave. The fact that patients will usually *accept* strong control at this phase of the psychotherapeutic relationship should not obscure the fact that the nature of the relationship has changed. The psychotherapist's reactions may, in fact, take on authoritarian overtones that are not apparent or appropriate at earlier or later stages. At such times the patient's attitudes toward control, authority, and domination will be strongly aroused. These must be anticipated, recognized, and appropriately dealt with by the psychotherapist.

THE MIDDLE PHASE OF PSYCHOTHERAPY

Objectives of the middle phase.   It has taken a long time to describe the objectives, techniques, relationships, and problems of the early phase of psychotherapy, even though we have focused as much as possible only on the self concept(s) of the patient's cognitive structure. Fortunately, we can use this foundation to explain more briefly the significant characteristics of the middle and terminal phases of psychotherapy.

We can define the objective of the middle phase with respect to the self concept quite simply. In this middle phase we are trying to eliminate the depreciated and phantasy self concepts as significant determinants of the patient's emotional and behavioral responses. At the same time we are attempting to complete the patient's awareness of the real self and to create reasonable standards for the evaluation of the real self. In the pursuit of these objectives we become involved in other subordinate (but nevertheless significant) tasks. For example, we may become involved in two projects relating to cognitive structure that have to do with minimizing the behavioral and emotional consequences of the depreciated self. One of these is to "time index" those aspects of the depreciated self that were once "true" of the patient but are no longer true of him. Secondly, we can further reduce the importance (especially the emotional significance) of these time-indexed aspects of the depreciated self by re-evaluating them in terms of the same "reasonable" standards that we want the patient to develop for evaluating the "real" self.

The phantasy self.   On the other hand, we may not spend much time in dealing with the phantasy self, per se. We anticipate that the time indexing and re-evaluation of the depreciated self (along with the possible exposure of part of the depreciated self as being imaginary or due to childish error) will considerably reduce the patient's need for his compensatory phantasies about himself. Working from the other side, we also anticipate that the patient's discovery of his real attributes and potentials will also serve to undermine the need for the phantasy self.

We should note here one more interesting aspect of the phantasy self. It is not unusual to find that certain characteristics of the phantasy self which the patient creates to compensate for imagined inferiorities happen to coincide with "real" attributes of the self. A common example would be this: a relatively intelligent child begins to feel "stupid" if he cannot live up to parental expectations, even though these expectations may be premature or excessive. Because he thinks of himself as stupid and such ideas are unpleasant, he may pretend that he is really intelligent but is just not interested in learning. In our relationship with him we will then try to convince him of the "reality" of the characteristic that he has "believed in" only because it made him feel better. We hope and anticipate that he may then be able to drop the pose of not being interested in learning.

Standards. We have mentioned previously that we are interested not only in strengthening awareness of and communication about the "real" self; we are also concerned with helping the patient to evaluate this "real" self by "reasonable" standards. In our estimation such "reasonable" standards can only be relative standards, that is, standards indicative of the characteristics, behavior, achievements of other persons comparable to the patient. For example, if we want to communicate with the patient about how intelligent he is, we can only do so in any meaningful way by comparing his abilities with the abilities of others of comparable age.

The need for comparisons of this kind may be obvious with respect to abilities, yet not obvious with respect to less tangible attributes, such as "beauty" or "morality." Yet we can point out to the patient that "absolute" beauty or "absolute" morality are as difficult to define as "absolute" intelligence. We can indicate that such judgments, when made in meaningful terms at all, are in fact comparative (who is more and who is less beautiful) and that even these judgments are relative to the ideas about beauty of a particular culture.

Specific self-evaluations. In addition to emphasizing the relative bases for self-evaluation, we may be further concerned with helping the patient to develop a more particularized and specific mode of self-evaluation. Instead of accepting general evaluations, such as "I'm too stupid," "I'm too ugly," and "I'm bad," we try to help the patient to be explicit about what particular attribute is excessive or deficient for what particular purpose relative to his own goals. This process might be conceptualized as one of helping to fill in the details of the self concept aspect of cognitive structure. The therapeutic value of such a process can be illustrated by example. A woman patient explains her avoidance of men by saying that she is unattractive. We ask what she means by this. She tells us that she has a bad figure. We ask what is bad about her figure. She tells us that her legs are not straight. In subsequent communication with the patient we do not "allow" her to talk about being unattractive, but require that she say what she means, namely, that *she believes* that her legs are not straight enough to be attractive to men. We can then deal with the reality of her belief, what measures might be useful to make her feel less embarrassed or self-conscious about this particular physical characteristic, what attractive characteristics she has, and so on.

The psychotherapist's role.   It should be obvious that in the middle phase of psychotherapy the roles of patient and psychotherapist have changed considerably. In the initial phase the psychotherapist is primarily receptive in the communicative process. When he assumes control, it is primarily for the purpose of eliciting more complete and more adequate communication from the patient. However, in the middle phase, the psychotherapist must indicate, either directly or indirectly, what he considers to be inaccurate or inadequate in the cognitive structure of the patient. Furthermore, his intent to make such changes as he considers necessary in the best interests of the patient is also obvious, whether or not it is explicit.

We cannot afford to assume that making these changes involves simply "giving information" or even the more complex process of "educating" the patient. The reason we cannot afford to make this assumption is because we are also involved with active emotional resistances on the part of the patient.

This may sound paradoxical, not only because he has come to us for help, but also because we are trying to get the patient to accept a *more favorable* concept of himself than he brings into the psychotherapeutic situation. However, we can usually find evidence for one or more of the following feeling problems to account for such resistances:

(a) a transfer or generalization of hostile feelings toward others who are perceived as attempting to control or dominate;
(b) negative feelings about relinquishing the "phantasy" self concept;
(c) anxieties that are associated with depending upon a new self concept that may not be reliable outside the psychotherapeutic situation;
(d) negative feelings regarding the effort and risks involved in readjusting behavior in accordance with the new self concept.

Because of these emotional responses of the patient (and to the extent that they exist and are manifested in a particular psychotherapeutic relationship), we cannot consider the patient passively receptive to any communication the psychotherapist may make. In order to achieve our psychotherapeutic objectives, it becomes necessary to make certain departures from objective modes of communication to the patient. The best way to describe these departures is to say that the psychotherapist becomes involved in the process of persuasion in his communicative interaction with the patient.

Persuasion.   We realize that the term "process of persuasion" is equivalent to other terms which generally have negative affective connotations, such as "selling" and "propagandizing," in the sense that the same principles apply to all these processes. We suggest that these negative connotations may be responsible in part for psychotherapists' neglect of principles of persuasion as means of increasing their psychotherapeutic effectiveness.

We suggest further that psychotherapists who have such negative reactions might consider the following "safeguards" for the use of persuasion in psychotherapy. First, the therapist should carefully examine his own motives for the use of persuasion. Second, the only justifiable motive would be to counteract the emotional resistance of the patient to the acceptance of concepts necessary for his own development and welfare. (This implies that the psychotherapist utilizes persuasion only when necessary and to the extent necessary to realize legitimate psychotherapeutic objectives. More specifically it implies that persuasion should be used only when less controlling techniques are not effective.) The third safeguard would be that persuasive efforts should usually be directed toward what the patient *thinks,* the choice of behavioral responses remaining the prerogative of the patient. It is quite conceivable, and usually should be the case, that while the psychotherapist is directly involved with trying to change a particular belief, he may also be responsible for helping the patient to develop and/or to consider a variety of behavioral responses. (This point is further developed in the next section of this chapter.)

THE TERMINAL PHASE OF PSYCHOTHERAPY

Objectives of the terminal phase.   This brings us to the terminal phase of psychotherapy, which is sometimes described in psychoanalytic therapy as "working through." We shall define the objective of this phase as being to elicit and to establish *behavioral responses* that are congruent with the *valid* self concept.

We are assuming that the patient has, prior to psychotherapy, premised his behavioral responses in part, at least, upon the various cognitive concepts which we have already described. Those responses that are associated either with the depreciated self concept or with the phantasy self concept must be considered inappropriate for the "real" self.

The simplest aspect of behavioral retraining is to have an undesirable behavioral response disappear as the inappropriate cognitive responses that evoke it are eliminated. However, this does not always happen, and even when it does we may still be concerned with the nature of the response that the patient develops in lieu of the "lost" one. In other instances, we may have to help the patient develop new and better (more appropriate) behavioral responses as the only effective way of eliminating old responses that tend to perseverate, although no longer congruent with the valid self concept.

We may, then, consider the terminal phase of psychotherapy as a period of behavioral retraining for the patient. There is considerable latitude as to how and to what extent this retraining process is carried out during psychotherapy, depending upon the needs and other characteristics of the patient. In certain cases, especially with more mature and competent persons, we may be able to leave most of this phase of psychotherapy to the patient's initiative, with minimal supervision and guidance from the therapist. With less competent patients we may feel it necessary to play a more active and directive role in this terminal phase.

The importance of others.   We must also consider that while we have concerned ourselves primarily with the self concept as an aspect of cognitive structure in the process of psychotherapy, this process also involves and is dependent upon other aspects of cognitive structure. We have already indicated how time indexing and standards are involved in reassessing the self concept. Parallel considerations apply to the concepts of "others." The primary distinction (although never a perfectly clear-cut one) is between "me" and "not-me." "Not-me" or "others" has a variety of aspects, such as the distinction between "personal" and "not-personal." The "personal" in turn breaks down into various categories, depending upon whether we are dealing with individuals or groups. We can consider groups in terms of behavior, mores, "culture," and so on. Obviously we must make as careful a selection as possible from the complexity of the patient's cognitive structure concerning "others," otherwise the process of psychotherapy could become impossibly long. Regardless of what specific aspect of "others" we select to communicate about, we can be sure that the patient's "ideas" about other people and other things are intimately related to the nature of his responses.

Alternative responses.   In addition to recognizing that a variety of cognitive responses may be involved in the evocation of a particular behavioral response, we should also note that any given stimulus complex (including cognitive responses) may have been associated with different behavioral responses at different times. Such conditions might give rise to a response hierarchy, the term "hierarchy" indicating that some responses are more likely to occur than others. When a patient is capable of responding in any of several different ways to a given stimulus situation, we may refer to such a situation as indicating "behavioral flexibility." Under these conditions the elimination of an "undesirable" response from the hierarchy would simply mean that the patient is "free" to "choose" some other response, or (more accurately put) some other response would then occur. In such instances the terminal phase of psychotherapy might be relatively short and involve primarily the psychotherapist's following the patient's behavioral developments in order to assure himself that the patient is in fact "adjusting well."

On the other hand, when no such alternative responses seem to be "available," the psychotherapist may become involved in a sort of teaching process that may be more or less complicated and prolonged, depending upon whether he aspires only to help the patient develop one behavioral response for dealing with a given situation or whether he considers it necessary to develop several different kinds of responses from which the patient will ultimately make his own choice. This decision in turn hinges upon such considerations as the patient's learning ability, the predictability of the patient's future environment, and the psychotherapist's confidence in his ability to correctly make decisions concerning that environment on the patient's behalf.

Problems of termination. The problem of literal termination is not even as conceptually neat as the rather complicated picture we have presented here as to the various possible natures and tasks of the terminal phase. One of the principal practical complications is that while we can clearly conceptualize three major phases to the psychotherapeutic relationship, unfortunately we tend to arrive at these phases at different points in time with respect to different major aspects of adjustment. For example, with adult male patients such major aspects of adjustment might involve separation from the parental family, completing an education, finding suitable employment, dating, and getting married. Not only will the sequence differ for different patients (we once had a patient who had "accomplished" marriage without having made much progress with any of the other adjustments), but it is almost inconceivable that there would not be a sequence in which some adjustments are completed—or at least initiated—before others.

Fortunately, in spite of the conceptual complications, the actual task of deciding upon an appropriate point for terminating the consecutive psychotherapeutic relationship can be decided without too much difficulty on phenomenological (rather than theoretical) grounds. (We specify "consecutive" in the above sentence to indicate that we prefer to leave the relationship "open" to later renewal should the patient's needs require it.) In order to appreciate this practical basis for termination, we should review briefly the relationship and feeling aspects of the various phases.

The point at which the "hidden" relationship becomes manifest in the initial phase represents the beginning of intense feelings for the patient. Depending upon the nature of prior relationships, especially the parental relationships, the feelings aroused consist in varying proportion of anxiety, hostility, and love for the psychotherapist. Furthermore, a definite "need" for the psychotherapist is manifested in many aspects of the patient's behavior, so that the therapist is quite aware that the patient has no intention of trying to get along without him. In the middle phase, the patient is less intensely emotional (or gradually becomes so), yet there may be no obvious lessening in his reliance upon the psychotherapist and the therapeutic relationship.

Feeling and behavioral criteria.   However in the terminal phase, two developments are likely to coincide. Just as the psychotherapist is beginning to wonder how much more he needs to do or ought to do with the patient, the latter begins to indicate in subtle ways that he is beginning to consider the same questions. The patient is also much more active in communicating with minimum assistance or "control" from the psychotherapist. For example, he often takes over the therapist's most directive functions in communication and makes his own evaluations and interpretations. In this way he indicates both symbolically and functionally that he is now capable of doing for himself what previously the psychotherapist has done for him.

Handling ambivalence about termination.   Just as the high school graduate will always experience some anxieties upon leaving home to attend college, regardless of how eagerly he looks forward to the college experience, so the patient on the verge of termination hesitates to sever the final cord of dependency. Understanding this ambivalence, we usually assume the initiative in discussing termination after we believe that we have clear-cut indications of the patient's basic readiness for it. In doing so we try to accomplish two objectives. First, we indicate our confidence in the patient's competence to make his own adjustments without our assistance. Second, we relieve the patient of his concern that we might interpret his desire for independence as a kind of personal rejection.

Having been assured that he is free to go, the patient not infrequently then indicates some reluctance to proceed with the separation. We may handle this by arranging for regular but more widely spaced appointments that continue until again the relationship "bogs down" for lack of sufficient functional value to the patient. Sometimes, however, this period of "trial separation" has quite a different outcome, as when it forces the patient to bring forward problems that he has withheld from the psychotherapeutic relationship for any of several reasons.

A valid termination is often signaled as well as any other way by a feeling of friendship and goodwill on the part of both the patient and the psychotherapist. Besides, the relationship is never "ended" as long as the patient and the therapist survive, since the changing situations and needs of the patient may create a desire for further help at some time in the future.

SUMMARY

In the introduction to this chapter we have tried to clarify certain aspects of the psychotherapist's responsibilities by pointing out that his responses are (initially) receptive (but not passive) and reactive (rather than active). We have also urged the need for an individualized approach to the patient. This makes talking about the psychotherapeutic process more difficult, but not impossible. In order to be specific, we have devoted ourselves in this chapter primarily to the task of changing the self concept by means of verbal communication.

The first therapeutic response in the initial interview is to express an interest in the patient and a receptive attitude toward his communications. This is useful in reassuring the patient about his value as a person. The patient often gives a clear picture of his own depreciated self concept by various kinds of response in this initial interview. Toward the end of the initial interview the psychotherapist responds actively in order to give the patient information that he needs about the continuation of the psychotherapeutic relationship.

The first aspect of the early phase of psychotherapy is one in which a communicative relationship is established. Actually, two relationships exist simultaneously. The "hidden" relationship is that which involves the patient's inadequacies and his dependence upon the therapist. Because of his problems the patient wants help, and he will be disappointed if he does not believe he is receiving assistance. However, since the patient's inadequacy and dependency are disguised in the ostensible relationship, the psychotherapist must be cautious about how he gives help.

During this aspect the therapist continues to manifest his interest in the patient and in what the patient says. He encourages the patient to go as far as he can in communicating about himself and his problems. This aspect ends when the patient has exhausted his communicative resources without having conceptualized his problems adequately or having developed adequate solutions for them.

The second aspect of the early phase begins as the patient's inadequacies are made apparent and his need for help from the psychotherapist is clearly recognized. This transition must be handled carefully, because it involves considerable anxiety for the patient. In addition to acknowledging his dependent need for the therapist, the patient must also face all the characteristics of his depreciated self concept and acknowledge the phantasy involved in his compensations for the depreciated self. As this dual process of "uncovering" proceeds, the patient manifests his anxiety in the form of resistance to the process. The psychotherapist may have to exert a significant degree of control if this phase is to be completed adequately. The patient's increasing awareness of his need for help usually makes him willing to accept this control. However, we may anticipate that he will have ambivalent reactions to control, which is an important reason why this is a particularly critical point in psychotherapy.

The middle phase of psychotherapy is primarily concerned with correcting the depreciated self concept. One way of doing this is to identify aspects of the self concept that are outmoded, that is, no longer valid (whether or not they were valid at some former time). Another general procedure is to encourage the patient to accept reasonable (normative) standards for self-evaluation. The psychotherapist also insists that negative self-evaluations be confined to specific characteristics.

If these procedures are worked out effectively, the patient is usually willing to relinquish compensatory phantasies about himself in exchange for a more valid (and favorable) self-evaluation.

The psychotherapist may find it either desirable or necessary to utilize techniques of persuasion in performing this part of the psychotherapeutic task. There seems to be little reason for the general prejudice against the use of persuasion in psychotherapy, provided adequate safeguards are recognized and observed.

The terminal phase of psychotherapy is concerned with the development of new behavioral responses that are congruent with the valid self concept and, therefore, most appropriate for the patient. However, the nature of these new responses will be determined by what the patient believes about and expects from "others," as well as by how he evaluates himself.

The psychotherapist is primarily concerned, during this phase, with helping the patient to develop a suitable array or "hierarchy" of behavioral responses to various general situations. The final determination of a specific response in a specific situation is made by the patient on the basis of the patient's own experience.

The *subjective* criteria for termination are usually experienced more or less simultaneously by patient and by psychotherapist. (Objective criteria are discussed in the final chapter.) It is appropriate for the psychotherapist to initiate discussion of termination when the patient appears reluctant to do so. Most patients experience some ambivalent feelings about terminating the psychotherapeutic relationship. However, the therapist understands this and may communicate that the relationship actually remains "open," depending only upon the patient's need for its renewal.

SUGGESTIONS FOR FURTHER READING

In these suggestions we shall attempt to direct the reader to both briefer and longer sources of information about the psychotherapeutic process.

We would suggest that the reader begin with Freud's *Collected Papers*, Volume 2: Clinical Paper XXXII (1). It will be instructive to compare this article with the modern viewpoint of Judd Marmor (2). Another good, brief treatment is Franz Alexander's (3), Chapter X. A picture of the sequence of events in psychotherapy that differs from our own is presented in Chapter VIII by Theron Alexander (4). Chapter V in Menninger's *Theory of Psychoanalytic Technique* (6) deals specifically with the problem of resistance, as does Chapter Five in Clara Thompson's *Psychoanalysis: Evolution and Development* (5). We also recommend the reading or rereading of Thompson's final two chapters.

For longer treatments of the psychotherapeutic process, we suggest Part II of *Principles of Intensive Psychotherapy* by Fromm-Reichmann (7). A more classical description is Part I of Reich's *Character Analysis* (8), of which Chapter IV should be most carefully considered. A good "stage-by-stage" description of psychoanalytic therapy is presented by Glover (9). Chapters I to XI are germane to the contents of this chapter and the chapter following.

Among nonpsychoanalytic points of view we also have a variety of resources. Chapters 11 and 12 in Ruesch (10) are particularly relevant. Both Ellis (11), Chapter 10, and Thorne (12) present excellent cases for the active management of the psychotherapeutic process by the therapist. For the reader who is not acquainted with the "nondirective" point of view, Nicholas Hobbs (13) presents this in briefer form

Frank (14) documents the case *for* the utilization of persuasion in psychotherapy. Chapter 8 should be read if the reader must be selective. Kubie (15), in Chapter XVII, represents traditional "antipersuasive" attitudes among psychotherapists.

Sullivan's brief Chapter 9 (16) should be read on the important and difficult subject of the closing phases of interviews.

Shands (17) provides an excellent overview of the entire psychotherapeutic process in Chapter XIV. We recommend it highly. We also strongly recommend the reading, at this point, of Harper's (18) final chapter, which will assist the reader in sorting out the various theoretical orientations represented by our other references.

REFERENCES

1. Freud, S. *Collected papers,* vol. 2. New York: Collier, 1963. (Basic Books, 1959.)

*2. Marmor, J. A re-evaluation of certain aspects of psychoanalytic theory and practice. In Salzman, L., and Masserman, J. (Eds.) *Modern concepts of psychoanalysis.* New York: Citadel, 1962. (Philosophical Library, 1962.)

*3. Alexander, F. *Fundamentals of psychoanalysis.* New York: Norton, 1963. (Norton, 1948.)

*4. Alexander, T. *Psychotherapy in our society.* Englewood Cliffs, N.J.: Prentice-Hall, 1963.

*5. Thompson, C. *Psychoanalysis: evolution and development.* New York: Grove Press, 1957.

*6. Menninger, K. *Theory of psychoanalytic technique.* New York: Science Editions, 1961. (Basic Books, 1958.)

*7. Fromm-Reichmann, F. *Principles of intensive psychotherapy.* Chicago: Phoenix, 1960. (University of Chicago Press, 1950.)

*8. Reich, W. *Character analysis.* New York: Noonday, 1962.

9. Glover, E. *The technique of psychoanalysis.* New York: International Universities Press, 1955.

10. Ruesch, J. *Therapeutic communication.* New York: Norton, 1961.

11. Ellis, A. *Reason and emotion in psychotherapy.* New York: Lyle Stuart, 1962.

12. Thorne, F. Directive and eclectic personality counseling. In McCrary, J. L., and Sheer, D. E. (Eds.) *Six approaches to psychotherapy.* New York: Holt, Rinehart and Winston, 1955.

13. Hobbs, N. Client-centered psychotherapy. In McCrary, J. L., and Sheer, D. E. (Eds.) *Six approaches to psychotherapy.* New York: Holt, Rinehart and Winston, 1955.

*14. Frank, J. D. *Persuasion and healing*. New York: Schocken Books, 1963. (Johns Hopkins Press, 1961.)

*15. Kubie, L. S. *Practical and theoretical aspects of psychoanalysis*. New York: Praeger, 1960. (International Universities Press, 1950.)

16. Sullivan, H. S. *The psychiatric interview*. New York: Norton, 1954.

17. Shands, H. C. *Thinking and psychotherapy*. Cambridge, Mass.: Harvard University Press, 1960.

*18. Harper, R. A. *Psychoanalysis and psychotherapy*. Englewood Cliffs, N.J.: Spectrum, 1959.

* Paperback edition.

Chapter 12 | *Changing Feelings and Emotions*

THE DEVELOPMENTAL POINT OF VIEW

Dealing with feelings. We have indicated elsewhere that changes in feelings and emotions are ultimately dependent upon changes in cognitive structure and behavior, including changes in the nature of communicative responses. In that sense how the patient feels after his therapeutic experience depends upon what cognitive changes and what behavioral changes have occurred in therapy or will occur as a result of therapy.

However, it is also true that the psychotherapeutic process may evoke strong feelings and emotional reactions from the patient. A significant aspect of the psychotherapeutic process is the emotional interaction between patient and therapist. This interaction enables the psychotherapist to become directly involved with the emotional responses of the patient and provides an opportunity for him to change these responses in ways that he believes will be helpful to the patient.

What emotional responses can the psychotherapist expect to encounter? What changes should he try to produce? How can he produce these changes? These are questions that are relatively simple, if the psychotherapist deals over and over again with the same kind of patient. These are questions that (perhaps) the psychotherapist can afford to ignore if he has a set routine of psychotherapeutic procedure that the patient must either be able to fit into or else be disqualified as a patient. Throughout this essay, however, we have argued for the broadest possible definition of "patient" and also for an individualized approach to each patient. There is no doubt that these two objectives greatly increase the difficulty of the psychotherapeutic tasks, especially when they are combined. We believe that these difficulties are resolvable. In the remainder of this chapter we shall present attempts at such a solution.

Developmental needs.   When we examine carefully the guiding principles which are used in our approach to psychotherapy, we conclude that these principles are determined by a certain conception of the developmental process. In other words, we usually or always find ourselves wondering: if this person had been raised under optimal conditions, what would he be like?

One must, of course, have some ideas as to what constitutes "optimal" conditions if one is to make this kind of evaluation. Our consideration then hinges upon four conditions that the child requires for normal growth and development. First, his physical needs must be met. Second, he must be accepted, approved of, and loved. Third, he must be expected and helped to develop competence. Fourth, he must be helped to develop adequate control over his behavior.

The importance of meeting physical needs seems to be self-evident. There is only one organism involved when we deal with any given person, and in this organism "physical" and "psychological" aspects are actually inseparable, although they can be separately conceptualized. Inadequate nutrition, exercise, sleep, rest, and protection from assault (whether mechanical or biological) are deficiencies that must have functional (psychological) consequences if they have structural (physical) consequences. Optimal physical health for a given person can be defined in terms of conditions that meet his basic biological needs without creating problems either of excess (as in overeating) or deficiency (as in vitamin deficiency or inadequate endocrine output).

We consider love (including acceptance and approval) a basic need for several reasons. First, it helps to ensure that degree of attention to the child's needs which will protect him from undue or traumatic anxiety. Second, it helps in mirroring back to the child the kind of evaluation that is conducive to the development of self-confidence. Third, the training responsibilities of the parents are many and demanding. Because parents are often deficient in both knowledge and skill, it is difficult enough for them to do an adequate job of training, even when they are well motivated. It is rather inconceivable that parents will do an adequate job if they are indifferent to or hostile to the child.

The "work" of the child is the development of competence. We live in a society where it is expected that every adult member will acquire certain basic skills, such as the ability to read and write. Going beyond these minimum requirements, we have good reason to believe that persons are happiest in adult life when they are able to utilize their innate aptitudes effectively for productive and creative purposes. Preparing the child for competent living in a technologically complex (and rapidly changing) culture is a difficult task. Errors are easy to make, yet such errors can have significant consequences for the personal happiness of the one who is being trained.

We add "control" as a separate need, because we consider it important to remember that the training of the child involves the child's learning *not* to do certain things, as well as his learning how to do other things. Beyond the basic matter of control (in the sense of inhibition of behavior) lies the broader problem of conformity, lined by the thorny hedges of "too much" and "too little."

With these basic requirements in mind, we look back and forth between the patient as he is when we see him and the conditions under which he has developed. When we look at the patient, we ask: "In what ways is he less than he might have been?" When we think we have some answers to this question, we may begin to look for those defects in developmental conditions that we expect to be correlated with deficiencies in the patient. Or, if we know about certain conditions in childhood that we would expect to produce adverse effects, we may look for corresponding deficiencies in the functioning of the person. The establishment of such expected correlations provides an empirical check on the validity of our theorizing about the patient and his needs for further development.

Developmental tasks.   A slightly different way to approach this problem of evaluation is in terms of the concept of "developmental tasks." In this approach we attempt to specify in a general way the characteristics of the newborn infant. We let these define the starting points of the developmental process. We then try to define corresponding aspects of the self in adults. These "adult" characteristics must, however, be defined with due regard for the innately determined characteristics of the person (sex, temperament, intelligence, aptitudes, and so on) and also for the cultural environment in which he will be expected to function as an adult.

We then attempt to assess the adequacy of the person's progress toward his ultimate status, taking his age into consideration. Such evaluations can only be made in terms of comparative judgments, that is, those which compare the patient with others of similar age, inherent characteristics, and cultural goals. When we conclude that development has been inadequate or deviant, we try to conceptualize what parental functions have been inadequately or incorrectly performed.

Our purpose in taking this point of view is not at all to saddle the parents with the "blame" for the patient's problems. Rather, we are trying to decide what has not been done for the patient that another person might conceivably do, or, what has been done incorrectly that another person might be able to rectify. In other words, our purpose is to decide what others might be able to do to help the patient to complete his developmental tasks adequately. Once this has been decided, there remains the further decision as to who shall play what roles or perform which functions in the corrective procedure.

Seldom will the psychotherapist himself be able to supply all of the conditions necessary for the most comprehensive corrective program, either because of his own limitations, or because of limitations of the psychotherapeutic situation (limited time, facilities, and so on), or because of the limitations of the therapeutic relationship. For example, the psychotherapist may not have the specialized equipment and skills necessary to diagnose and treat endocrine deficiencies. He may not have the time, knowledge, or facilities to engage directly in the formal education of the patient. Or he may lack "authority" or other attributes of a relationship necessary to "discipline" the patient. However, if he assumes responsibility for dealing with the psychological problems of the patient, the psychotherapist should find means to provide for those needs of the patient that he himself cannot supply directly.

In other words, the psychotherapist assesses the developmental needs of the patient. Then he attempts to provide for the meeting of these needs. Certain aspects of this task may or must be "farmed out" to others who are qualified to cope with them. Those aspects of the task that the psychotherapist believes he can best perform himself constitute the basis for the psychotherapeutic relationship and help to define the nature of that relationship.

THE PATIENT'S FEELINGS AND EMOTIONS

Evaluating feelings. A wide variety of feelings about the psychotherapeutic relationship is encountered among patients. We also find different feelings about the relationship in the same patient at different stages of the relationship. The observation and correct identification of the patient's feelings (or accurate inferences about what feelings might exist) is quite important to an understanding of the patient's adjustment. Knowing what his feelings are also helps us to know what we must help him to do by way of improving his adjustment.

The developmental point of view is a helpful orientation for observing, inferring, and understanding the patient's emotional responses. First of all, it provides an orientation that is applicable to all patients, regardless of their chronological age. Second, it often enables us to understand the feelings of the patient by considering his developmental needs and how adequately or inadequately they have been met in prior relationships. Furthermore, an analysis of the patient in these same terms can be most useful in suggesting where our emotional relationship with the patient will begin, what the nature of that relationship will be, and what changes in it must take place before we can consider the psychotherapeutic process reasonably complete.

The pattern of feeling development.   As far as relating to others is concerned, everyone is initially completely dependent. The child accepts what others do for him by way of meeting his needs without question and "loves" them according to how well they interpret and satisfy those needs. There is no question of functioning independently to satisfy his own needs, except as a matter of intrinsic motivation, as when the infant indulges in spontaneous movement, rests, cries, falls asleep, and so on. The infant is not aware of any need to earn the care he receives by doing things to please others or by meeting their needs in other ways.

Ambivalent feelings toward others grow out of experiences of frustration that they impose either purposely or inadvertently. At this stage the parent is a "good parent" when he meets the child's needs directly and a "bad parent" when he does not do so.

In spite of this ambivalence, the child still maintains his dependent orientation toward the parents. This dependent orientation is in part due to the fact that it involves less effort and in part due to his lack of confidence in his own ability to provide for himself.

Gradually, however, this situation changes. At first the child only has to cope with the fact that his parents are refusing to do things for him which they believe he is able to (and should) learn to do for himself. Such refusals, however, finally lead to an awareness that eventually he will become more or less completely responsible for his own welfare. At the outset, this awareness is vague and general and might be expressed in such terms as "I'm going to be a daddy when I grow up." As the years go by, this awareness becomes more definite and concrete. For example, "when I grow up" may become defined in terms of "when I graduate" and can be specified in terms of a certain number of years. And while all aspects of "being a daddy" may not be clearly defined, they usually include the requirement that the male be able to support himself and, eventually, others.

This increasing awareness and definition of future function creates a new aspect to the "good parent, bad parent" evaluation of others. This new aspect is in conflict with the dichotomy based on the desire for immediate and direct need gratification. As the child develops anxieties about his ability to function in an independent role, others will be evaluated as "good parents" when they help him to reduce his anxiety by assisting him in becoming more competent. Others may also be evaluated as "bad parents" when they neglect or interfere with the development of such competence. However, being "good parents" in helping the child to develop his own competence is incompatible with being "good parents" in the sense of providing immediate need gratification. Regardless of which function the parents are actually concerned with, there is a necessary ambivalence on the child's part that is attendant upon the frustration of the other need.

When the parents are persistent in their demands for the development of competence, and to the extent that they are helpful in the development of competence, the child actually develops a greater or lesser capacity to provide for his own needs. As he does so, he is no longer forced to rely upon others. As his needs become less, he is also able to evaluate others more objectively. Finally, he "escapes" from the problem of his ambivalent feelings toward this original relationship by becoming less emotionally involved and by establishing new relationships.

Understanding "transference."   The nature of and the reasons for the responses (both emotional and cognitive) that the patient brings into the psychotherapeutic relationship as a matter of "transference" or generalization can be most easily understood in terms of the developmental sequence that has just been described. The assumptions that make this feasible are given below.

We assume that the patient "has problems" or is functioning unsatisfactorily because some of the basic conditions required for development were inadequately or improperly supplied. The patient has not been able to diagnose the nature of the deficiency, or, if he has done so correctly, he has not been able to find those conditions that would enable him to complete or correct his inadequate development.

The patient comes to the psychotherapist as a person who can help him to complete or improve his competence in obtaining satisfaction. Regardless of whether this is openly acknowledged at first (see Chapter 11), it must be true. The need of the patient for help and his selection of the psychotherapist as his helper automatically places the therapist *in locus parentis*. Therefore, the cognitive and emotional responses to the psychotherapist must take up at a point where previous "helping relationships" have left off. It is difficult to conceive of any other possibility.

The psychotherapist now has two parallel and correlated means for evaluating the patient. Where he can accurately judge the immaturity of the patient, he should be able to infer or anticipate the nature of the patient's transferences. If, on the other hand, the nature of the transferred responses is obvious, he should be able to infer or anticipate the patient's degree of immaturity. When the therapist has more or less direct evidence on both points, he can check the validity of his evaluation in terms of whether his estimate of the patient's maturity is congruent with the nature of the patient's transference responses.

Transference problems.   The extent to which transference responses create problems in the psychotherapeutic relationship is determined by the developmental status of the patient. If the patient is relatively mature and relatively competent (and the psychotherapist is performing his task properly), the distortion involved in the perception of the therapist may be relatively slight. This is because the relatively competent patient is able to accept a reasonable image of the "good parent." All he expects of the therapist is that he be accepted by the therapist and actually helped to deal more effectively with his problems. The transference problems of such a patient are not likely to involve intense feelings or to be too difficult to resolve. The principal feeling problem is the ambivalence created by the desire for assistance, on the one hand, and reluctance to accept a dependent role relative to the psychotherapist, on the other hand.

The more difficult problems relating to transference occur in those cases where the patient has evaluated himself as very inadequate and incompetent. Such a person feels he needs a very perfect "good parent" who knows all, can do anything, and will do everything for the patient. This type of patient accepts a therapeutic relationship only if he is able to convince himself that the psychotherapist actually meets his specifications of being omniscient, omnipotent, and all-giving. Once having made such an evaluation, his emotional response to the psychotherapist is proportional to the "magical" qualities he attributes to him.

It is rather obvious that this latter type of relationship will present more difficulties, both for the patient and for the psychotherapist. In private practice and in most clinics the psychotherapist immediately contradicts one aspect of the cognitive transference by asking a fee for his services. A characteristic of "the good parent" is that he provides his services out of love for the child. The less mature patient "resists" recognizing the reality of this demand from the psychotherapist. Some of his ways of resisting are to attempt to obtain services without paying a fee, to haggle for a lesser fee than he is able to pay, to be late in paying for the therapist's services, and to stay on beyond his allotted time. To allow the patient to succeed in any of these maneuvers gives the patient immediate gratification. Unfortunately, it also serves to perpetuate the transference responses rather than helping the patient to accept and adjust to this particular aspect of reality.

The patient's cognitive transference which involves the illusion of unconditional acceptance is contradicted when the psychotherapist indicates that he expects the patient to make efforts on his own behalf.

The "good parent" image of the very immature patient includes the characteristic of not requiring the patient to grow or to develop competence in order to ensure the continuation of the relationship. As soon as the psychotherapist makes it clear that a condition of the relationship is that the patient will make efforts to improve his adjustment, the patient feels anxious (because of his lack of confidence in his own growth potential), frustrated, and angry. The insistence upon growth cannot, therefore, be made obvious until such time as the patient's need for the relationship has been well established and is strong enough to prevent the patient from breaking off the relationship.

Another contradiction of the patient's transferred image of the "good parent" occurs if the patient anticipates direct emotional gratification that the psychotherapist does not provide. For example, if the patient expects sexual interaction, he will feel frustrated and angry when denied such gratification by the psychotherapist. The way in which such a denial is handled and explained, however, can make a considerable difference in the patient's feelings about the refusal.

WORKING WITH EMOTIONS IN PSYCHOTHERAPY

Dealing with feeling problems.   The "problem" feelings in psychotherapy, as in other relationships, are the unpleasant feelings; the problem emotions are anxiety and hostility. We have just indicated some of the problems that may arise as a result of the conflict between the patient's wishes for unconditional acceptance or for direct emotional gratification and the psychotherapist's inability or refusal to grant these wishes. There are many other such conflicts that may arise in the course of psychotherapy. For example, the patient would like a quick and easy solution to his problems. This the psychotherapist cannot supply, unless the patient's problems are very simple. The patient dislikes and would prefer to ignore his depreciated self concept; the psychotherapist may insist that a thorough knowledge of this self concept is essential. The psychotherapist tries to get the patient to give up less efficient modes of adjustment for more efficient ones; the patient insists that he cannot attempt this because it makes him too anxious.

The psychotherapist's ability to cope with such negative feelings as these and other situations may generate is determined entirely by the patient's positive feelings about him. To put the matter in its simplest and most general terms, the patient's "love" for the therapist must be maintained at a higher level of intensity than the anxieties that the psychotherapeutic relationship creates at any given time. Otherwise the patient will terminate the relationship. The patient's need for the psychotherapist, combined with his fear of him, must be adequate to forestall hostile attacks of such intensity that the psychotherapist is unable to tolerate the relationship. For these basic purposes of "managing and maintaining" the psychotherapeutic relationship, it is not necessary to distinguish between "transferred" and "earned" emotional responses of the patient.

The problem of "resistance."   Basically, the psychotherapist is involved in the training and retraining of the patient, so that he is more effective in obtaining what he wants out of life. The patient has his own reasons for wanting to change the pattern of his behavior, if only or fundamentally because he is dissatisfied with the emotional results of the existing pattern.

Each patient, however, has his reasons for not being able to change or not wanting to change. Basically these can be reduced to two: either he cannot conceive of any better ways to cope with his environment, or he is anxious lest attempts to change result in failure or lead to a still more unsatisfactory state of affairs. In a sense, he can only "move" (improve his adjustment) if the psychotherapist will indicate a superior way to respond (if necessary) and will help to relieve his anxieties about making changes.

In this context we would have to suggest that encountering "resistance" in psychotherapy is simply another way of saying that the psychotherapist has not performed one or the other of these two functions properly.

All other aspects of "resistance" can, we believe, be accounted for in terms of the normal effort and skill required to establish new habits, break old habits, or substitute one habitual way of responding for another. In this sense "resistance" on the patient's part will be inversely correlated with the psychotherapist's skill as a trainer or educator.

We shall make a somewhat more detailed analysis of "problems of persuasion" and "problems of education and training" in the material that follows. We suggest that the reader consider these as our attempts to understand and to cope with "the problem of resistance."

Problems of persuasion.   Sometimes the only problem and often a significant problem is that the patient feels anxious because he is not able to meet certain standards of behavior or performance he believes he must be able to achieve. He believes this because he has been given these standards by others, who have also conveyed the impression that failure to meet these standards will make him unacceptable to others.

When the standards are reasonable in terms of the person's ability to perform, the psychotherapeutic problem is to help the patient to develop the necessary traits, skills, and adjustments. However, when the standards have been or are unreasonable, the psychotherapist must be involved with the task of establishing reasonable standards.

How "axiomatic" his standards seem to the patient and how convinced he is of the necessity for meeting them is often evidenced by the patient's more or less obvious demand that the psychotherapist accept and agree with these standards and simply concern himself with helping the patient to live up to them. If the psychotherapist hints that the standards themselves may need revision, the patient may react either with hostility or with anxiety. The patient "knows" there is nothing wrong with the standards. He has been given these standards and told that meeting them was essential by others (usually the primary social conditioners) at a time when he was dependent upon them and when, because of his dependence, he had reasons for assuming that they were omniscient. If the psychotherapist thinks otherwise, then the psychotherapist may well be leading him into some sort of behavior pattern that would ensure his being rejected by others.

How "sure" the patient is of the validity of his standards (and, therefore, how anxious and resistant he will be to attempts to change them) will vary according to the competence of the patient. The more mature patient, who has already developed enough competence to begin to question such standards on his own initiative, is not particularly difficult to convince. The less mature and less competent patient, however, may never have considered questioning these standards. He is the one who is particularly disturbed when the psychotherapist does so.

We have referred before to the matter of "timing" in psychotherapy. Now we have an opportunity to illustrate what we mean by timing. The more competent patient may be willing to grant from the outset that the psychotherapist is a more reasonable and competent judge of standards than his prior social conditioners have been. With such a patient one can begin a discussion of this topic at any time that is relevant or that suits his psychotherapeutic purposes.

This is not true with the less competent, less mature, or more anxious patient. It is not until cognitive and emotional transferences combined with more realistic responses to the psychotherapist have given him more prestige in the patient's eyes than the original social conditioners had that the patient is able to consider changes in standards without undue anxiety about the results of such changes. When the psychotherapist has *less* prestige, he will find it difficult or impossible to persuade the patient to change his standards. When the psychotherapist has prestige value roughly equivalent to that of the primary social conditioners at the time when they first suggested *their* standards, then the patient will have conflicting feelings about the subject of changing standards and may attempt to avoid the subject in order to minimize such feelings.

The psychotherapist has a choice of strategies with respect to this particular problem and with respect to problems of persuasion in general. If he is dealing with a relatively competent patient, or if his psychotherapeutic procedure is to consider the development of competence as one of the first "jobs" to be accomplished, he may use persuasion only as a means to the development of further competence. Decisions about values, standards, and goals may then be left largely or entirely to the initiative of the patient. If, however, the patient is immature and incompetent and if the revision of values, standards, and goals is considered fundamental to other aspects of the psychotherapeutic task, then the psychotherapist will find it necessary to use techniques of persuasion in order to effect such revisions.

Now we return to the point that whether or not the psychotherapist succeeds in his efforts at persuasion will depend entirely upon his prestige as an authority figure relative to the prestige of the original social conditioners. He must, then, be quite accurate in his assessment of the patient's emotional and cognitive responses to him. If he makes his suggestions at a time when his prestige is sufficiently great, he will succeed; otherwise he will not.

This is one example of what we mean by saying that the psychotherapist "uses" the emotional and cognitive relationship of the patient for psychotherapeutic purposes. Please note well that for purposes of persuasion it is quite irrelevant whether the emotional and cognitive responses of the patient are "realistic" or "transferred."

Problems of education and training.   The psychotherapist often encounters situations where the patient could function more effectively if he had additional information or more adequate skills. The problems involved in dealing with such situations differ considerably depending upon the reasons for the patient's deficiencies.

These reasons can usually be classified into three categories: (a) the patient has been unaware of his need for further education; (b) the patient has not had an opportunity to learn, although aware of his need; (c) the patient has considered himself unable to learn, although aware of his need and having the opportunity to learn. An example of the first kind of problem would be the patient who is a poor communicator, but who is not aware of this. An example of the second type would be the patient who feels handicapped because he does not know how to behave on a date. An example of the third type would be the patient who is bored by the kind of work he has been trained to do, but who thinks he is too stupid to learn to do work that would be more interesting.

To the extent that (unwarranted) self-evaluations of inadequacy or incompetence are responsible for the patient's failure to obtain necessary education or training, the psychotherapist may be involved with the problems of persuasion which we have just discussed. In other words, the psychotherapist will have to find some way of changing either the self concept or the standards by which characteristics of the self are evaluated before any further progress can be made.

When this problem has been dealt with (or if it does not exist), we can then shift our attention to the four conditions necessary for learning, namely: motivation, cues, response, and reinforcement. Let us now look at how and to what extent the emotional responses of the patient to the psychotherapist are involved in providing each of these.

Are there any ways in which the psychotherapeutic relationship can be used to enhance the patient's motivation for learning? Actually, there are so many of these that we shall only be able to suggest some of the more important ones. The psychotherapist can increase motivation by pointing to specific benefits of learning and stressing the value of these benefits. (His prestige in the eyes of the patient will have much to do with the success of this type of activity.) The psychotherapist can increase motivation by his suggestions that what is to be learned will not be as difficult to learn as the patient may believe—again, a kind of suggestion in which the psychotherapist's prestige or authority value for the patient is important. The patient's motivation for constructive efforts can be enhanced more directly by his desire for the psychotherapist's approval and/or by his anxiety about loss of the relationship if he does not make an effort. The strength of such auxiliary motivation will, of course, be proportional to the general value of the relationship for the patient.

In order for the patient to learn there must be adequate cues to elicit the response that he is supposed to make and to learn. Any of the communicative techniques we have described in Chapter 10 can be used for this purpose. The responsible psychotherapist will be able to recognize what parts of this aspect of the educational needs of the patient can be met more efficiently or practically by other persons than himself. So far as the psychotherapist *is* involved, however, the patient's confidence in the psychotherapist's "authority" (in this instance, the psychotherapist's competence as an instructor or the validity of his information as an educator) is obviously important in determining how readily and appropriately the patient will respond.

We would point out that in this aspect of the learning situation, the extent of the patient's transference becomes a matter of some concern to the psychotherapist. Since the psychotherapist has no reason to regard himself as infallible, he should always be more or less concerned about the possibility of misinforming or misdirecting the patient. The more the patient regards the psychotherapist as an absolute authority (and the less, therefore, he is inclined to question the therapist's opinion or to utilize his own judgment), the more cautious and conservative the psychotherapist must be with respect to the adequacy and accuracy of the cues he provides. The reason for this should be obvious: under these conditions the patient will tend strongly to blame himself for any difficulties attendant upon the learning process or for any unfavorable outcomes. If the fault is actually the psychotherapist's, the patient's self-blame represents an unwarranted addition to his "problems." (The psychotherapist can, of course, mitigate the adverse consequences of his own errors by his willingness to admit them and to accept responsibility for them.)

The patient cannot learn without making the necessary responses (those to be learned) for himself. The most fundamental condition for meeting this requirement for learning is that the patient be *allowed* to respond. This is the reason why the psychotherapist cannot do all the work of psychotherapy and why the patient must be required to make an effort on his own behalf. It is also the reason why the psychotherapist must keep his own activity in the psychotherapeutic situation to the necessary minimum at all times. As we have suggested elsewhere, the "necessary minimum" will vary according to the competence of the patient.

The emotional aspect of this part of the learning process has to do with the patient's feelings about receiving direct gratification as opposed to developing competence. The most dependent patients consider themselves as being unable to do anything for themselves and expect the psychotherapist to do everything for them. An immediate, obvious, and complete denial of this expectation would make it impossible for the patient to continue the relationship, both because of his self-evaluation that he cannot meet the expectations of the psychotherapist and because of his resentment of the psychotherapist's lack of consideration. The psychotherapist must, in fact, have a special sensitivity to the patient's self-evaluation and a considerable accuracy in assessing it. (It is of critical importance that the psychotherapist *not* confuse his own estimate of the patient's ability with the patient's evaluation of himself.) The psychotherapist can then safely use the tactic that all parents use, namely, he makes it clear that his continuing acceptance, approval, and assistance are dependent upon the patient's efforts to develop competence on his own behalf. In other words, he uses the emotional value of the relationship to help resolve the patient's ambivalence or to counteract his anxieties.

Those who are familiar with the literature on psychotherapy have probably encountered the term "dosing the patient's anxieties." The concept can be usefully applied to the delicate process of evoking responses from the patient. If the psychotherapist's demands are excessive or premature, the patient develops strong anxieties and may leave the therapeutic situation. If the psychotherapist is not demanding enough, the psychotherapeutic process is unduly prolonged.

The value of the psychotherapist in reinforcing the patient's responses is obviously going to be a function of the feelings the patient has about him. Depending upon the nature and intensity of these feelings, the therapist's recognition, approval, praise, or other acknowledgments of the patient's performance have more or less reinforcing value for the patient. Once again we are concerned with a situation where the "real" or "transferred" basis for the patient's feelings is a matter of no significance.

However, the kind of reinforcement that the psychotherapist can safely use is very definitely determined by the state of the relationship at any given time. For example, in the early stages of the relationship, specifically in the period before the patient has developed any considerable acceptance of the psychotherapist on either a "real" or a "transferred" basis, the use of negative or punitive reinforcements can only serve to retard or prevent the development of such acceptance. Consequently the psychotherapist uses criticism or disapproval at this stage only if and when it is absolutely necessary for some other therapeutic purpose. On the other hand, the psychotherapist has more freedom in the use of such negative reinforcements when the general relationship is emotionally "stronger."

However, two principles remain true under all conditions. First, punishment is only useful for producing inhibition or avoidance; it cannot be used to reinforce the development of new responses. Second, punishment always involves the liability of creating some negative feelings both about learning and about the person who is helping him to learn. For this reason, positive reinforcement should always be used when possible, with "punishment" reserved for those situations where reward is inappropriate or ineffectual.

Persuasion compared with emotional intervention.   It has probably occurred to the reader by now that there are no hard and fast distinctions between "persuading" the patient and "helping him to learn." The psychotherapist's success in either venture will depend to a considerable extent upon the competence of the patient, the patient's cognitive and feeling responses to the therapist, and the psychotherapist's skill in determining what the patient needs and what the patient can do at any given time. Furthermore, the psychotherapist is limited to the same communicative techniques in either instance, although his reliance on certain techniques or forms of communication will vary, depending on whether he is more concerned with persuasion or with the direct facilitation of learning.

To illustrate the different emphases involved, we shall turn our attention to a subject that was mentioned only briefly in Chapter 11: changing the patient's concept of others.

The "problem" involved in the patient's concept of others is basically that he tends to lag behind in his "time indexing," so that he thinks of contemporary others and of his relationships with them as if they were the same as the persons and relationships about which he has learned at earlier stages of development. The psychotherapist wants to help him to become more discriminating and to bring his concept of others up-to-date, so that they are a realistic representation of the persons and relationships in his present environment.

When the psychotherapist uses persuasion, he is attempting to substitute new ideas for old. Let us see what he might do in the following situation.

First, he could question whether persons in the patient's contemporary environment actually expect the same kind of characteristics and behavior that the patient's previous social conditioners have expected. He could question whether contemporary others are as cognizant of or as concerned about the patient's behavior as previous social conditioners have been. He could question whether the approval or disapproval of contemporary others can affect the welfare of the patient as much as did the approval or disapproval of his primary social conditioners. He could also question whether the patient's compensatory efforts to please or impress others are the most effective means of gaining the approval of contemporary others.

Such efforts at these obviously represent a direct "attack" upon the patient's existing cognitive structure. They will also readily fit any reasonable definition of "persuasion," such as Doob's (1) or Frank's (2).

Now let us look at examples of how the psychotherapist might attempt to change the patient's concept of others by himself responding in a different way to the patient.

How does the psychotherapist respond to the patient's verbal exposures of his sins, faults, weaknesses, and deficiencies? Rather than responding punitively (as previous social conditioners might have), the psychotherapist is interested in such exposures, he helps in the process of uncovering, and he approves of the patient for his efforts in this direction. Furthermore, he responds differently by helping the patient to make a more realistic evaluation of his shortcomings, so that usually the patient feels better for having "spoken out."

So far as the patient's compensatory efforts are concerned, the psychotherapist responds in a different way than previous social conditioners have done by exposing (and, by inference, condemning) their "unrealistic" nature. He assures the patient that these compensatory efforts are *not* responsible for the pyschotherapist's acceptance of the patient. He indicates both his disapproval of these efforts and the reason for his disapproval, by pointing out their inefficient and self-defeating aspects. By contrast, the psychotherapist gives obvious expressions of approval for efforts on the patient's part to define a valid self concept and to react to others in a "realistic" way.

In these more direct interventions, the psychotherapist is not trying to persuade the patient to believe that others are different so much as he is "proving" that they are different by the nature of his own responses to the patient. He is not telling the patient directly how he should think, feel, or behave. Rather he is helping the patient to think, feel, and behave differently by providing novel (for the patient) motivations and reinforcements. We could also say that he is changing the patient's "expectancies" about the behavior of other persons.

Too often in discussions of psychotherapy those who prefer persuasive techniques argue with those who prefer direct intervention, and *vice versa.* Rather than evaluating persuasion *versus* direct intervention on an "either-or" basis, we would point to the obvious conclusion that they represent complementary orientations, or somewhat different means for accomplishing a particular objective. When the emphasis should be upon one and when upon the other involves complexities of theory and technique that are beyond the scope of our present concern. Therefore, we shall cut the Gordian knot by saying that the psychotherapist should use the approach which is most effective with a given patient at a given time.

"Working through the transference." The psychoanalytic literature on psychotherapy is heavily larded with references to "working through the transference" or "working through the transference neurosis" (see Freud [3], Reich [4], Fromm-Reichmann [5], and Thompson [6] for various examples). "Working through the transference" is apparently regarded by most authorities on psychoanalysis as the final and most valid description of the basic process of psychoanalysis, as contrasted with such lesser and subordinate processes as "catharsis," "the development of insight," and "dealing with resistance." (The first two of these subordinate processes, incidentally, are generally considered to be Freud's first and second ideas about the basic process in psychoanalysis.)

Since we have used such terms as "emotional and cognitive transference" and "the transferred basis for feelings" ourselves, we would like to make explicit our definitions of the terms "transference" and "working through the transference" and give an interpretation of how they apply to the process of psychotherapy.

It is a bit awkward to define "transference." It is simple to define the verb "to transfer," because we would simply equate it with "to generalize," as Dollard and Miller (7) do. "Transference" as a noun implies "something" that is transferred. In psychoanalytic theory it is not always clear what that something is, although most frequently it seems to be a feeling or an emotion.

The concept of "generalization" is a familiar one in learning theory. This term implies that any of a variety of similar stimuli may evoke the "same" response, even though the response has been habitually associated with only one of these stimuli. The principle of generalization applies to any kind of response, whether cognitive, physiological, or behavioral.

We have used the term "cognitive transference" to refer to the patient's tendency to think of the psychotherapist (or other persons) as having the same *characteristics* as persons whom the patient has known previously. We have used the term "emotional transference" somewhat loosely to refer to the feeling qualities of cognitive responses plus the corresponding behavioral response tendencies that are generalized from previous to new relationships, particularly the psychotherapeutic relationship.

We do not use the term "neurotic," but we can translate it readily for purposes of communication by saying that the patient's transferences to the psychotherapist are "neurotic" to the extent that they lead the patient to believe the psychotherapist possesses characteristics which he does not have and to the extent that they cause emotional responses in the patient which are unrealistic in terms of the therapist's actual behavior toward the patient.

We would say then that a patient has "worked through a transference neurosis" to the extent that he perceives and thinks of the psychotherapist in terms of the psychotherapist's actual characteristics and to the extent that his feelings toward the psychotherapist represent a reasonable response to the psychotherapist's actual behavior.

From this point of view the term "working through the transference neurosis" is not so much a general description of or prescription for the psychotherapist's efforts, as it is a description of their ultimate goal or purpose. Even from this point of view, however, the term leaves something to be desired. It seems to imply (note the singular article, "the") that it is only or primarily the patient's relationship with the psychotherapist with which we are concerned.

Nothing could be farther from the truth. The psychotherapeutic relationship is only a training ground and a relationship *pro tempore*. It only exists so that it may cease to exist, as is true—in a very basic and "good" sense—of the parents' relationship with their child. If the psychotherapist does his work properly, his reward is that the patient no longer "needs" him, although the psychotherapist may garner a certain amount of "real" affection and appreciation for performing adequately his helping function. (Children and patients are notoriously "ungrateful," however, for the very good reason that they do not have adequate means for evaluating the significance of the "helpers'" contribution nor the effort it involves until they attempt to function as helpers themselves.)

We emphasize this point for a very specific reason. It is to remind the reader that the psychotherapist should be *primarily* concerned with how adequately and realistically the patient handles his relationships with persons in his extratherapeutic life. While the nature of the therapist's experience with the patient is a general guide to how well the patient functions in other relationships, we suggest that specific evaluations of these other relationships should very definitely be a part of the psychotherapist's responsibility and that an objective which should guide the psychotherapist at all times is the improvement of these other relationships.

We do not, of course, assume that psychoanalytic therapists think any differently about this matter than we do. We have, however, found their statements of theory confusing at times. Our intent has been to spare the reader this same confusion.

THE PSYCHOTHERAPIST'S PROBLEMS

The psychotherapeutic contract.   Throughout this book we have tended to use the terms "patient" and "person" interchangeably, especially when referring to events outside of the psychotherapeutic situation. This has been done purposely in order to emphasize to the reader that the only distinctive characteristic of the "patient" is that he is a "person" who is involved in a psychotherapeutic relationship.

There is also another person involved in the relationship: the psychotherapist. The primary distinction between these two persons depends upon the nature of the "contract" between them (see Menninger [8]). This contract specifies that the person designated as "the patient" will pay the person designated as "the psychotherapist" for the performance of certain services, or at least that the psychotherapist is to be compensated in some manner.

The services specified in the contract can be most simply defined as "helping the patient to grow." More specifically, the service may be defined as "helping the patient to function as effectively as he can, considering both his inherent limitations and the nature of the environment in which he must function."

What specific responsibilities does the psychotherapist assume by his acceptance of this contract? Reverting to the simpler definition above, we would say that he becomes responsible for supplying the conditions necessary for growth.

We have already specified the conditions which we consider essential for growth earlier in this chapter. These are: (a) adequate attention to physical or maintenance needs; (b) love (acceptance, approval); (c) help to develop competence; (d) help to develop an optimal degree of control over behavior.

When the psychotherapist assumes the psychotherapeutic contract, he assumes responsibility either for meeting the patient's "growth needs" himself or for seeing to it that they are met by others. This responsibility does *not* vary according to the competence of the patient, as some psychotherapists seem to believe. The competence of the patient is only relevant to the means that can or that will be used to meet these needs.

Unfortunately, the contract cannot specify an exact minimum of acceptable performance on the part of the psychotherapist. We can only delineate characteristics or limitations which significantly *decrease* the probability that the psychotherapist will be able to fulfill his part of the contract, or designate characteristics which *increase* the probability that he will be able to fulfill it.

Bases for failure.   We have studied literally hundreds of instances of "failure to provide for adequate growth," including the failures of parents, psychotherapists in training, psychotherapeutic colleagues, and our own. From this experience, we have developed a fourfold classification of the reasons for such failures.

The first basis for failure is that the helper is inadequately informed or trained for producing the kind(s) of growth his contract with the person being helped calls for.

The second basis for failure is lack of interest or motivation to perform the services required.

The third basis for failure is for the helper to attempt to satisfy his own *emotional* needs in such a way that his behavior interferes with the growth of the person being helped.

The fourth basis for failure is for the helper to attempt to satisfy his own *ego* needs in ways that interfere with the growth of the person being helped.

The first type of error would seem to be self-explanatory, as would the second. However, we would like to point out that this second basis for failure implies that the "helper" must have adequate "feeling" reasons for performing his services to the best of his ability. This clearly does *not* rule out the possibility that these "feeling" reasons might include positive feelings about the person being helped.

The third basis for failure indicates where the line must be drawn in terms of the "helper's" emotional involvement with the person being helped.

The fourth basis for failure could have been included with the third, since all considerations are parallel for these two, and also because the "ego" needs of the helper can ultimately be defined in terms of emotional needs. We have stated it separately primarily because the psychotherapist frequently uses this category in evaluating the shortcomings of other helpers, especially parents, and often finds it applicable to himself as well.

Evaluating the psychotherapist.   The reader will undoubtedly agree that some of the decisions involved in evaluating the psychotherapist's reasons for failure would require a high degree of discernment and objectivity. Such discernment and objectivity are all the more difficult when the person being evaluated is one's self. Yet the psychotherapist must be able to make such self-evaluations accurately. How can we be sure of his ability to do this?

Observing the psychotherapist in the course of his training is the usual basis for assessing his ability to function adequately in his specialized role, including his ability to assess and correct his own errors. This training may include a psychotherapeutic relationship in which the future therapist is "the person being helped." Such prolonged, intensive, and intimate evaluation is surely a desirable safeguard. It becomes an absolute necessity when other means of evaluation indicate that the prospective psychotherapist is making significant errors in procedure that he is unable to detect or to correct.

How "good" in this respect must the psychotherapist be? Again, unfortunately, we cannot set exact quantitative requirements, and we cannot expect perfection. What we have to do instead is to describe certain specific characteristics and suggest that the closer the psychotherapist comes to meeting these standards, the better are his chances for fulfilling his part of the psychotherapeutic contract.

Characteristics required for successful performance.
    (1) The person has a realistic appraisal of himself as he is con-

temporarily. This includes both his strong points and his weak points, so far as his ability to function is concerned. We believe that he is motivated to continue the revision of this self-evaluation on the basis of future experience, and is capable of doing so.

(2) The person is able to make a realistic appraisal of others, especially with respect to their attitudes, expectations, and intentions where he is concerned. This means, among other things, that he is aware of his own tendency to generalize from past experience in new situations and relationships, and that he makes due allowance for this tendency.

(3) The person has access to information about all significant aspects of himself through an adequate awareness of his own feelings and habitual modes of response. Even when he is not "conscious of" certain habitual responses as they occur, he has learned his own patterns of reacting to situations from an analysis of previous behavior. He has also achieved sufficient integration of cognitive structure so that all relevant information at his disposal is considered in the determination of a given response. In order to maintain and increase his effectiveness, he avoids the use of repression as a defense against unpleasant feelings and the tensions associated with conflict.

(4) The person possesses skills in communicating that are effective enough to enable him to interact with and relate to others as he wishes. This means, among other things, that he is capable of conveying to others accurately his own subjective qualities, desires, and experiences.

(5) The person is free from excessive emotional constraint. He is able to realize and to express appropriately his own feelings and needs.

(6) The person is able to control the behavioral expression of his feelings, impulses, and needs in such a way that his cognitively defined objectives are not compromised. This includes the ability to avoid those forms of behavior that will evoke unnecessary or excessively hostile reactions from others.

(7) The person has "cognitively available" various ways of responding to the most common and the most significant situations that he is likely to encounter. He also has some conception of which responses will "work best," but he is able to revise such conceptions on the basis of actual experience.

We cannot leave the reader without a word of warning and a suggestion. The warning is that these standards come perilously close to being the kind of absolute standards that we have criticized as not being appropriate standards for the patient. They represent extremely high standards for any kind of "helper," including psychotherapists. It is intended that they should be used primarily to define ideals and directions of development. We must still depend on judgment to decide when a helper functions "well enough."

With this warning in mind, we suggest that the reader may also regard these standards as the additional criteria for termination which we mentioned and promised in Chapter 11.

SUMMARY

In this final chapter we have concerned ourselves primarily with what have become the classic and principal topics of psychoanalytic theory about psychotherapy, namely: resistance, transference, and counter-transference.

We have proposed that there is an obvious reciprocal relationship between competence and dependency. The less competent the person is (or believes himself to be), the more he tries to rely upon others for the satisfaction of his own needs. As the person becomes more competent, he becomes correspondingly less anxious about his ability to meet his needs through his own efforts.

This leaves him free to become involved in relationships on the basis of preference, rather than on the basis of necessity. It also leaves him free to relate to others on a realistic basis. By this we mean that he no longer has to distort his perception of others to make them fit the dimensions of the "good parent," nor are his expectations of them distorted by his own needs or presumed inadequacies. He is also freed from the necessity to perform special services for others in order to ensure their acceptance and assistance. He is no longer obliged to maintain superficial "social personalities" as a means of appearing sufficiently valuable or desirable to warrant the acceptance of others. Finally, he no longer has to distort his perception of himself, because he no longer needs his compensatory phantasies.

From this point of view "working through the transference neurosis" can be defined in terms of the patient's becoming more competent and being able (because of the resulting reduction of his anxieties) to relate to others in a realistic manner.

The "psychotherapeutic contract" specifies that the person known as the patient is hiring the person known as the psychotherapist to help him in this task of "growing up." The patient then "transfers" or generalizes to the psychotherapeutic relationship his more or less distorted perception of prior social conditioners. The patient goes through his habitual maneuvers in attempting to please the psychotherapist. The therapist is also reacted to as having the characteristics of the "good parent," including the "good parent's" magical ability to give to or do for the patient whatever the patient needs or wants. The amount of distortion involved in these "transferences" is inversely related to the patient's evaluation of his own competence.

The psychotherapist has to do several things in order to "work through" the transference distortions. He may have to bring the patient "up-to-date" on how much competence he has already developed. He may have to help the patient to develop more competence. The therapist may also have to change the patient's standards for evaluating himself, if the standards the patient is using are obviously unreasonable.

The "resistance" of the patient to making such changes will be directly correlated with (and will serve as an index of) the patient's anxiety about making these changes. This anxiety, in turn, can be most closely related to the patient's confidence in the psychotherapist and to the patient's confidence in himself. When (and where) the patient's confidence in himself is low, his confidence in the therapist must be correspondingly high if he is to follow the therapist's program of growth without undue anxiety and resistance.

The psychotherapist must be able to maintain the patient's anxiety at a level low enough to ensure the continuation of the patient's efforts to grow. Therefore, it is incumbent upon the psychotherapist to plan the sequence and the timing of growth steps so as to minimize the patient's anxieties and his avoidant tendencies. How rapidly the patient will then develop will be a joint function of his capacities as a learner and the psychotherapist's effectiveness as a helper. How much time will be necessary for the psychotherapeutic process will depend upon these same factors, plus how much growing the patient has to do before developing a reasonable degree of competence.

The techniques that the psychotherapist uses as a helper encompass a tremendous variety of possibilities, ranging from supplying necessary information, through persuasion, to direct emotional intervention in motivating and reinforcing the patient's efforts. The therapist is expected to be able to determine and to use the most effective technique for achieving a particular result.

The psychotherapist's ability as a helper will depend upon his knowledge and skill, upon his motivation, and upon the extent to which his own emotional needs interfere with his effectiveness. The problem of "counter-transference" is concerned with the last of these three conditions. The psychotherapeutic contract clearly specifies that the psychotherapist may not satisfy his own emotional needs in any way which interferes with the patient's growth toward competence. In order to meet this condition of the contract, the psychotherapist must himself have a considerable degree of competence in being aware of and in being able to satisfy his own emotional needs.

SUGGESTIONS FOR FURTHER READING

We are inclined to believe that at this point the reader will either do no further reading at all, or else he will be ready for the serious continuation of his education. For this purpose we would suggest the following reading program.

We would recommend that he read first Harper's (9) excellent summary. Following this he would read Freud (3), Reich (4) (Part I), Menninger (8), Fromm-Reichmann (5), and Thompson (6), preferably in that order.

Dollard and Miller (7) will supply a bridge between psychoanalytic theory and general psychology, and also provide a more detailed treatment of many topics that we have only dealt with briefly in this book. Rotter (10) is valuable for the same purposes.

From this point the reader should be able to find his own way by referring back to our suggested readings and references in previous chapters.

REFERENCES

1. Doob, L. W. *Propaganda*. New York: Holt, Rinehart and Winston, 1935.

*2. Frank, J. D. *Persuasion and healing*. New York: Schocken Books, 1963. (Johns Hopkins Press, 1961.)

*3. Freud, S. *Therapy and technique*. New York: Collier, 1963. (Basic Books, 1959.)

*4. Reich, W. *Character analysis*. New York: Noonday, 1962.

*5. Fromm-Reichmann, F. *Principles of intensive psychotherapy*. Chicago: Phoenix, 1960. (University of Chicago Press, 1950.)

*6. Thompson, C. *Psychoanalysis: evolution and development*. New York: Grove Press, 1957. (Nelson, 1950.)

7. Dollard, J., and Miller, N. E. *Personality and psychotherapy*. New York: McGraw-Hill, 1950.

*8. Menninger, K. *Theory of psychoanalytic technique*. New York: Science Editions, 1961. (Basic Books, 1958.)

*9. Harper, R. A. *Psychoanalysis and psychotherapy*. New York: Spectrum, 1959.

10. Rotter, J. *Social learning and clinical psychology*. Englewood Cliffs, N.J.: Prentice-Hall, 1954.

* Paperback edition.

NAME INDEX

Adler, A., 16, 30, 33, 71, 160
Alexander, F., 19, 30, 33, 273, 274
Alexander, T., 273, 274
Allen, F., 130, 131
Allport, G., 227
Axline, V., 131, 248, 249

Bach, G., 27–28, 31, 34, 222, 227, 248, 249
Becker, E., 227
Birney, R., 58
Blum, G., 15, 33
Bridges, K., 41
Brammer, L., and Shostrom, E., 29, 34, 248, 249
Brown, J., 131
Buhler, C., 13, 33

Cannon, W., 58, 59
Cantril, H., 12, 32
Carmichael, L., 18, 33
Chase, S., 94, 105, 106

Dollard, J., and Miller, N., 11, 23, 26–27, 31, 32, 58, 59, 83, 84, 105, 106, 131, 157, 158, 203, 204, 248, 249, 299
Dollard, J., *et al.*, 32, 34, 58
Doob, L., 124, 131, 299

Ellis, A., 28–29, 31, 34, 157, 158, 180, 181, 273, 274

Fairbairn, R., 11
Ferenczi, S., 18
Frank, J., 105, 106, 248, 249, 273, 275, 299
Freeman, G., 58, 59
Freud, A., 20, 30, 130, 131
Freud, S., 32, 33, 58; on anxiety, 203, 204; evaluation of his theory, 9–14, 30; and learning theory, 11–12; on objectives of psychotherapy, 227; patients of, 7–8; and psychology, 3–9; as a psycho-

therapist, 8; structural concepts of, 12–14; technique of, 4–5, 8, 248–249, 273, 274, 299; training, 3–4; on work attitudes, 45–46
Fromm, E., 19, 30, 33, 42
Fromm-Reichmann, F., 227, 248, 249, 273, 274, 299

Glover, E., 273, 274
Graves, R., 173
Guntrip, H., 11, 18, 33
Guthrie, E., 62, 84

Hamilton, G., 130, 131
Harper, R., 15, 31, 33, 274, 275, 299
Hayakawa, S., 29, 84, 94, 105, 106
Hilgard, E., 43, 58
Hobbs, N., 273, 274
Horney, K., 17, 30, 33, 42, 203, 204
Hull, C., 11, 32, 40, 43, 58
Hurlock, E., 59

Iscoe, I., 106

Jackson, L., 131
Jacobi, J., 33, 84
Jersild, A., 58, 59
Johnson, W., 29, 34, 94, 105, 106, 180, 181
Jones, E., 32
Jourard, S., 180–181
Jung, C., 16–17, 30, 71

Klein, M., 11, 17–18, 30, 130, 131
Korzybski, A., 29, 84, 94, 105, 106, 125, 151, 158
Kubie, L., 274, 275

Lewin, K., 12, 41–42, 44, 58
Lippmann, W., 106

Marmor, J., 106, 273, 274
Maslow, A., 227
May, R., 227

SUBJECT INDEX

Acting out, 176

Addiction, 219

Adjustment, and communication, 210; problems of, 80–81

Adolescence, and evaluation of parents, 171; transference in, 175

Adolescent patients, characteristics of, 118–121; problems of working with, 120–121

Adult patients, communicative problems of, 121; *see also* Patient, Patients

Affective connotation, 86–87

Aggression, and frustration, 42

Anxiety, 10, 42, 184–187; dosing, 289; free-floating, 186–187; in resistance, 285

Attitudes, definition of, 97–98

Awareness, loss of, 77, 150

Behavior, conscious determinants of, 72

Behavior language, 88

Catharsis, definition of, 36; Freud's theory re, 36–37; as a psychotherapeutic objective, 36–37

Child patients, communication of, 116–118; *see also* Patient, Patients

Classification of patients (*see* Patients)

Cognition, and emotion, 28–29

Cognitive differentiation, lack of, 177–178

Cognitive distortion, of parental image, 160; of self concept, 159–166

Cognitive structure, 60–61; evaluating deficiencies in, 151; habitual nature of, 62–63; integration of, 68–69; probability factors in, 214; and reality, 70–71, 159; rigidity of, 63–64; *see also* Rigidity

Communication, accuracy of, 211–213; accuracy of, re feelings, 212–213; with children, example of, 231–234; class differences in, 127–128; competence in, 210; as a defense, 236; effect of culture on, 126–127; hypnosis and, 235; need for flexibility in, 93; nonverbal, 90–92, children's preference for, 239–240, importance of, 241; openness of, 211; problems of, in early phase of psychotherapy, 256; psychotherapeutic objectives regarding, 210–213; psychotherapist's, involuntary, 238–239; and psychotherapy, 152–155; and relationships, 152; restriction of, in psychotherapy, 236; Rosen re, 21; sex differences in, 127; social expectancy in, 149–150; social inhibition in, 149; Sullivan re, 19; technique of, in psychotherapy, 241–246

Communicative distortion, re marriage, 139–142; re parenthood, 144–148; re vocation, 142–144

Communicative intent, 115

Communicative stimulus, defined, 85, 115

Communicative taboos, death, 138–139; feelings, 133; politics, 136–138; religion, 135–136; self, 134–135; and self evaluation, 163–164; sex, 132–133

Communicator, defined, 85; child patient as, 116–118

Compulsion, 219

Conformity, 28

Consciousness, nature of, 74–75; retreat from, 77, 150

Contacts, with patients, frequency of, 19–20

Control of behavior, and standards, 176–177; as a psychotherapeutic objective, 216–217

303